Fish Won't Let Me Sleep

Fish Won't Let Me Sleep

The Obsessions of a Lifetime Fly-Fisherman

JAMES R. BABB

Skyhorse Publishing

Skyhorse Publishing books may be purchased in bulk at special discounts for sales promotion, corporate gifts, fund-raising, or educational purposes. Special editions can also be created to specifications. For details, contact the Special Sales Department, Skyhorse Publishing, 307 West 36th Street, 11th Floor, New York, NY 10018 or info@skyhorsepublishing.com.

Skyhorse® and Skyhorse Publishing® are registered trademarks of Skyhorse Publishing, Inc.®, a Delaware corporation.

Visit our website at www.skyhorsepublishing.com.

10 9 8 7 6 5 4 3 2 1

Library of Congress Cataloging-in-Publication Data is available on file.

Cover design by Tom Lau
Cover illustration by C. D. Clarke

Print ISBN: 978-1-5107-0981-2
Ebook ISBN: 978-1-5107-0982-9

Printed in the United States of America

Contents

PART ONE

Blue Horizons

Sleeping we imagine what awake we wish;
Dogs dream of bones and fishermen of fish.
— Theocritus

1. *Roamin' the Gloamin'*

I<small>T BEGAN SIX AND A HALF MONTHS INTO THE</small> new century.

The world hadn't ended when the calendar rang up three zeroes, to the relief of many and the disappointment of a few. Gasoline cost $1.26. The stock market was expanding like a jaw full of Bazooka and so was the quiet sport of fly-fishing, the former driven by a new fad called the Internet and the latter by Brad Pitt's wounded eyes and soulful fly-casting in the 1992 movie *A River Runs Through It*.

I had been a fly fisherman since the age of five and a fly-fishing writer for the past five years. My name was on the masthead of a prestigious American hunting and fishing magazine, I'd written a few features for an even more prestigious British sporting magazine, my first book of fly-fishing essays had been kindly reviewed in both the US and the UK, and my second book was under contract and due at the publisher in December.

A few days before I'd celebrated my fifty-first birthday at a bankside party on the River Avon in Wiltshire, a scene torn from a Constable painting of a Trollope novel complete with a stone bridge, a silver braided trout stream, and the misty spires of Salisbury Cathedral. Late the next evening I'd cast dry flies with new friends for wild brown trout on Sydling Brook in the flinty ancient hills of Dorsetshire, and early the next morning I boarded a train bound for Edinburgh and Inverness, a rendezvous with another friend and a rented Vauxhall Astra. A day later I found myself staring at the ceiling of a five-hundred-year-old Scottish hotel surrounded by burns and rivers and lochs where in the morning I would cast flies to wild, never-knew-a-hatchery brown trout. And for the first time ever, I couldn't sleep.

Maybe it was excitement; maybe it was worry. Maybe all those doom-and-gloom prophets really knew what they were ranting about: that the globe is warming due to our relentless industrialization, that the wild is disappearing due to our relentless proliferation, that the fish are under threat from ocean acidification, from headwater deforestation, the fish without which a fisherman cannot plausibly fish and thus cannot comfortably exist.

Maybe it was performance anxiety. Would I suck at fishing Scottish burns and lochs as badly as I sucked at fishing wild English chalk streams? I'd spent my whole life fly-fishing, yet it had been until recently a parochial experience confined to the bouncing freestone streams of my native East Tennessee mountains or the cold hard waters of Maine, where I'd set down roots at the impressionable age of twenty-three. Now I was fifty-one and newly established in a promising career in a burgeoning industry. Maybe I felt that a hillbilly like me didn't belong in such sophisticated company, in such storied surroundings. Maybe I was horrified that my quiet little sport had begun to burgeon in uncomfortably mercantile ways. Or maybe it was just the unrelenting light that wrapped me in the hotel's duvet like a burrito, my brain racing my pulse toward some unknown illumination.

Maybe it was that damned gloaming.

Gloaming?

Before that night I never understood its meaning. My dictionary says it comes from *glom*, twilight, and that it's akin to *glowan*, to glow, and that it has been broadly adopted from Scots dialect to mean the dusk of approaching night—those few brief moments between light and dark that romantically illuminate evenings worldwide.

My first encounter with true gloaming came in the extreme northwest of Scotland in the primordial gneiss and quartzite mountains of Sutherland, where gloaming describes that never-say-dark interlude between sunset and sunrise—between, say, ten at night and three in the morning, when in June it never quite grows dark but only less light, and that light an eerie enveloping glow, as though all the world had been swallowed by a ghost. In Sutherland it could be called nothing else but gloaming, and gloaming could describe nothing else once seen in its native land.

We had shoved off into the gloaming after a late supper at the Scourie Hotel—painter C. D. Clarke and me and our new friend Fraser Campbell, a Highlander who, like us, was mad about wild trout because wild trout live only in beautiful places.

We had arrived at Scourie Hotel in late evening—C. D. from a few weeks of salmon fishing on the Spey and the Tweed; me from three weeks of trout fishing in Wales and Devon, Dorset, Hampshire, and Wiltshire; Fraser from a hard week assembling drilling rigs on the northeast coast of Scotland. After our ale and our taties and neaps and our haggis, that "great chieftain o' the Puddin'-race" so maligned by those who have never eaten the true article, we drove from the hotel through wandering lanes lined with shaggy black-faced sheep and long-horned cattle to nearby Loch Stack, where we had the 58.35-degrees-North version of a solstice sunset to see.

In the gloaming, the fierce geologic upheavals of Ben Stack and Ben Arkle and distant Foinaven glowed gray and amber and gnawed great hunks of cloud from the belly of the sky to feed the silver burns bouncing into Loch Stack's broad golden bowl. Trout rose, dimpling Arkle's mirrored face. Red stags and hinds moving down from the hills lifted their heads and stared our way regarding us, as we did them, as interesting scenery.

The scenery itself was beyond interesting—bog and heath and bare rock, more like Labrador than the storybook image of Scotland. Which isn't surprising, for if you could suspend physical laws and roll your eyeball straight down the parallel of latitude running through Scourie, a tiny coastal village some two and a half hours of enthusiastic motoring north-northwest of Inverness, you would find yourself looking not at my home in Midcoast Maine, which you might expect from the Gulf-Stream-moderated climate, but at the northern end of Labrador's Torngat Mountains. This isn't surprising, either, because the two coastlines once were one, torn apart some million years ago when the continents themselves went roaming.

Sutherland looks like Labrador because it *is* Labrador only with paved roads, ruined castles, and seventeenth-century hotels with real ale and good food and steam heat and en-suite rooms, meaning you needn't share a lavatory with a constipated Glaswegian who shaves his back in the tub.

And it has trout, of course. Which is why C. D. and I had come all this way, haggis and steam heat and interesting scenery notwithstanding.

Of course without the scenery, fly-fishing the wild Highland burns—fly-fishing anywhere—would be nowhere near so romantic as it is. And romance, let's face it, is the fuel that propels most fly fishers away from busy urban desks and into the uncertain wild. Certainly it's what propelled us—a professional painter, a professional writer, and a certified fly-fishing instructor and ghillie whose day job is building drilling rigs—into the extremes of wild and romantic northwest Sutherland.

Having drunk our fill of scenery, we drove slowly back to Scourie through the gloaming, dodged apparitional sheep lounging on the narrow single-lane track, exchanged stares with more stags, and looked enviously into the River Laxford, a small Glenmorangie-colored freestoner dashing from Loch Stack to the sea. The Laxford is synonymous with salmon—*lax* means salmon in Old Norse. The Norse settled here in the Eighth Century and called it South Land—Sutherland; for centuries the River Laxford's anglers bore Norse names. Nowadays most flyrodders on this exclusive bit of water bear names like Lord This or Lady T'Other with an occasional HRH.

One of those lords, the Duke of Westminster, owns all the land hereabouts as far as you can see, some twenty-five thousand acres of which His Grace leases to Scourie Hotel along with upward of two hundred fifty lochs and lochans and a half dozen burns. This quiet, unpretentious lodge has had its present fishing for more than a century and, for a modest fee, lets romantic commoners such as we come stay a while to indulge our fancies.

Even a leveler hillbilly like me can swallow the economic rationale behind that.

*   *   *

The morning finally came bright and shining, and when Fraser and I finished our eight-o'clock breakfast—with blood pudding, second only to haggis in culinary Highlandic rhapsodies—I was, thanks to my in-room coffee maker, buzzing through a caffeinated fog.

The weather didn't feature fog, but a fickle mix of bright sun, rushing clouds, and a stiff easterly wind herding intermittent showers was grand for dramatizing scenery, less so for catching fish.

We began, Fraser and I, where most fishing expeditions begin—in the sweet spots, the obvious targets, one being the deep eddy where Loan Burn enters Loch Stack, a place where Fraser said he had taken good trout many times before. But in the bright sun the fish wouldn't take, and the burn near the loch was low and slow. Despite a wet spring elsewhere in Britain, northwest Sutherland had gotten only half its allotted rainfall, and the burns were showing their bones.

So after exchanging pleasantries with a pair of tweedy M'Lady picnickers launching an assault on Arkle with their ghillies, hampers, and springing springer spaniels, we headed upstream and tossed dry sedges with nymph droppers into what few pockets and runs looked deep enough to hold fish. We took a few lively six-inch browns—wild and beautiful feasts for the eyes: butter-yellow flanks sprinkled with cinnamon and berries and backs of whole-wheat toast smeared with Marmite. But the romance of the wild notwithstanding, they *were* the size of sardines.

After a sharp cascade Loan Burn began to stair step up Arkle's broad shoulder and changed, as many small streams do upon encountering closely spaced contour lines, from piscatorially uninteresting gravelscapes with scattered six-inch fish into a long chain of plunge pools, some deeper than a nine-foot fly rod and most of a sodden inquisitive arm yet never more than two fly rods wide. As we fished our way up the mountain and the weather cleared, we began to pick up much better trout: twelve, thirteen, fourteen inches. By lunchtime C. D., who had gone off early to perform his own professional duties and paint the morning light on Ben Stack, joined us, and now we were three, leapfrogging up the mountain, taking turns fishing pool after pool, and taking trout after trout.

The scenery was so imposing that it was nearly impossible to concentrate on our little sedge flies bouncing down the burn, so vast and sweeping, in the mountain-bordered moor, as to defy not just description but imagination. It was like fishing in a postcard, in a symphony—an endless concert of fast-moving water playing over rock and peat, spanning the range from soft intimate chamber music to demonic panpipes and crashing dissonant bombast with too much timpani.

The fish could be equally imposing. Once, from a cliff-top vantage point, I saw a gate-mouthed brown trout nudging twenty inches dart from beneath a midstream boulder and swallow C. D.'s nymph then spit it right back out without even moving his indicator dry fly. C. D. cast again and again, and the big trout came out again, though by now he wasn't chasing the nymph but the flocks of eight-inch trout that rose from the head of the pool to mob C. D.'s fly. He caught one, too. The big trout, I mean. Not C. D.

I looked back down the burn at the long chain of fast pockets where we'd taken good trout, and the deep mysterious pools where we'd taken only smallish trout, and wished now at least one of us had fished all those miles not with a dainty floating caddis imitation but with a giant swimming streamer fly that to a big trout would look more like a groaning platter of haggis and taties and neaps than like a matchstick of celery daubed with peanut butter.

I remembered—in this setting it's impossible not to remember—Robert Burns's masterful poem "The Hopeless Lover":

> *The trout within yon wimplin' burn*
> *Glides swift, a silver dart;*
> *And safe beneath the shady thorn*
> *Defies the angler's art.*

In this neck of the woods, I suppose Burns ought to have the last word on burns. But of course Burns hadn't had giant weighted streamer flies to dive beneath the shady thorn.

Alas, by the time this logic penetrated my dry-flies-are-the-coolest-ever skull, it was full evening; the burn had been for some time subdividing into smaller and smaller threads, and the estate's equipment shed and our car had shrunken in the distance to a speck of barely discernible white set into a vast panorama of gray and green and brown. With lunch and residual caffeine having long worn off, the promise of a memorable evening meal at the hotel weighing on our collective minds, and a good night's sleep very heavily on mine, we set off across the moors and struck cross country through the string bogs and peat hags and scattered bones of winter-killed sheep and deer toward a distant trail—happy for the walk through the gathering dusk and

> *the long Scots miles,*
> *The mosses, waters, slaps, and stiles,*
> *That lie between us and our hame.* (Robert Burns, "Tam o' Shanter")

I did sleep that night, at least for a while, perhaps because unlike the wild braided chalk streams of southwest England, these mountain streams were something I could efficiently fish, familiar territory despite their exotic setting. The next morning I was all for going back to Loan Burn for some depth-charge Woolly Buggery of those furtive silver darts, but as we were to be at Scourie only a few days and I was here not to indulge my fancies but to do my job, it seemed more journalistically appropriate to go try something completely different. So after breakfast we donned backpacks and headed up the other side of Arkle's bare granite shoulder to follow a rough deer track through the peat and bog and shingle to Loch Stalker.

The wind blew as 'twad blawn its last;
The rattling showers rose on the blast;

But the hour-and-a-half climb and modern fleece and water-proofs kept us warm and comfortable, at least until we stopped at the loch to rig our rods and the infamous Highland midges that had trailed us along the track finally caught up and set to work.

The Highlands get much bad press because of its weather and those midges—*Culcoides impunctatus*, in Eggheadian terms. "Scourie," said a rambling Londoner I chatted with on the train between Exeter and Edinburgh, "I was there once. Dreadful place. Cold and wet and the midges horrible. Why would you go there?"

I told him I live in a place like Maine and go to places like northwest Sutherland precisely because they are cold and wet and the biting bugs are horrible. And because it isn't always cold and wet and the bugs aren't always horrible, and sometimes it's sunny and warm and the bugs are in hiding. But none of these minor inconveniences really matter, I said. Because it's the rumor of these climatic and insect-ridden horrors that keeps the Scottish Highlands, Labrador, northern Maine, northern Quebec, and other still-pleasant places sufficiently empty to be interesting even in these burgeoning times, when humanity expands at exponential rates and newly minted fly fishers hatch like Highland midges, and our quiet little sport becomes, for want of a better description, a bit noisy.

* * *

We piled, the three of us, into a polyethylene rowboat, which would have looked more at home holding three scoops of ice cream and a split banana, and headed off into rainy, blowy Loch Stalker to practice the curious art of British wet-fly fishing.

Basically, you tie on three gaudy wet flies of different improbable color combinations and cast downwind while drifting along. You retrieve in quick spasmodic jerks and animate the bob fly, the one closest to your hand, with a high rod so it dances across the surface like a caffeinated four-year-old.

It's difficult to believe these wild Scottish brown trout are the ancestors of the university-educated snobs who count elbows and arseholes before deigning to accept our entomologically exact offerings on the Madison or the Beaverkill, Little River or the Firehole. Because in Sutherland, my precise American-style imitative tactics caught far fewer fish than simply chugging along a Silver and Teal or a Blue Demon or a popular bristly bob fly whose name I've forgotten but looked exactly like a miniature toilet brush.

In five or six hours of not-particularly-intense fishing we caught some three dozen browns between ten and fourteen inches, and because we were under orders to help clear out some of Stalker's oversupply of small trout to make way for larger ones, we kept a dozen for the larder.

They were bright as new pennies and ranged the spectrum from burnt toffee to crown jewel gold, brilliantly spotted in white-circled carmine, with white-verged fins and wildly leaping dispositions—nothing big, but plentiful and wild and beautiful and coming freely to the fly in a stunning amphitheater walled in by gaunt gray Arkle and its granite acolytes.

Back at the hotel we joined the hoary custom of ensconcing our catch on the slab—a marble mausoleum at the entryway where the day's various catches are laid out like Tsunami victims and labeled by slayer, water of origin, and intention: *Babb/Clarke/Stalkers/Breakfast.*

As the fish lie in state, guests gather to discuss the means of their demise and reminisce about other demises they have presided over or witnessed. It's all so antiquely British it makes one wish to call oneself one and wear tweed breeks and a flat cap, have cream tea at four, keep your pecker up, drive a three-wheeled Morgan on the wrong side of the road, and go all John of Gaunt about scepter'd isles and such when you describe how your Bloody Butcher offed a fat brace of brownies from the Duchess Loch.

The English guests found it amusing that C. D. and I had cleaned our own fish at the loch. They leave them in the round—the better to admire them, I suppose, or perhaps it's a legacy of conquerors being coddled by the conquered. I clean my own fish, I told a decorous elderly gentleman with twinkling eyes and a clipped Oxbridge accent, not from any transoceanic spirit of self-sufficient democracy but simply because to my colonial palate they taste better if gutted before they bloat. But then you have to remember it's only in the past few decades that the English have come to regard food as a delight and not as a judgment for unspecified sins. This doesn't apply to Scotland, of course. In Scotland food has always been important even if some—haggis, for instance—make you feel briefly ill when you learn how it's made. But only briefly because, offal or not, the proper article is *wordy of a grace, As lang's my arm.*

* * *

The night passed in slow rotisserie revolutions and perhaps an hour's scattered sleep. In the morning we were scheduled for Loch Stack, at one time the finest salmon loch in all Europe and still widely noted for its salmon, sea trout, and fine resident browns. After breakfast we set off from the pier in a classic clinker-built rowboat with transplanted Welshman Rob Jones at the oars and our anticipation at a high level after seeing some big trout from Stack laid out on the hotel slab. We'd dressed for the weather predicted—wet and blowy and cold, just what you want for fishing the loch—and so of course the morning clouds quickly burnt off into a Coleridge day, hot and sunny and still, and the few fish that showed early on our painted ocean disappeared as quickly as our layers of wool and fleece.

In a land starved for warmth and sunshine, both are roundly cursed in Sutherland, at least by anglers, for when the sun is bright the fish lie low, and the dreaded Kleggs sally forth. Kleggs are a larger, slower, dumber, and vaguely more decorative edition of North America's horseflies, with glowing emerald eyes and a nasty bite that makes you think you've been stabbed by a hot soldering iron. Fortunately, they're easily evaded or murdered by the alert, and they can't overwhelm you by the sheer weight of numbers as the midges can.

The midges, seen only in damp lowering weather, are the itchy harbingers of good fishing—which isn't what we had on Stack. C. D. caught a twelve-incher and that was it, though in the early morning before it cleared we saw several fine sea trout in the three-pound range leap into the air and insolently flip us the pectoral.

We cast throughout the day—C. D. more than me, for I was a man of letters here to do a job, and every thousand fruitless casts or so I sat, fiddled with my notebook, and pretended to write while listening to the distant trickle of Loan Burn, its depths still unplumbed, the last I knew, by a depth-charging streamer fly just as the sun slips down behind Arkle and the earth begins to glow.

> *Gie me the hour o' gloamin' gray,*
> *It maks my heart sae cheery O . . .*

As the song says, "When the sun has gone to rest, that's the time that I like best." It might have been written for a brown-trout fisherman with furtive silver darts in mind. Or it might have been written for a fly-fishing writer officially entering his middle years, who for the first time in his life has found he can't sleep, and couldn't say why.

2. *The Promised Land*

A FISH PORPOISED FIFTY FEET AWAY MOVING right to left with its dorsal and caudal fins separated by a vast expanse of back. I shot the big fly ten feet to the left toward a likely intercept.

Three twitches and the line stopped dead then headed south, gathering momentum like a train leaving the station. With half my backing peeled away, I tightened the big fly reel's drag, and the heavy aluminum skiff began moving upwind like a super-tanker getting underway.

"E's towin' us, by the Jaysus!" said guide Mark Caines. "I never been towed by no fish!"

I have, but it was a bluefin tuna off the coast of Maine. This was a brook trout. A big brook trout on Crooks Lake and the upper Eagle River in Central Labrador—the wilderness fly-fisher's Promised Land, where I had come as a pilgrim in my first-ever entry into the world of professional fish-writing.

* * *

It was 1995. Two months before, right-wing lunatics bombed a fed-eral office building in Oklahoma and killed 268 people, including fifteen from a children's day care center. Gasoline cost $1.10. The

American economy was growing at an unprecedented rate despite a series of boneheaded government shutdowns. And I, the newly minted angling columnist for *Gray's Sporting Journal*, was sitting in an Air Labrador Twin Otter feeling its way through thick overcast and rain toward Crooks Lake—a thin sheet of brown water like countless other thin sheets of brown water in this vast, humbling wilderness of black spruce, peat moss, and permafrost.

We dipped below the five-hundred-foot ceiling for a peek, pivoted on one wingtip, and dove for the lake—a neat bit of pin-the-tail-on-the-donkey that's far more entertaining than the typical commercial flight and a great exercise for the sphincter muscles. After a flurry of spray and a collective unclutching of butt cheeks, we coasted into the mouth of an inlet toward a tiny dock backdropped by a pair of ramshackle red buildings and a solid wall of tangled black spruce.

Crooks Lake Lodge is the only camp on this obscure lake, sixty miles southeast of Goose Bay and twenty miles from its nearest neighbor. Aggressively unostentatious and as comfortable as worn-out jeans, it looked and felt just like the northern Maine logging camps where, only twenty years before, I had briefly made a sort of living delivering truck parts from Bangor. There was a rumbling generator, hot showers, smoldering mosquito coils, and endless platefuls of logging-camp food. "Everyone gained ten pounds," I read from the lodge's guest book.

It was familiar, it was friendly, and it was unintimidating—it was home. At night I dreamed of pork roasts and onion rings, lemon pies and molasses cookies. I was haunted by rutabagas, and the gravy runs through it. A fly-fishing trencherman would go to Crooks even if the fishing were mediocre.

Which it wasn't. A learned biologist setting out to design the perfect habitat for aquatic insects and brook trout would probably devise something very much like Crooks Lake and the Eagle River. Crooks sounds twenty-seven feet at its deepest and averages ten feet deep. Its bottom is sand and mud thickly encrusted with overlapping layers of car-sized boulders—a fecund insectiary that manufactures limitless clouds of caddis, mayflies, stoneflies, and midges; at any one time a dozen species might be hatching. A trout need only swim around with its mouth open like a baleen whale vacuuming up krill.

The fish average better than three pounds, and five-pounders are thoroughly unremarkable. There are almost psychedelic caricatures of brook trout, fat as pigs and strong as oxen. They have to be because they share the watershed with monstrous northern pike. Of the many large trout our party of five took over a week of diligent fishing, one in ten bore the scars of previous encounters with these ferocious alligators of the north. The slow and the weak are eaten. For people and fish alike, Crooks Lake is mostly about eating.

* * *

With northeast winds gusting to twenty knots and a cold rain slanting in, we headed downlake in big tin skiffs to the river. Together we were Bill and Wayne, a couple of Boston-area computer execs on their second trip here; Fran and Arnie, a pair of GE retirees who've made other Labrador trips and found them wanting; me, a northwoods junkie, wild brook trout fetishist, and wide-eyed pupating professional fish-writer; and guides Lee Peddle and Mark Caines.

Ultimately, it's the guides who make or break a trip like this, and these guys were two of the best. Lee is a talented fly tier whose brown-flash Hexabugger, tied to imitate the big *Hexagenia* mayfly nymphs that throng the lake and river, turned out to be the killer fly for the week. Mark is an inquisitive naturalist and voluble conversationalist who unobtrusively puts you onto fish and leaves you believing it was your own brilliance that took them.

Arnie told us of a trip to northern Labrador where the guides were dismayed he hadn't brought a big spinning rod and a five-of-diamonds spoon. To them, fly-fishing was a waste of time. Not at Crooks. It isn't strictly fly-fishing only, but it's definitely the focus. To preserve this extraordinary fishery, anglers are restricted to artificial lures with single barbless hooks, and except for a weekly fish fry of mid-sized male trout suffering from pike or hook damage, it's all catch and release—although Those Who Must may take home one trophy.

Bill, Wayne, and Lee decided to fish the necklace of pools at the outlet; the rest of us headed downriver a half-mile to the next set of pools. Fran and Arnie were soon into good fish on small Elk-Hair Caddis, but I was after big brook trout, and since I was a professional fish-writer who lives in Maine and thus knows all about big wilderness brook trout, I flung huge multicolored streamers and didn't get a touch.

Finally Mark waded over with a small spun-deer-hair caddis. "They likes dry flies in the river," he said.

And they did. Two casts later I was into a broad-breasted hen-fish of about four and a half pounds—at that time the biggest brook trout I'd ever taken. A few casts later, I began a long string of broken records: a broad brown back rolled slowly over the little fly and I latched onto a bulldozer—a slow, steady, relentless peeling away of line. I could only hang on and try to nudge her out of the current.

When she finally came to net, Mark brought out the digital scales: an ounce under six pounds, her bright orange belly the width of my hand—the kind of trout that makes you forget all about the wind and the mosquitoes and the cold driving rain.

The next day, in the same rain in the same spot with the same fly, I took another fat female that scaled six pounds exactly, and a short while later I took her twin brother. It was enough to spoil any angler—especially a brand new professional fish-writer who wasn't just catching his largest-ever brook trout deep in the Labrador wilds but had also only then realized he was at the friggin' *office*.

* * *

We fished the river through midweek with each of us taking a half-dozen or better brookies averaging three and a half pounds daily, mostly on dry caddis or Lee's Hexabuggers. An autopsy of

a pike-damaged mid-sized male headed for the skillet revealed a
pint of multicolored caddis pupae nicely matched by an old-fashioned cast of soft-hackle wet flies that the fish literally fought
over. The river was a fly fisher's dream—pools and riffles, bends
and runs, hatches and big rising fish. But Mark patiently pointed
out that the really big fish were in the lake. As usual, he was right.

On Wednesday everyone else went downriver, and Mark and
I headed for the lake. By supper time I'd taken a dozen fish from
four to five and a half pounds by sight-casting to the nymphing
trout that rippled the surface. Thursday I took a baker's dozen
better than four pounds. By now we were joined by the Wayne
and Bill show, who were often into doubles, with their alpha male
corporate war whoops audible for miles.

Friday morning I took three four-and-a-half-pounders, a five-
and-a-half-pounder, and the six-and-three-quarter-pound fish
that towed our sixteen-foot skiff upwind for fifteen minutes—
unofficially the largest trout then taken at Crooks Lake. Sated
with trout for the first time in my life, I became curious about
pike, and we headed up the inlet stream by the camp. In less than
an hour a big red-and-chartreuse streamer landed a half-dozen in
the five- to six-pound range—savage, slashing fish that left little
doubt why so many trout bear scars. Earlier in the week, a northern at least four feet long chased a fly right to Wayne's rod tip, and
he couldn't decide whether he was disappointed or relieved that it
didn't eat his fly.

None of us were relieved to see Saturday arrive; it was time
to return to jobs, bills, politicians, the evils of modern life, and
the necessity to write this all down in a way that wouldn't seem
too golly-gee or self-important. As we awaited our floatplane, Bill
and Wayne were making plans to return next summer. Arnie was
already making reservations. "This is the experience I've looked
for my whole life," he said. "I'll be back as often as I can. I just
wish I'd found it sooner." Me too.

Soon, the old Labair Otter's big radial engine yanked us into
the sky, and we headed back across the Mealy Mountains to
Goose Bay and civilization. That night in the Aurora Motel, with

NATO Phantom jets howling in the background, I reread excerpts copied from the lodge's guest book. "Best trip I've ever had." "Best trout fishing I've found in nine states and three provinces." "Finest staff I've ever had the privilege of meeting." And my favorite, "I've fished all over the world in the last thirty years and the only time I got this excited was when I first caught a brookie at six years old."

That's the magic of fishing these far-flung places. For a week you can be six years old again—an excited kid with a full stomach and a bright, flashing brook trout straining at the end of a long line. Sooner or later, someone will realize how addictive this is and invent a twelve-step program to cure its sufferers.

3. *Someone Like Us*

Human brains are peculiar machines. The same protoplasmic supercomputer that simultaneously processes sight, audio, and complex muscular instructions so we may walk and talk and compile shopping lists might also randomly substitute an inconsequential event from childhood for the important reason we walked to the corner store.

Which is how I found myself in Tozier's Market staring blankly at milk and butter and baking powder and seeing mostly a black-and-white photograph of Ted Trueblood's sons fishing for trout in an overgrown Idaho creek.

Precisely how I wormholed from a twenty-first-century Maine market into a 1950s copy of *Field & Stream* interests me less than what was written under the photograph where I landed, which after almost half a century I approximate as: Trueblood's kids found fishing for big stocked rainbows in the main river a bore and the small wild trout in the tributary a challenge.

Whoa, I remember thinking way back then. *There's somebody else like us.*

In our small East Tennessee town, the few kids our age who trout fished used not flies but whole-kernel canned corn, and they'd no more leave a pool full of feedlot rainbows to chase six-inch brook trout up some snaky holler than they'd abandon a platter of church-supper fried chicken for a communion wafer of gluten-free bread topped with a smear of dairy-free cheese.

Trueblood, for you younger readers, was the fishing editor of *Field & Stream* magazine between 1941 and 1947. Then, as near as I can piece it together, he looked up from his desk one day, realized he lived in New York City, and raced back home to Idaho, where he fished, camped, hunted, and wrote about it.

When *Field & Stream* arrived at our house each month, we'd lose ourselves in Trueblood's sensible, practical, elegantly unpretentious articles about camping in canvas tents, cooking over open fires, and fly-fishing with no-nonsense flies. The Truebloods, in other words, were just like us: my fly-fishing father, my fly-fishing brother, and fly-fishing me.

In retrospect, I'm guessing the synaptic short-circuit that zapped me out of Tozier's and into the 1950s began on a press trip—one of those deals where a tackle manufacturer invites a few fish-writers to come admire their new toys in a tax-deductible context. The best of these are low-key—here's our stuff, there's the river, supper's at eight. The worst pair you with a hovering marketeer who keeps insisting you admire the fly rod du jour in the same way a car salesman keeps insisting you buy the clear-coat paint protection and undercoating package.

This was one of the good trips—four or five writers who all knew each other and a couple of tackle wallahs that we all liked because they were way more interested in fishing than flacking. Here's our stuff, there's the river, supper's at eight. Hallelujah.

It was a spot Trueblood & Sons would have recognized: a beautiful stretch of spring-fed river winding through a broad green valley surrounded by stereopticon vistas of the Rocky Mountains. What Trueblood wouldn't have recognized, but has become all too recognizable in these horrible times, was that this was no longer a stretch of river people like us could simply wander into and fish.

This river was private property reserved for a select group shopping for their own seventeen-acre slice of the New West. If they liked what they saw they'd sign on the dotted line, and a team of artisans would build them a rustic log cabin with granite counters, heated towel racks, and gas fireplaces operated by remote controls. On pleasant evenings when no one felt like cooking they might visit the development's central lodge for a magnificent meal, perhaps a massage, some ten-dollar cigars on the screened porch, and an after-dinner single-malt served by a respectful young person wearing a shining face and a spotless apron. Winters, they'd hie off to the nearby mountains to ski or to the nearby town for an art opening at a self-consciously rustic gallery followed by *buffalo bourguignon* and *pommes boulangère* at a self-consciously rustic restaurant where respectful young people with shining faces and spotless aprons attended their every whim. In summers, they'd ride polite horses on groomed trails and drift flies through two miles of gold-star trout stream where every trout could grace the covers of glossy magazines. No need to venture out. Life is beautiful right here.

There's nothing wrong with that, of course. Few things are more ridiculous than a class-resentment rant coming from someone trying to earn a living by guiding the sort of fly fishers who can afford to hire guides or by selling paintings of fish, sculptures of elk, handcrafted cane rods, or fiddly little stories about flyfishing to the folks with the money to buy them. Still, when every year a new crop of No Trespassing signs sprouts along yet another stretch of gold-star trout water, you begin to wonder where the children and grandchildren of today's guides and painters and rod builders and sculptors and fish-writers will find a place to fish free and wild and utterly uncivilized, where they can learn their difficult hands-on crafts in places of true inspiration.

Not on that stretch of river anymore. But, you can't help but admire the developer for choosing the spot with its deep dark pools and runs, sweeping bends, and fertile riffles. It is, as the brochures promised, a little piece of paradise.

Yet there's something troubling about a place where the fish, like the residents of Lake Woebegone, are all above average. After battling yet another grossly obese twenty-inch rainbow to the bank and watching the gossamer tippet part just as I reached for it, I began to suspect that in the quiet of night, when good little anglers are all snug beneath their high thread-count sheets, the Purina fairies might come and shower the river with kibbles. And then, in the ghostly gray dawn, the trout might line up against the bank while small silent gnomes pluck flies from their jaws to be resold to the fortunate folks who'd lost them.

Not that the trout were easy to catch. Show them a spider-webby 5X tippet and they'd wither you with scorn. Downshift to 6X or even 7X, present them with precisely the right fly tied just so, placed just there, drifted just that way, and they might condescend to eat it.

Of course this level of difficulty is exactly what a serious angler wants in his trout. But there were so many of them—one rising every five or six feet—and they were such experienced fighters, knowing just how far to push their lactic-acid envelopes before resigning themselves to a brief wallow at the bank and a civilized release. As Huck Finn said of life with the Widow Douglas, "Everything's so awful reg'lar a body can't stand it."

Fortunately, the tackle wallahs knew our hearts and minds, and early the next morning we lit out for the territory, dropped the last Range Rover astern within an hour, and fetched up an hour later in a tumbleweed town ruled by rusty pickups and hulking combines.

We checked in with the local fly shop and acquired a couple of grizzled guides, a dozen flies, and some take-out sandwiches of the lunchmeat-on-a-bun species. Then we drove down a network of ever-dustier roads and finally crossed the cattle guard of a sprawling ranch where the fly shop had a lease. We drove past the equipment sheds, the corridors of baled alfalfa, and the ramshackle ranch house that even a lowly fish-writer might afford if it were, say, on one acre and didn't have gold-star trout water running through it. A mile more of bouncing and weaving and chewing dust, and we parked.

The rolling plains stretched in all directions toward blue distant mountains. Winds gusting to forty knots blasted the sage and our eyeballs as we picked our way through the cow pies to a wild, lonely river. Our progress was monitored by hundreds of beef cattle—some curious, some worried, a few noisily indignant that we weren't at all the sort of people they were accustomed to seeing.

The fish were hard-caught—one of those situations where you see the seam you want to hit forty feet across the river, so you cast twenty feet upstream and to the left in hopes that the fierce western wind will push the aerodynamically unhelpful hopper-dropper combo somewhere near the right spot. It reminded me of an elderly friend's description of his teenage years shooting hopefully at Messerschmitts from the belly of a B-17.

Even when we hit what we were aiming at, we weren't guaranteed a strike. In sharp contrast to the coddled trout back at the dude ranch development, these fish were scarce, spread out, and a whole different level of wary. But when we connected, they fought like tigers and broke us off not from their dull porcine weight but from their unrelenting savagery.

The sight that will stick, maybe as long as the image of Trueblood's sons fishing that little finger of Idaho trout water, was fellow fish-writer Ted Leeson tossing a hopper into an eddy beneath a bridge and a rainbow about the size of the ones back in civilization grabbing it once, twice, three times before finally slaughtering it and running upriver and downriver and across the river and into the air and down to the bottom and into the reeds and then back into the air and back to the bottom again, all the while shaking its head like an overworked Ayrshire at an ox-pulling. When Ted finally released it, the rainbow was still snapping at his fly like an alligator who means to have that yappy little cockapoo and couldn't care less that it's attached by a leash to an immense woman wearing neon stretch pants and screeching like a fire alarm.

It was all so beautifully uncivilized, exactly what makes wild trout fishing so compelling for people like us. But it also made me wonder if, a half-century hence, there'll still be uncivilized places to fish—and if there'll be any of us left who care.

4. *Redefining the Envelope*

W<small>HAT I ENJOY MOST ABOUT FLY-FISHING IS</small> its breadth of possibilities—from a simple day wet-wading a neighborhood trout stream with tattered boots on their fourth set of felt soles and a rod that was cheap twenty years ago to a private-water extravaganza with waders that cost more than my first car and a rod that cost more than my first house.

Because I yam what I yam, I am most familiar with the first extreme, but I don't let my egalitarian ethos come between me and the latter when opportunity calls. Which it did some years ago in the form of a press trip to the farthest edge of fly-fishing I've encountered in all my years of investigating the furthermost quintile.

If you read the right sort of magazines or get the Orvis catalog, you probably saw those Nomads of the Seas ads—"Patagonia by Land, Sea, and Air"—with the stirring photographs of the Motor-Vessel *Atmosphere*, its candy-apple red Bell 407 airlifting anglers into the you-can't-get-there-any-other-way Chilean backcountry and the onboard fleet of drift boats and jet boats and one of those big fifty-knot Zodiac inflatables meant to quietly insert lethal doses of Navy Seal into the badlands.

Military precision was my first impression of the *Atmosphere* as its crisply uniformed staff lined up at Parade Rest to welcome us aboard in Puerto Montt, Chile, the lovely tourist and fishing town perched between the foot of the Andes and the head of a series of island-sheltered bays stretching southward toward the Straits of Magellan.

A decade previous, en route to Jim Repine's lodge on the Futaleufu River near the Chile-Argentine border, I flew over this same coast, staring out the twin-Cessna's window at the roadless green mountains sliced by thin blue lines rushing toward the sea and thinking, *They look like trout streams, but how would anyone ever fish them?*

About the same time, an energetic young fly fisherman/fighter pilot/hotelier/financier named Andrés Ergas was wondering the same thing. And figuring it out. All he'd need was a 150-foot ship purpose-built for ferrying fly fishers and their families from stream to shining stream, inserting them into inaccessible areas via helicopter and jet boat, with the ship traveling by night and arriving at new rivers by dawn's early light, and the happy anglers all the while imbibing unvarnished nature and unmatched Chilean cuisine.

Any of us might dream of something like that. But Andrés, with military precision, dogged determination, and vast piles of family money, pulled it off. The result was a fly-fishing expedition so far over the top that it redefined summit.

Of course when rising to the evening hatch of hors d'oeuvres and paying homage to the *Atmosphere's* formidable wine cellars, it's possible to lose sight of just why Andrés built that ship. But in the morning, wadered-up and boarding the chopper, there was no doubt—it's all about the fishing.

Still, on our first morning it was nearly impossible to suppress the feeling that this was a different kind of mission as we raced upriver at 200 feet and 120 knots with the jungle-covered mountainsides whizzing by almost close enough to touch and the intracranial iPod involuntarily wailing *Die Walküre*. I say nearly because *Pumping Iron* author Charles Gaines and I were traveling neither to Odin's Hall with Brünnhilde and her heavyset sisters nor to a hot LZ with Robert Duvall and the First of the Ninth but to a splendid laguna to meet a drift boat and a personable guide that had been ferried in by helicopter while we lingered over our eggs Benedict.

These feelings of mission creep persisted as the morning progressed. I knew we were trout fishing because we were catching trout, but as José rowed us around this pond-in-the-river surrounded by soaring mountains and the kind of alien jungle through which one expects revenant tyrannosaurs to soon come stomping, it didn't feel like trout fishing.

Partly this was because we actually seemed to be bass fishing—Charles tossing immense Chernobyl-ish bugs into dinner-plate pockets in the reed beds and me tossing big scary buggery-looking things that cratered the reed beds with a *ker-sploink*—and partly because the heavyset browns and rainbows we were catching looked like potbellied Florida largemouth who'd thought it would be a hoot to show up at a Halloween party dressed as trout. Whatever, it was great fun even when battling Patagonia's relentless roaring-forties wind, though given the conditions I'd have traded a slice of last night's *foi gras* for a capful of weedless bass bugs and, if pressed, even thrown in my pillow mints to boot.

After a few more days of chopper flights, weed-bed whacking, and a float trip down a narrow winding river fraught with equal numbers of underwater snags, back cast snags, and big snaggletooth brown trout, we awoke one morning to find ourselves anchored in the appropriately named *Bahia Pescadora* with legions of gulls, cormorants, sea lions, and porpoises feeding on phosphorescent shoals of *sardinas* attracted by the ship's lights.

After breakfast, *Forbes* writer Monte Burke and I piled into one of the jet boats with Che at the helm and headed up the Tic Toc River, which began all Creature-From-the-Black-Lagoon with a jungle full of squawking parrots and, through the magic of elevation, morphed into a Montana trout stream complete with glaciers and snow-capped mountains.

At a likely looking rapids we dismounted and waded in—mutinying against the locally favored tactic of casting bugs to backwater reed beds in favor of drifting nymphs and dries precisely where and how we would have drifted nymphs and dries on the Madison or the Delaware. And there they were: lots of big rainbows and a few bigger browns, including one I'd guestimate well northward of six pounds that escaped when fish and fisher simultaneously realized that fisher was well past his divin'-in-after-'em-over-the-waterfall years.

Coming back downriver into the bay, we saw a pair of humpback whales blowing and spiraling in their strange playful fashion, and we bobbed around on the gun-gray sea to watch.

Thanks to the constant swelling of cold rich currents from the Pacific intermingling with the inrush of nutrients from the many mountain rivers, Chile's vast semi-sheltered sea is among the world's great concentrators of sea life. At one time we had six humpbacks swimming around, under, and beside the boat, and we were all humbled to biological insignificance by the sight of several blue whales, the largest creatures to live on earth, majestically oscillating past us a doable double-haul away. Standing eye-to-eye with blue whales, which are down to a mere 1 percent of their pre-whaling-days population, is a conflicting and visceral experience—so many of those unforgettable nineteenth-century whaling stories, so many magnificent creatures unceremoniously turned into lubricants and corset stays, so many possibilities for their future with this recently discovered nursery off Chile's southern coast.

On the way back to the ship we saw a Hitchcockian cloud of birds hovering over an *Exxon Valdez* oil slick with Andrés' boat hovering around the edge. I was wondering if one of the whales had gone all Moby Dick and sunk the ship and these were its sole remains upon "the great shroud of the sea," when a pair of silver rockets hit the sky and flung back the sun: sierra mackerel chasing sardinas.

Andrés, the largest ten-year-old I've ever met, unleashed his contagious enthusiasm and decided that we ought to catch one, and that I, as the press trip's token saltwater guy—dodging the fact that much of my saltwater experience involves not tarpon, billfish, and speed-burning tuna but lobster traps, gillnets, and bottom-feeding long lines—should be the one to come onto his boat and try it.

Always one to answer when opportunity calls, I tied a big streamer onto a doubled length of tippet and cast into the oil slick. Within two strips I was hooked up but noticed that (A) I was fishing a trout-sized six-weight rod and (B) this sierra was twice the size of the eight-pounders of the same species I'd found to be rough customers on a big honking twelve-weight a few years before off Cabo San Lucas. It was touch and go for a while with these toothy mini-wahoo on such dinky tackle and no wire tippet, but I finally finessed one in, then so did Andrés. And this is how one of the Pacific's tastiest ceviche ingredients found its way onto the M/V *Atmosphere*'s menu and saltwater fly-fishing onto its long list of optional activities.

In a land of such incredible trout fishing, it's easy to overlook other fly-fishing opportunities, but the waters off Chilean Patagonia are among the richest in the world with immeasurable schools of krill, the shrimplike crustacean that forms the forage base for everything from these limitless schools of sardinas to the huge blue whales themselves.

"Just think," I said without thinking. "Those blue whales out there probably hoover up six million krill every day. Krill are just shrimp, like a bonefish fly tied on a size-two hook. Just imagine what you might catch with a three-fly cast of Crazy Charlies."

"Yeah," Andrés said looking, like me, at the distant spouts of blue whales lofting into the sunset like pale ghosts on a flooded continent, "just imagine."

5. *Around the Fire*

A<small>T LEAST ONCE EACH FISHING SEASON ON RIV-</small>ers and streams and lakes and ponds from sea to shining sea, small groups of old friends gather together in familiar places at familiar times to replay familiar scenes and renew their connections with, well, everything.

As my particular crowd goes, I'm a newcomer. Will, Marcel, and Shawn have made this trip the third week of June for more than thirty-five years; Norm and Barney's intermittent visitations date back that far, as well; Chucky, now pushing thirty, began coming here as a small boy; Tom became a regular about four years before me; and I began coming during the first Clinton administration.

We straggle in to camp on Maine's West Branch of the Penobscot from our homes in Vermont, Massachusetts, and Maine and pitch our tents in the same places, tie off the tarp where we always tie it off, build the fire where we always build it, and cook the same meals we always cook—Marcie's boiled Vermont ham and pea soup, Shawn's T-bones and venison sausages, Chucky's burgers and dogs, my rectal-rooter chili, and our annual odds and ends of game birds, ducks, moose, and deer. We drink a bit in the evenings, some of us sometimes more than we ought, and we tell the same stories, laugh at the same jokes, and marvel at the same endless idiocies of modern existence.

It's a fairly raucous crew with a relentless focus on two shared goals: catching large landlocked salmon on flies, and making our fellow campers laugh hard enough that beer squirts out their noses. In mysterious ways this grounds our year with an emotional anchor none of us would feel comfortable talking about but all of us would miss were it not there.

John Gierach and his circle of old friends have one of these annual events, as well, and in the interests of scientific comparisons I tagged along in September 2004 to their yearly campout in Roy Palm's backyard on Colorado's Frying Pan River.

It was a familiar scene: old friends straggling into camp from homes in Boulder, Colorado Springs, and Lyons, pitching their tents in the same places they've always pitched them, tying off the tarp where they always tie it off, building the fire where they always build it, cooking the same meals they always cook—Mike's spicy fire-roasted chicken, John's elk chili, Ed's elk stew, and A.K.'s bacon and eggs. There's a bit less drinking in the evenings than with certain elements of our crowd, but again the twin goals of catching tough fish and cracking up your fellow campers take precedence, and underpinning the relentless humor is the same baffled bemusement at the endless idiocies of modern existence.

The campsite is right alongside the Frying Pan, which cuts cold and clear and beautiful through an album-cover canyon carved from sandstone as red as an Irish setter—a perfect blend of riffles and runs and pools and eddies sculpted partly by nature and, at least on his half-mile of water, partly by Roy, who rolled some rocks, shifted some gravel, and reimagined a revised ecosystem with the twin goals of nurturing fish and humiliating fishermen, both of which it does admirably.

June on the Penobscot can be cold and rainy one day and withering hot the next, and September in the Colorado Rockies is no different. A chill rain sent us shivering into our tents early the first night, and we awoke entombed in snow. The next few days we floundered about in felt-soled wading shoes encased in great galumphing basketballs made of snow and mud, and we'd fish the water around Roy's place for a few hours then head back to camp and hover over the fire, smoking ourselves like bacon until someone thawed a bit and, nominally dry, would wander over to the campground pool and see faces eating flies and pick up his rod to start working out line. Then we'd follow along one by one, dispersing up and down the river and working through the various pools and riffles, in our various ways, to catch a few fish, some of them very nice. But we inevitably headed back to the warmth of the fire and the relentless campaign to force fluids from our camp-mates' nostrils.

Ultimately the weather improved and the fishing did, too, and we spread out into the public water upriver because fishing only private water seems somehow wrong for the likes of us and perhaps too easy—even though it's anything but easy to fish the home waters of an authentic old-time Western fly-fishing legend like Roy Palm, who could catch trout on a dry fly in a storm drain if he put his mind to it.

A.K. went to a popular pool below the dam unofficially called The Toilet Bowl, where crowds of fishermen cast for immense indifferent browns that loaf about like great dappled zeppelins snarfling in *mices* shrimp by the bucketfuls and ignoring flies by the squadrons. But not, of course, A.K.'s flies.

Ed and Mike fished the lower end of a long stretch of riffles and runs, and John and I fished the upper end, and we all caught trout that weren't huge but which anyone with a proper sense of perspective would describe as very nice indeed. The fish were difficult enough so that each required a specific plan and usually a fly change—sometimes many fly changes, each progressively smaller until we bottomed out around size twenty-six; roughly the size of that semicolon. And sometimes, no matter what we did or how long we messed around with tippets and flies and drifts and mends, the fish simply could not be caught, which is precisely as it should be.

Once, John and I were fishing opposite sides of the same pool, and we each caught three very fine and very tough browns, colored up like brook trout with bright red adipose fins and muscular flanks as yellow as cheddar. I caught mine on a Pale Morning Dun, which were hatching on my side of the river, and John caught his on a Blue-Winged Olive, which were hatching on his side of the river. I tried a BWO and caught nothing, and John tried a PMD and caught nothing, and as we were less than twenty feet apart at the time, this illustrates both the obduracy and the entertainment value of the Frying Pan's persnickety trout.

The last day turned out to be so satisfying, no one fished after supper despite plenty of bugs on the water and plenty of faces rising to eat them. It isn't that we'd spent the day catching whole crowds of enormous fish. We caught somewhere around a dozen each, for a guess, that averaged fourteen inches, for another guess, and ranged up to eighteen or so inches, for another guess. And they were mostly caught on teeny-tiny dry flies, for more of a certainty, by casting to fish seen rising and deliberately targeted. They were all difficult, and they all came on public water that doesn't get fished so much as it gets relentlessly hammered by people who know what they're doing, and all the fish were selective in maddeningly satisfying fashions.

So we sat around the fire that last night warming our hands and recounting the day, rolling burritos from leftover elk chili and toasting them in the flames, and talking about fish we'd caught or hadn't caught, trips past when the wind blew so hard that cottonwood limbs crashed down all around, the time they'd had to sleep in their trucks because outlaw bears were vandalizing the countryside, the rude awakening I'd had the night before when two outlaw mice slit through the fabric of my borrowed tent and were fist-fighting over a granola bar an inch from my nose, and whether the best name for a blues-rock band made up of geriatric fly fishermen who've spent five damp days crouching unwashed and unlaundered around a cottonwood fire would be Smoked Goat or Bad Haggis.

The next day the camp came down as it always comes down, and as they always do, everyone speared their best fly into the wall of Roy's outhouse, autographing it and dating it and leaving it for the mice to defoliate over the winter, a pleasant closing ceremony that in my own crowd has its parallel when Chucky returns our campsite's presiding pink plastic flamingo to the hollow tree where it spends the winter.

That's basically how all these annual events go, as near as I can tell. Modern-day anglers restlessly travel the globe fishing new places, catching new species, meeting new people, imbibing new experiences, and endlessly looking for, well, something. But at least once a year we all seem to convene our core circle of friends and strictly follow a familiar script written less in our heads than in our hearts—a brief sabbatical from the endless idiocy of modern life, where the fish make fun of you and your friends do, too.

6. *Fish Camp*

IT OCCURRED TO ME, WHILE BANGING NAILS into the new screened porch we were building for Jim Lepage's camp up on Maine's Caribou Lake, that the desire for a little place near the water where we can get away from it all is a powerful driver of human behavior.

These days, with so many of us living in cities and suburbs and enduring tedious commutes to jobs that we sometimes love but more often simply tolerate and occasionally outright despise, it's no wonder that we carry in our hearts a shining vision of a cottage upon a hill overlooking a pond where herons wade, a lake where mountains invert their visages, an estuary where ospreys soar, or a river that flows past in an endless cycle of renewal.

For anglers, this fuzzy paradisiacal image has a sharper focus. We want our little home away from home to front on a pond where trout rise, a lake where bass swirl, an estuary where stripers blitz, and a river where salmon swim in from the sea in their own endless cycle of renewal. I've met a lot of anglers over the past six decades, and the only ones who didn't long for their own little place on the water were those who already had one.

Back in those hazy days between infancy and first grade, I remember another summer when men gathered to bang nails: my father and his fishing buddies in our big backyard turning a pile of lumber into the first fish camp on East Tennessee's Tellico River.

It was Bob Orrin's cabin. He bought the materials and, being a nuclear engineer, he designed it: two connected cubes with pyramidal roofs, a hard-shell version of the World War II army headquarters—and hospital—tents where these men had so recently expended their youth. It would be prefabricated in panels, trucked to Tellico on rough wagon roads and abandoned narrow-gauge railroad beds, and erected alongside the river to become a different kind of headquarters for this band of brothers.

All I remember of its building was the sound of hammers and saws, but I can never forget the stories—the mashed thumbs, the wandering saw cuts, the teetering load on the borrowed truck, the assembly on the riverbank where everything so carefully engineered to fit precisely together didn't quite, and the men on the ladders saying, "I wish I were a eng-a-neer. This morning I didn't even know what one was, and now I *are* one."

On our visits there I remember thinking it must be the finest thing in the world to have not one house but two, and the best of them nothing like Bob's nice house four doors down from ours with its deep carpets, pine paneling, and the very first television I ever saw. Instead, Bob's cabin had kerosene lanterns, bunk beds, an outhouse, and, best of all possible things, a wild river running a few feet from its doorstep. The cabin glowed with magical possibilities that a regulation middle-class house in a regulation middle-class neighborhood could never hope to acquire—shiny new television or not.

Long before entering first grade and learning that life has many paths and we are free to choose which ones to follow, I had decided that one day I'd build my own cabin on a distant, wild river. But for one reason or another I never quite did.

I did build a house—banging nails, sawing lumber, and teetering on a ladder wondering why things weren't fitting together as precisely as I'd eng-a-neered them. And although the house doesn't overlook a wild river, it's a five-minute walk from a small pleasant trout brook that forms our back boundary for most of a heavily wooded mile. For thirty years it was our little place away from it all, a cottage upon a hill at the edge of a small Maine town of 2,600 souls, our front yard a blueberry field that turns red with the frost, and our backyard an unbroken evergreen forest.

But these days forests near small towns don't stay unbroken. I was up at my friend Jim's on Memorial Day weekend partly to help him and his son Brian with their porch and partly so I could no longer hear the sounds of machinery across the small pleasant trout brook. The new owners of the adjoining ninety acres were peeling away the trees and the very earth itself, and the soggy, boggy neighboring woodlot was transitioning from the home of deer and partridge and turkeys and foxes into an antiseptic subdivision containing as many as forty-five regulation suburban houses.

This left me thinking that our compromise scheme of living year-round in a hybrid between a fish camp in the woods and a proper house at the edge of a proper town had its short-range charms and its long-range flaws. And I wondered whether I'd gotten too creaky to think about building some nice little place near the water where I can get away from it all now that there's something to get away from.

When I sit home by the fire I wholeheartedly agree with that famous waterfront cabin builder, Henry David Thoreau, who wrote that "there is some of the same fitness in a man's building his own house that there is in a bird's building its own nest." But teetering on a shaky ladder banging nails into Jim's porch brings to mind the all-enveloping experience of building a house, and I figure I'd rather spend my remaining years fishing than banging nails—or, worse, working far into my dotage to earn the money to pay someone else to bang my nails.

Not that there's a shortage of fish camps whose nails have already been banged. Check the ads in the back of huntin' and fishin' magazines and, depending on the targeted demographic, you'll find everything from a medieval castle on Scotland's River Spey to a tar-paper shanty on Mud Pond. There is a camp out there for everyone who wants one—or at least for everyone who can afford one, which isn't always the same thing.

Lately I've been lingering over these ads and imagining a little place on a river in northern Maine, New Brunswick, the Gaspé, or Labrador. I'm not sure I'm ready or even able to buy, but meanwhile I'm lucky enough to have friends like Jim whose fish camps I can sometimes borrow in return for a bit of nail banging, outhouse shifting, and all those other enjoyable tasks that make proper fish camps so much more than simply a place to sleep.

A proper fish camp is a bit like obscenity: difficult to define but you know it when you see it. Certainly my brother's cabin fits the description—a small cottage teetering on a steep hillside not ten minutes' brisk walking from the riverbank where our father and his friends built Bob's cabin all those years ago. Because modern fish-writing forces us to be travel-writers as well, some of us know people outside our ordinary spheres who own riverside castles—their walls lined with first editions and their kitchens staffed by culinary-school graduates wearing spotless white. But the camps of my everyday peers uniformly fit the old-fashioned archetype: rustic structures built by friends and furnished with castoffs from family homes. Odds and ends of dead animals and fish adorn the walls. Old sporting magazines molder in corners along with camp diaries that track day-to-day activities stretching back into the misty past. The plumbing is rudimentary to nonexistent. The kitchens smell of bacon and eggs and beer. Dust balls of cast-off fly-tying materials blow across the floors like Texas tumbleweeds.

But no matter how humble or elegant, from shack to castle, there's always an open-air porch where everyone spends their time away from the river sitting and talking and listening to the loons and the whippoorwills far into the night.

That's exactly what I was doing when I wrote these words back at Jim's camp in early August. But this time I was alone. Jim was working at his job with Orvis in Vermont. His son Brian was at his job guiding fly fishermen in Colorado. And I was sitting on the screened porch, into which I banged those nails, watching Mount Katahdin gnaw its way through the clouds of a passing thunderstorm, watching a rainbow arc across Caribou Lake,

watching a family of black ducks paddle by, and listening to the
loons eerily declaring their territories: *It's mine, mine, mine.*

Another thunderstorm was making in from the west, and the
battery-powered radio called tomorrow a washout with triple-
digit temperatures, violent wind, and drenching rain. Not a day
for fishing even though my favorite river was only twenty minutes
away.

But then the best thing about fish camp is you don't really have
to fish. You need only sit there on the porch and listen to the
loons, and without any striving or shame at your indolence you
can be who you really are, sitting there in a little place on the
water at the edge of the great woods, and "front only the essential
facts of life, and see if I could not learn what it had to teach, and
not, when I came to die, discover that I had not lived."

7. *Home Away from Home*

Aᴺʏ ᴛɪᴍᴇ ᴀ ᴘʀᴏꜰᴇssɪᴏɴᴀʟ ꜰɪsʜ-ᴡʀɪᴛᴇʀ complains about his job, the world is rightfully licensed to kick his butt until he shuts up and realizes he isn't exactly leading a life of quiet desperation out there on the Deschutes, Tay, or Golfo Duce.

You may not get rich fish-writing, unless you define a shift manager at McDonald's as rich, but you do acquire a wealth of pleasant experiences. Except one: although you get to visit incredible places, you rarely get to revisit incredible places. To keep fish-writing fresh, you must constantly pursue new horizons.

Good anglers don't do this. If they find a good spot, they go back. If they find a great spot, they go back again and again. And if they find a spot that in mysterious ways defines who they are, they try to figure out ways to make it their home, or at least their home away from home. Page through the guest book of a great fishing lodge and you'll read countless variations of "Our tenth trip back, and we're already booked for next year."

In my seventeen years as *Gray's Sporting Journal*'s resident fish-writer, I got to do some pretty cool fishing, from flirting with albatross and battling giant trevally on Midway Island in the North Pacific to fishing Atlantic salmon like a proper toff on Scotland's Royal River Dee.

And then there's Three Rivers Lodge on the Woods River in central Labrador. I fished there with my fish-writer friends John Gierach and A.K. Best back in 2001, and in an article called "As Good as it Gets," I wrote that not only had we enjoyed our best-ever trout fishing at Three Rivers but that we'd also enjoyed our best-ever lodge experience—we felt less like guests than like long-lost family come home for the holidays. Of all the places I've been, Three Rivers is the one that most calls me back.

And so, in the climatologically challenged summer of 2004, I finally answered. The same cold and rainy weather that had decimated Bar Harbor hotel bookings had also generated waves of vacancies in northeastern fishing lodges. And because fish-writers fill vacancies the way matter fills a vacuum, mid-August found me heading up Maine's Route 201—Moose Alley, as it's locally known for its astonishing concentration of fatal car-moose collisions—toward the Quebec City airport and the late flight to Wabush, Labrador, stopping en route at a Maine pull-out to collect a properly scheduled guest at Three Rivers called Bob.

Among other things I learned about Bob on the long drive north was that he'd recently beaten an especially unpleasant breed of cancer and now meant to live to the fullest the life he'd almost lost, starting with a budget-busting first-ever trip to a Labrador lodge where he'd read how three fish-writers named Gierach, Babb, and Best had enjoyed their best-ever trout fishing in long lives filled with trout fishing.

Now that I think of it, another minor drawback of fish-writing is a nagging feeling of responsibility. After all, you're always recommending readers try fishing some new way, with some new rod, or in some new and often expensive place. But what if you're wrong?

So as I followed the route of the Revolutionary War expedition of 1,100 Continental troops led by pre-turncoat Benedict Arnold and kept watch for 1,100 pounds of collision-minded moose, I worried that this particular expedition, which began with such great expectations, might end in a similarly disappointing fashion.

The next day, after a 158-mile flight from Wabush loaded with two caribou hunters, two fishermen, and enough food to feed Arnold's starving army, the familiar old de Havilland Beaver blatted its way alongside the Three Rivers dock, and I crawled out into a familiar and welcoming world: camp-cook Frances Barry hugging me like my mother, saying "right on" every three sentences, and issuing orders to freely raid the refrigerator "just like you was to-home," and camp manager, and Frances's husband, Kevin, still ruggedly woodsman-like and philosophically patriarchal and quietly hilarious, along with a new crop of young guides from Newfoundland eager and efficient and genuinely glad to see us.

The only thing that seemed different was the angle of the dock to the shore, which Frances explained by showing snapshots of the eight feet of snow that still covered the cabins when they flew in on June 18 to open up. "The river's dropped three feet since then," Kevin said, "but it's still up a good two feet over normal."

The Woods River runs out of Quebec and into Labrador at around 55 degrees north in a great sprawling arc of seeps and ponds and horizon-bending lakes toward the immense Smallwood Reservoir. Here and there the lakes pinch in to drop through geological stepping stones, and it's in these rapids that the brook trout congregate—partly to feed and partly for protection from the huge pike that prowl the lakes. I was thinking that with the water so high the fishing in these rapids might be very different this year than in the dry and magical summer of 2001. But I didn't say anything to Bob, figuring that a fish-writer who might've created unrealistic expectations ought to keep his misgivings to himself.

Sure enough, the first few days of fishing were slow, with miserable, rainy, windy weather. What few good trout we caught were so stuffed with sucker minnows they could barely move, and the pike were marauding throughout the swollen rapids and were, unlike the trout, hungry. I caught a three-pound trout that looked freshly gnawed by a Kodiak bear, and when I slipped her from the hook she swam away with the forlorn resignation of a designated victim certain of her fate.

I've fished the north enough to understand that bad weather is more the rule than the exception, but after a few days of slogging through thirty-knot winds and lashing rains to cast heavy flies toward trout that were more scared than hungry, Bob became weighted down by his own sense of forlorn resignation, very visibly feeling that once again elements beyond his control were about to rob him of an enjoyable life.

That was the last I saw of Bob for four days because, owing to another cancellation, I found myself heading north for a change of venue that we'll get to in the next chapter.

When I got back to Three Rivers, the sun was out, the birds were singing, and Bob was all smiles and laughter—a man no longer weighted down by unrealized expectations but buoyed aloft by joy. While I'd been gallivanting around the cold soggy north with Marco the pilot and Kevin Junior in the Beaver, Bob had been enjoying great weather and great fishing at the lodge and catching, among dozens of other braggable fish, a brook trout that taped twenty six and a half inches long and eighteen inches around, which the Provincial fish charts calculate to weigh 10.73 pounds—the trophy of a lifetime by any measure. Bob's recounting of the battle could almost be a book in itself.

On our last day, Bob and I fished the appropriately named Rick's Surprise, a tiny finger running between two arms of the river and resembling in every way every ten-foot-wide trout brook every one of us has ever fished: tea-colored water; bathtub-sized plunge pools connected by bouncy little runs and skittering riffles, undercut banks guarded by tangles of willows, and a thick forest of spruce and tamarack.

In a morning of intense fishing I caught close to a hundred brook trout in the six- to eight-inch range—about what I might expect on a similar stream in the deep backwoods of Maine. But I also caught a couple of two-pounders, a three-pounder, a four-pounder, and an honest six-pounder that led me on a drag-ripping, rock-hopping dash a hundred yards downstream before Cliff the guide finally got a net under him.

As we released that trout, a howl floated down on the wind, and we splashed upstream to find Bob kneeling in the tiny creek and cradling a seven-pounder, a great snapping monster with bristling fins and pumpkin flanks. An ear-to-ear smile split Bob's face, lit from within like a Rembrandt portrait.

The last night, with the boats and the Beaver double-moored in the camp's lee against a glancing blow from Hurricane Charley, we gathered together in the lodge and, with the winds howling and the rain lashing, had a serious northwoods party.

After supper, Jordan the guide appeared with three beers in one hand and a guitar in the other, and he sat down and launched right into *Tight-Fitting Jeans* and *Saltwater Cowboys* and rapid-fire stories involving Newfoundlanders who find the answer to life's mysteries by shoehorning a 454-cubic-inch Chevy V8 into their Ski-Doo. Hurricane Charley was howling accompaniment at the windows, and the assemblage of guides and guests and staff and friends were finding their own answers to life's mysteries by singing along and stomping their feet to the old Newfie favorite, *Are You Happy?*

I looked around the table, and if anyone on earth has ever been happy it was Bob, a man who had been looking for his own answers to life's mysteries and for a home away from home, and now had found both.

8. *Romancing the Falls*

"**R**OMANCE," SAID THE AMORAL MRS. CHEVELEY in Oscar Wilde's *An Ideal Husband*, "should never begin with sentiment. It should begin with science and end with a settlement." This is not quite how my ten-year romance with Helens Falls played out.

My first encounter came through the science of radio in a northern Quebec caribou camp, where a deflating inflatable and wrath-o-God weather had sent guide Chris Turcotte and me searching for food and shelter; instead, we found vandalizing bears and a shredded tent. Four long days we waited for flying weather and the rescue Otter while living on salvage from our abbreviated float trip of the Lefevre River and crumbs of culinary radio chatter between Marlene, who cooked for the arctic char camp at Weymouth Inlet, and her mother Shirley, who cooked for the Atlantic salmon camp at Helens Falls.

"Oh, t'wedder's awful," Shirley told Marlene. "T'sports was catchin' lotsa salmon, but den t'weather turns ugly and now t'sports is hangin' round t'kitchen an' gettin' underfoot, and dere's been seven bears here doin' t'same. One had 'is face pressed right up against t'dinin' room window, all slobberin' an' moanin'."

"Shoot 'em," said Marlene. "Remember las' year when they had t'kill t'polar bear come sniffin' round up here?"

"Well," said Shirley, "they comes 'roun moi kitchen I'll get after'm wit' t'broom. So what you got on for suppah?"

This was the part Chris and I were waiting for. We had our own bear stories. What we didn't have was food.

"Oim makin' roast turkey and cheesecake. You?"

"Oi've got stuffed pork chops and lemon pie."

Chris looked down at the salvaged salami from which he'd been trimming furry green spots. I looked at the oil heater, where our sole half-loaf of waterlogged bread lay drying.

"Mmmmmmmmmmmm," we said in our best Homer Simpson voices. "Helens Falls."

Fast-forward nine years, and I was sitting in a half-century-old de Havilland Beaver flying down the rugged valley of the George River and heading for Helens Falls, an entirely accidental zigzag from a brook trout trip to Three Rivers Lodge in central Labrador.

As the story goes, Sammy Cantafio of Ungava Adventures invited Three Rivers partners Kevin Barry Junior and Robin Reeve to come visit Helens Falls with the idea of forming some sort of business relationship—an extra-cost option for sports who might want to fly north to Helens Falls to fish some of North America's best Atlantic salmon water or fly south to Three Rivers to fish some of North America's best brook trout water.

This all sounds properly businesslike until you factor in Marco Valcourt, who piloted the Three Rivers Beaver and subtly and perhaps underhandedly instigated this expedition, and Trina Wellman, who cooked at Helens Falls and on whom, unbeknownst to everyone including Trina, Marco had romantic designs.

And me? Well, I was just along for the ride—a last-minute seat-filler for Robin, who was recalled to Massachusetts to settle some business affairs.

Settlement? Thank you Mrs. Cheveley.

* * *

It's a long flight from Three Rivers to Helens Falls. We stopped en route to fish Arctic char on Mistastin Lake, a large asteroid-impact crater so sacred to the Innu that they can't even look at the small croissant-shaped island at its head. After a cold, wet afternoon of fishing for Arctic char, icing several to take back to Three Rivers, we flew on into the gray dusk to Lac Cananée, where we spent the night at a caribou camp Marco's father used to own. In the morning we topped off the Beaver's gas tanks from fifty-five-gallon drums by dipping with a five-gallon detergent pail and straining the gas through panty hose of unknown provenance, and then we flew off into the mist, skimming just beneath the clouds at three hundred feet above the unending Arctic landscape until we found the George River. For two hours we followed it downriver, turning left and right as the river willed, until finally we zoomed over the falls and past Cantafio's famous salmon camp that I had been longing to see for the past nine years.

Marco circled, scouting the swirling eddies below the falls for a smooth place to set down the Beaver, and as we pivoted on one wingtip I frantically filled my tattered notebook with adjectives in a vain attempt to capture the setting's sheer romance.

Helens Falls—sources differ on the presence or absence of an apostrophe, and some even dispute the possessive s altogether, perhaps alluding to the original Greek tragedy—are more a series of falls stretching over several miles than a single sharp drop, and the river looks less like standard-issue Atlantic salmon water than a high mountain trout stream somehow grown to the size of the Ohio or the Tennessee, flowing through as wild a country as you will find on this earth yet possessing a tender, almost delicate beauty that veils, but doesn't entirely conceal, a savage core.

We climbed the stairway from the roaring falls up onto the gravelly bench, past a cluster of neat frame cabins and into the magnetic dining room, which was as large and bright and comfortable as Chris and I had imagined it years ago while we were quietly starving in a weather-bound caribou camp. Inside, its picture windows looked out on a vista that could stop your heart.

From the kitchen emerged the smells of cooking that drew both bears and t'sports from far and wide, and then Trina—like the original Helen, a heart-stopper and voyage launcher in her own right—entered from the kitchen bearing a platter of sandwiches and mint-chocolate-chip brownies so rich you could happily infarct at the first bite. Trina didn't look like a typical northwoods camp cook, who tend to be as rugged, burly, and raw as bears; she looked like a ballerina, as refined and ethereal as her cinnamon rolls—a proper Helen of the Falls.

Kevin and I exchanged glances, understanding finally why Marco the Lothario and unrepentant gourmand had engineered this trip. But we weren't here, camp owner Sammy Cantafio reminded us, to ogle his cook and eat all his food. We were here to fish for salmon, or at least Kevin and I were—or at least I was, Kevin having business affairs to settle. So after a quick and elegant lunch we pushed off upriver and powered through the falls in a jut-jawed old freighter canoe through some of the most dramatically magnificent water you could ever hope to see.

* * *

The romantic thing about Atlantic salmon fishing is its utter uncertainty coupled with the wealth of unsupportable theories that attempt to explain the uncertainty. As serious anglers all know, Atlantic salmon don't eat anything in freshwater, but they do take flies—though not for reasons anyone entirely understands. This maddens the scientific wing of angler-dom just as it delights the romantically inclined. Discovering the precise why of the thing is to improve efficiency at the expense of sentiment. What begins as enigma becomes merely ant-like industry that crushes the thrill of surprise beneath a ream of informative instruction and relentlessly repeated activity.

I have fished Atlantic salmon a fair amount and know too well why they're called both the fish of kings and the fish of a thousand casts—the wild, exclusive water they inhabit and those wild, heart-stopping leaps you see just often enough to keep you coming back but not so often that you ever feel entitled. So I was more than a little surprised, my first afternoon on the George, to hook and land a couple of tail-walking eight-pound grilse and a fourteen-pound salmon as bright as a silver ingot, as well as to hook and not land two others in the ten- to twelve-pound range thanks to the brutal current and my wimpy seven-weight trout rod. And I was even less surprised the next morning to find the salmon completely indifferent to the fly they had wanted so badly the previous afternoon.

The river level didn't change. The weather, soft and misty and autumnal, didn't change. My persistent presentation of small dark wet flies didn't change. Only the salmon changed, and the mystery of why they suddenly changed is part of why we fish for them. Whatever is most difficult becomes most interesting, if you're doing it right. A properly romantic fly fisher doesn't want his fish to come easy; he wants them playing hard to get.

And they were. Once, imagining yesterday's teeming river somehow gone barren of fish, I waded onto a barbell-shaped boulder of pink and gray serpentine polished to glass by a current so overwhelming that it shot chest-high waves into my face, and a hen salmon close to three feet long swam across my bootlaces—a flashing silver heartthrob pursuing a hot date who ignored me as part of the landscape, the inevitable fate of all middle-aged men.

Young and handsome Marco—politely, cordially, but firmly rebuffed in his own great pursuit—shortly scored compensation in another when he landed a high-jumping male, bright from the sea and heading uphill from twenty pounds.

Kevin, too, tied into a couple of good fish, his first Atlantic salmon despite living his whole life in central Labrador. Finally my morning's drought was broken by a pity strike from an electrocuted grilse, and just as I released him it was time to head downriver, pile back into the Beaver, and set a course for home while stuffing ourselves along the way with a liberated pan of Trina's cinnamon rolls so light they nearly floated away. As did, for various reasons, our hearts.

As we buzzed the camp at Helens Falls, Marco waggling the old Beaver's wings like some madcap Waldo-Pepper barnstormer from the biplane days, I pressed my face against the window and wondered if I'd ever again see what I had waited so long to see and saw all too briefly.

* * *

Sometimes if you sit back and allow life to develop its own map for the future instead of trying to impose your own myopic views, things have a way of settling out, because a year and two weeks later on a sunny morning in late August, I was climbing out of an Air Inuit Twin Otter and heading down the trail from the airstrip toward Helens Falls. This time I was going salmon fishing not for an afternoon and a morning but for a whole week thanks to a midwinter invitation from Sammy and a fortuitous cavity in my editorial calendar the very week he had free.

Trina waited in the dining room dispensing hugs and brownies, and we—we being two retired doctors from New Jersey, a real-estate guy from Manhattan and another from Boston who were traveling as a pack and had been here before, and two guys from New Brunswick who can only be described as salmon bums and hadn't been here before—sat down to eat, fill out the paperwork for licenses, and engage in the usual pregame banter of fish camp.

Then it was into the canoes, up the river, and back into the rhythmic waltz of Atlantic salmon fishing: cast, cast, cast, *step-step-step*; cast, cast, cast, *step-step-step*. *Whaaaaaaaaang*!

For such an immense river, the George is surprisingly easy to fish. Most of the salmon lie close to the bank; only a few lies require casts longer than fifty feet, and most can be covered with a thirty-foot lob. Only a few pools require deft wading, and many can be fished in knee boots. It's a bit of a hike to the top of the falls and the last pool, but the first pool is only ten feet from the boat landing. In many ways, the George is almost remedial salmon fishing.

Not that this helped us catch fish our first afternoon. Frenchy—one of the New Brunswick salmon bums who lives on the Miramichi and fishes it daily—landed a good one using a very large and flashy fly, a counterintuitive approach for this river, where the fish are said to prefer small dark flies, riffle-hitched and waked like water-skiers. But then, with Atlantic salmon, slavishly following conventional science is only wise if sentiment fails to direct you elsewhere.

The trouble, as usual, was the weather: bright and warm and unapologetically sunny, which for salmon fishing is good news but for salmon catching isn't. What we wanted were clouds and drizzle and wind, and as Marco the pilot found out last year, when you really want something is exactly when you don't get it.

* * *

Yet we didn't suffer for salmon over the warm and sunny week. Everyone caught fish, from Peter, who was fishing for only the second week of his life, to Frenchy—he insists on being called that, honest—who has fished virtually every week of his life.

I, who fish a fair amount, caught two grilse in the eight-pound range right off by riffle-hitching a small Black Bear-Green Butt through the pocket water near the bank. To see me in action with that first grilse, however, you would never believe I've fished a day in my life.

Sammy, who was guiding me—or interfering with me or amusing himself with me, depending on your viewpoint—was laughing too hard to breathe as the fish, brought in too hot and too soon, set about amusing himself with me, too. I reached for his tail, and he darted between my legs and jumped head-high behind me. When I reached again for his tail he darted back through my legs and jumped head-high in front of me. Just as he was making his third pass through my legs, crossing the tee on the clove hitch, Sammy grabbed him by the tail and prevented what might have been the first hog-tying of a salmon fisher by a salmon in angling history.

After lunch Sammy and I took the canoe across the river to the east bank and walked up the old portage trail, a path followed by centuries of caribou and caribou-hunting Inuit and, a hundred years ago that very August, by a young woman from Ontario called Mina Benson Hubbard.

Back in 1903, Leonidas Hubbard, a New York-based editor for *Outing* magazine, tried to find these falls and thence Ungava Bay in a long canoe expedition by following much the same route from Labrador that we flew last year in Marco's Beaver. Only Hubbard's expedition didn't make it to the George. Hubbard took a wrong turn in the braid of channels leading from Northwest River into Michikamau Lake and starved to death. He left behind, back in the States, a young wife.

Mina Hubbard felt that her husband and his sense of direction had been unfairly maligned in *Lure of the Labrador Wild*, a book written by another expedition member, Dillon Wallace, and so in 1905 she set out to make things right by completing her husband's expedition to chart the inland path from coastal Labrador to Ungava Bay. Moreover, she did so while racing a parallel expedition led by Wallace.

And she won, leading the expedition the whole way and writing, in 1908, a remarkable book called *A Woman's Way Through Unknown Labrador*, and describing for the very first time this land of terrible beauty.

"And still the river roared on down through its narrow valley, at Helen Falls dropping by wild and tempestuous cascades, and then by almost equally wild rapids, to a mile below where it shoots out into an expansion with such terrific force as to keep this great rush of water above the general level for some distance out into the lake. Here we made the longest portage of the journey down the George River, carrying the stuff one and a quarter mile."

Walking along this trail a century later, I found it difficult to think about anything except Mrs. Hubbard and the kind of romance that will spur a young woman to lead an expedition through untracked land at a time when society compressed young women into roles typically allowing no leadership at all.

At least it was difficult to think about anything else until the portage trail led back down to the river, with a whole new array of pools and seams holding great salmon awaiting their own

romantic spur to goad them out into the current and on upstream
to fulfill their biological imperatives.

And yet we didn't catch a thing, Sammy and I, although we
saw plenty of fish. But with the river so high, we couldn't get a
good drift or wade out to the right spots on this eastern shore, as
geologically and topographically different from the west bank as
though the George were an ocean separating two continents.

It fell to Frenchy and Steve, on their last day and with water levels down a couple of feet, to come fish the east bank's tough pools
and to take five bright salmon, including the fish of the week, an
eighteen-pounder that tail-walked like a tarpon, and to lose the
fish of the year, a twenty-five-pounder, according to Chris the
guide, that bulldogged Steve for half an hour before finally disappearing downstream—trailing his entire fly line.

As for my last day, unattended and wandering beneath a welcome new veil of clouds, I decided that after a week of waking
riffle-hitched wet flies in the glaring sun and catching two or
three eight-pound grilse each day—and getting skunked yesterday—that I ought to diverge from accepted science and rely
entirely on sentiment.

I opened my fly box and spied in a dusty corner an electric
green cigar with a hackle wound through it that looked less like
a proper fishing fly than like something ejected from the Jolly
Green Giant's nostril: a small Green Machine leftover from a trip
to the Miramichi.

After lunch I knotted one on, greased it to float, and headed for
the topmost pool. On the third swing, a fourteen-pound cockfish
nailed it and tore the pool to foam. As I tweezed out the fly and
watched the salmon melt away, I remember thinking: *All right. I'm
onto something here.*

Which of course meant that I wasn't, as for the next hour I
waked the Green Machine across splendid water without one pull.
But at least I had the whole river to myself with Frenchy and Steve
on the east bank, Sammy off in the Cessna to Kuujjuaq to attend
to business, and everyone else gone char fishing in the nearby Ford
River. With no salmon showing I reverted to type and trout fished

my way down to the canoe, dead-drifting the little Green Machine in all the places I would be if I were a brook trout.

And there they were. By the time I reached the canoe I'd taken better than a dozen bright orange brookies to twenty inches and a bonus grilse of maybe six pounds. Down at the boat pool at a dark little eddy within a foot of shore, I cast toward a perfect brook trout lie, and the instant the fly hit the water a twelve-pound salmon plucked it from the surface and rocketed across the river.

After releasing him and resting the pool—well, resting me, more accurately, as the salmon was fresh from the sea and wild as a wolf—I cast again to the same spot, and five salmon rose simultaneously for the fly. An eight-pound grilse got there first, but as he somersaulted across the pool and came to hand, fiercely snapping and freshly peppered with sea lice, it was hard to be disappointed even though he barely won the race for the fly against three salmon around twelve pounds and another that easily bested twenty, according to my notebook—though in my sleepless dreams he's gaining weight by the week.

And in those same dreams I envision somehow engineering a return to Helens Falls, and in this dream I do everything right. I always arrive in the dining room just as Trina's evening platter of gravlax makes its first appearance and before it makes its rapid disappearance, and when we see bears they're always picturesquely sequestered on the far side of the river. I always cast perfectly and fish my drifts precisely. I choose the right fly by knowing my quarry's mind and not by simply following conventional wisdom or my own unsubstantiated whims. I land what I hook and hook what I cast to, and it's always the biggest fish that takes my fly. And when I cleanly release those big salmon they all swim away unmarred, psychically or psychologically, by the experience.

In my dreams of Helens Falls, sentiment and science combine to form the very core of romance, and there is no talk anywhere of a settlement.

Of course that's how I fish in my dreams, not in real life. For an honest assessment of my fishing I must borrow a line from Mrs.

Cheveley's polar opposite, brave Mina Hubbard, "The work was imperfectly done, yet I did what I could."

* * *

"I did what I could." It's such a keen, useful phrase from an intrepid soul like brave Mina Hubbard and such self-important bloat from that most un-useful of all possible parasites, a professional fish-writer. And yet . . .

Once upon a time I went to Helens Falls in northern Ungava, and I did something worthwhile, because eight years after my last visit there I received an e-mail from Trina. She wrote:

> I'm sure you don't remember me. I used to work as a cook at the beautiful Helens Falls salmon camp on the George River in Quebec, Canada. You visited us there in 2005 and later wrote an article for *Gray Sporting Journal* called "Romancing the Falls." If you remember this, then you must remember the Beaver pilot who flew you there, Marco Valcourt. The article was great, by the way. I read it a few months after it was published and thought it was quite flattering, especially the part that suggested Marco had romantic designs on the cook. To make a long story short, Marco and I started dating in the spring of 2008, we fell very much in love, which was easy because you spilled the beans about our love through writing this article. I never thought it could be possible for a guy like Marco to like me, but after reading your article I did, and it helped to move things to another level for us: Ha!
>
> I thank you for that. Your article has been such a big part of my love story with Marco that I've shared it with *many* people we've met over these past five and a half years. Although, today, I'm saddened to the depths of my being to tell you that Marco has passed away. He died suddenly on September 20, 2013, of a massive heart attack, when we were both working together at a caribou camp in northern Quebec. I just ordered a copy of Gray's Feb/March 2006 issue to have in my

safekeeping your wonderfully written article that I will keep with me forever in memory of my beautiful Marco. So thank you so much for that. I believe if it weren't for your article I may never have believed he could have loved me and I possibly would have missed out on the absolute best part of my life, which was spent with him.

Thank you,
Trina

9. *Gros Saumon, Petite Rivières*

T HE EARTH IS A BEAUTIFUL PLACE, BUT SOME places are more beautiful than others: Maine's Penobscot Bay, East Tennessee's Cherokee National Forest, Montana's Madison River Valley, Scotland's Grampian Mountains, Quebec's Gaspé Peninsula. I live on the first, was born and raised near the second, and the others I visit as often as I can.

So I needed little convincing when my friend C. D. Clarke suggested we spend a prime chunk of June salmon fishing the lovely little rivers that vein the outermost end of the Gaspé. We'd meet in the parking lot of the York-Dartmouth-St-Jean ZEC, bum around on our own for a few days, and then head down the coast to the Malbaie River Lodge near the tourist magnet of Percé with its famous limestone arch, knick-knackeries, and whale-watching vacationers wearing cable-knit sweaters bedaubed with salt spray and *fruits de mer.*

And we very nearly did meet in the parking lot of the regional salmon-fisheries office, except that I'd lost track of time driving from New Brunswick, where my cell phone helpfully reset itself to Atlantic Time from Eastern Time, into Quebec, where my cell phone didn't speak French and didn't realize that French-speaking Quebec had found yet another way to diverge from English-speaking Atlantic Canada by adhering to Eastern Time.

So when I arrived at the rendezvous at the agreed-upon hour there was no C. D. to be seen, and when one whole hour and half of another had crawled past the agreed-upon hour and the skies grew ever darker and my eyes ever heavier and my patience ever thinner, I slunk off to the familiar old Motel Adams visible from the ZEC's parking lot and went to sleep.

Or very nearly. Because before I'd done much more than wash off ten hours of road grime and slide beneath the covers, there came a great whacking and hallooing at the door, and there was C. D., looking as always just like Clark Kent and talking a mile a minute about the great salmon he'd rolled at sunset on the York and how he'd been loath to tear himself away from the first actively interested fish he'd seen on a very hot, very sunny, and very ungenerous day, and he figured that I'd figure he was into fish and thus wouldn't mind his being a half-hour or so late, although neither of us had yet figured out why I kept insisting he was an hour and a half late.

And besides, he reminded me, it wasn't as though I'd never been late to one of these long-range meet ups. Although the first time, meeting at a barn dance high in the Chilean Andes, wasn't my fault so much as it was the airline's fault—if airline is the right word for an aging twin-screw Cessna with an eagle-faced Incan teenager in the pilot's seat. And the second time, meeting at the train station in Inverness, Scotland, wasn't my fault so much as it was British Rail's fault. I mean, it's *always* British Rail's fault, isn't it?

But the next morning, meeting again at the ZEC office in the pleasantly un-touristy little village of Gaspé, being late was my fault because I hadn't yet figured out that I'd left a whole hour lying in the middle of the bridge that crosses the Matapédia River from New Brunswick onto Quebec's beautiful Gaspé Peninsula.

Beauty is in the eye of the beholder, of course. Although writers are always gushing on and on about the beauty of this and the beauty of that, beauty isn't something words successfully capture. So while I struggle to describe objects of a different kind of beauty

to the fidgety young woman behind the counter in Tim Hortons—
"duh caffy oh lay, uh, grandy, uh, et un bignay, hmmmmm, un petty
pain, hmmmmm, un crossant du chockolatt. Pardone? Uhhhh,
all three, er, uh, (holding up three fingers) toot twa. Bone!"—and
while C. D. paces back and forth in the ZEC parking lot pointedly
looking at his watch, I invite you to Google C. D. Clarke to see
what I mean by the Gaspé's beauty. Because C. D. is an artist, and
artists don't describe beauty: they create beauty *from* beauty.

C. D. had already created one beautiful thing today, or at least
he'd lucked into it, which for an artist is pretty much the same
thing. He'd entered our names in the ZEC's forty-eight-hour lottery, and we'd drawn Beat Three on the York—two gorgeous, picture-perfect pools, Bluff and Mississippi, for two rods only, and
the two rods only were us.

For folks unfamiliar with Quebec's idiosyncratic approach to
salmon fishing, each salmon river, or in some cases a group of
rivers, is controlled by a local conservation organization called a
ZEC—Controlled Exploitation Zone, to reverse it into English.
The ZECs manage both the fish and the fisheries and apportion
access to prime water via annual preseason lotteries, forty-eight-
hour lotteries, and daily draws on unlimited water. Everyone has
an equal chance, more or less, at the hotspots, and not all the
hotspots are on the limited sections.

Although it's home to some of Quebec's largest salmon, the
York looks like a medium-sized trout stream, never more than
an easy fly-cast across. Its banks are heavily forested with cedar,
spruce, aspen and pine, and it cuts through the kind of rugged
mountains you'd expect to find at the head of the Appalachian
spine. Along its thirty-eight-mile length of fishable water are seventy named pools divided into eleven sectors, with seven limited
to preseason or forty-eight-hour lottery winners and four sectors
unrestricted and available by day ticket. As is the case throughout
Quebec, guides aren't required for visiting anglers, though if you
don't know the country they are recommended.

It being my fifty-seventh birthday and all, I took first pass and
fished very rustily and unsuccessfully down through the pool. I

saw one salmon of about twelve pounds leaping in that scoping-
out-the-terrestrial-world way they have, but I was utterly unable to
get him to scope out my Green Machine, which had been good to
me before on the George, the Miramichi, Quebec's North Shore,
the Gaspé, and even in Scotland. And then C. D. started in with
his favorite Gaspé fly, a silver-bodied white Muddler originated by
one of Quebec's most experienced salmon guides, Austin Clark,
head guide at Malbaie River Lodge.

At the head of the pool I had just fished, C. D.'s line stopped in
its third drift and tightened. C. D. lifted and then, as the cliché
goes, the battle was joined. At first we thought it was the twelve-
pounder that spurned my Green Machine, but over the next half
hour of decidedly un-salmon-like behavior, it steadily grew in
size. It didn't jump. It didn't roll. It simply powered upstream
and peeled off all C. D.'s line then most of his backing, with rod-
wielding C. D. and camera-wielding me splashing along in its
wake.

Usually, hooking an Atlantic salmon is like hanging onto a
jet-ski. Not this salmon. It was more like being towed by a tugboat. When he finally began to roll and we could bring him into
shallow water to tail him, I found I couldn't lift him by the tail
with one hand. When we measured him against the rod then later
measured the rod, we found he slightly exceeded forty inches and,
extrapolating, likely exceeded thirty pounds. He was a marvelous
gift from the river for C. D., though it was *my* birthday.

Later I fished down through the pool again and rolled the
same twelve-pounder repeatedly. He'd splash at the fly in the
streamy water at the head of the pool, but he wouldn't take a
Green Machine, a borrowed White Muddler, or even a desperation Butterfly. He'd rise to them as they swung past his lie, but he
wouldn't open his mouth, which I thought ungenerous behavior
on a person's birthday.

I continued fishing while C. D. set up his easel and painted
Bluff Pool in all its iridescent glory, the early summer wildflow-
ers lining its banks just beginning to pop, while C. D.'s Brittanys,
Winchester and Remington, the grandson and great-grandson of

author Ben O. Williams's famous bird dog Winston, sat patiently with their matching red tethers while supervising our fishing and briefly being astonished that a large sleek otter could swim upstream on his own fishing expedition without including two very good dogs in the adventure.

We were both fishing light spey rods, I should mention, not because this little river you can cast across with a four-weight requires them but because they allow you to cover more water with less effort. When you watch someone who knows what they're doing, the spey rod's advantages quickly become evident. There is no wasted effort; the fly is always in the water fishing and not whistling back and forth to gain velocity, and there are few current seams the long rod can't mend your fly into or out of. The constant changes of direction that would require a false cast or two with a nine-foot single-hander need only a nudge with a twelve-foot spey rod.

When the light finally left the water and C. D. had finished his painting, we resumed fishing in earnest by rotating through the pools and trying different flies—some of them more effective than others at momentarily discouraging the leaping salmon from further leaping—but none proved effective at encouraging them to take.

Still, who could complain about an entire day on two private pools on one of North America's best salmon rivers with fish to see, fish to cast to, and one fish of a lifetime landed? Certainly not anyone who's spent much time fishing for Atlantic salmon. The fish of a thousand casts is, in my experience, more like the fish of ten thousand casts. Yet I can't stop fishing for them or thinking about fishing for them or planning to fish for them or dreaming about them throughout countless sleepless nights. I'd do this even if I knew I'd never catch another. Atlantic salmon fishing has all the symptoms of a disease, one of those expensively terminal affairs that entertains your doctor, infuriates your insurer, and ruins your family.

The next day, freshly supplied with caffeine and empty calories at Tim Hortons, we bought day tickets for the unlimited water and began at Petite Saumon on the York, a lovely bit of bendy river that sees the first fish up from the sea and which proved, beneath a searing sun and blow-dryer winds, utterly barren. Seeking shelter from the elements and cooler water, we migrated upstream after lunch to Gary Pool, a series of sharp ledge drops in a nearly sunless canyon of layered shale, which looked like a cross-section of a very large and very old Tim Hortons croissant, with one pool deep enough to submerge a loaded log truck.

Gary is a five-minute trot downhill from the road and a twenty-minute trudge back uphill to the car. Like the other pools managed by the Gaspé ZEC, it's clearly labeled with good parking, a clean outhouse, picnic tables, and stairs with railings so geezers like me can hobble down to the river.

Just above the falls at the head of the pool I hung a nice salmon around fifteen pounds that rolled for a waking Green Machine and then a few casts later enthusiastically ate a borrowed White Muddler, but he was quickly over the falls and porpoising downstream like Flipper pursued by Orca, and I couldn't hold him in the current with a fifteen-pound leader, nor could I follow him down the bank without soaring off in airborne pursuit like Peter Pan. Forty-five exciting seconds passed before my fly reel's spool began to peek from beneath the backing, and I snubbed the line and broke him off.

I could have held him, maybe, with a thirty-pound leader and a big hook buried in bone. But it would have been a cruel battle against those falls, one he likely wouldn't have survived. In these troubled times, when Atlantic salmon populations are everywhere imperiled, I would far rather lose a salmon than *lose* a salmon, if you know what I mean.

* * *

Finally, C. D. and I migrated down the coast from our rented caravan in a campground near the town of Gaspé to our official destination of the Malbaie River Lodge, and after settling in and gorging on brilliant Gaspésian cuisine we headed back up to the

York with guide Gordy Drody. We cast and cast and cast and cast in stifling heat and threatening thunderstorms and didn't see a fish all day.

The next day, a guest called Ken and I had exactly the opposite experience at Falls Pool on the Dartmouth while guided by young Draper Clark, Austin's son. Under a cold, steady rain and a colored, rising river, we saw an almost endless parade of fish, none of which we could manage to catch, of course, but at least we were seeing them—as many as four dozen fish to thirty pounds or better cycling through the pool. I had three or four follows and two or three pulls, and that was that. Ken, a well-experienced steelheader from Oregon on his first Atlantic salmon expedition, didn't get that.

But fish were jumping and leaping and rolling as far as we could see, and we showed them every salmon fly we possessed. Then we broke into Ken's steelhead flies, but the fish refused even these novelty items, the like of which I will bet real money those fish had never seen or even suspected.

Other folks at the lodge did varying degrees of well, however. With his favorite White Muddler, C. D. had a thirty-two-pounder, grudgingly and exactingly measured by his acerbic guide, and a fifteen-pounder on a dry fly with a cane rod, which goes into a whole different level of classic salmon fishing. Two other guys hooked five and landed three, which left Ken and myself in sole ownership of the daily skunk. But someone must excel.

The next day I made up for it—or at least lodge-owner Bill Greiner saw that I made up for it by delivering me and Joe, who comes from Maryland to the Gaspé for a couple of weeks each summer, to Maison Blanc high up on the York.

Up here the river transforms into a Rocky Mountain Trout Stream with regulation riffles and runs familiarly rimmed with coniferous spires. But I've never fished a Rocky Mountain trout stream where my first fish of the day, a ten-pounder that rose beautifully to a dead-drifted Bomber, is considered small potatoes. Such power, such grace, such sheer dogged athleticism. It makes you wonder how anyone handles one of this river's big fish.

And there are very big fish in these little Gaspé rivers, out of all proportion to their size. This, and the undiluted beauty of the surrounding country, forms the core of the Gaspé's charm.

When you catch fish like these Atlantic salmon, whether great hulking thirty-pounders or my lithe little ten-pounder, you don't care how many thousand casts go unrequited just as long as there's a chance at one. For a week or more of constant fishing, even one is enough reward—particularly on the dry fly with a savage take from that lobster-claw mouth and that head-shaking run and those trademark Atlantic salmon leaps that defy gravity and physics and twist in the sun like *le grand finis* in the Cirque du Soleil.

Twenty minutes later, in the same riffly run, Joe connected with a twelve-pounder on his White Muddler—another running, dashing, leaping fish that was improbably large in this intimate setting. Then we moved down into the main pool, broad and deep and absolutely stiff with salmon of all sizes, overseen by the ZEC guardian's tiny white cabin that watches over the pool and supplies its name.

Bill and I perched on the bluff overlooking the pool and watched Joe toss increasingly bizarre flies into the deep water beneath our feet. Joe was occasionally moving fish and once got a savage follow from two fish well northward of twenty pounds and one approaching forty. It looked less like a documentary on the quiet sport of fly-fishing and more like one of those Discovery Channel specials about tiger sharks slaughtering albatross in the surf; the salmon pursued the racing fly right to his rod tip and looked as though they meant to drag Joe back into the depths. One of them was certainly big enough.

After lunch, with Bill puppeteering the attack from above, Joe finally hit the right stripping speed—fast enough to tempt the salmon up from the depths but slow enough so they'd expend the energy to try and catch the fly—and he landed another twelve-pounder.

Meanwhile, I fished the swirly seam of water chuting into the pool with my favorite Atlantic salmon rig, a riffle-hitched Green Machine, and inadvertently connected with one of the White

House Swine, the oversized salmon that haunt the pool's depths and sometimes move up into the shallow riffles from, I'm guessing, vague feelings of ennui.

As Bill realized what I'd gotten myself into, he crossed the river to assist. Over the next half hour we alternated between grasping the tippet, reaching for the tail, and looking anxiously as bare metal began peeking again through the last turns of backing. A half-mile downstream, the leader wrapped around a pile of beaver cuttings with Bill and I standing a forearm's length away, and we watched the hook pull free and the salmon lurch back into the depths. It was longer from dorsal to tail than my ten-pounder had been from nose to tail. Were it not for the fear of the post-event growth that affects all lost fish and most caught ones, I'd call it an honest thirty pounds and probably closer to thirty-five. By next year I might be able to boost it to forty, but that's as far as self-delusion will safely take me.

Later in the afternoon, as Joe and Bill pestered the pool pigs with stripped flies, I took another nice salmon on a hitched Green Machine—a series of rough-and-tumble into-the-backing runs, a quick hustle down the bank to get him into deeper water, and a head-shaking jump into the rays of a magazine-cover searchlight bursting through the clouds. I tailed and released him and estimated him at fourteen pounds, decidedly less than half the size of the earlier fish but somehow more satisfying because it was quickly landed and released unscathed, all by myself with no adult supervision.

The day ended as beautifully as it began, with a sunset the color of smoked salmon and an enormous fall of sherry spinners. Joe took a twenty-pound salmon on his third cast from the top pool: beautifully caught, beautifully played, and beautifully released, a perfect end for a perfect day.

* * *

The next day was far more typical of Atlantic salmon fishing than the previous day's slice of perfection—though, like all days spent fishing, it had its own version of perfect.

The luck of the draw sent C. D. and me back to Falls Pool on the Dartmouth on a misty, cool, and promising day. A few salmon hung at the pool's tail-out when we arrived, and as the day progressed, the pool slowly and steadily filled with salmon—new fish moving in from downriver and old fish dropping down from their attempts to vault the falls but thwarted by the low water. Just like the fishermen.

By evening more than two dozen salmon were in the pool—rolling, leaping, putting on a Discovery Channel salmon show, and doing everything but taking flies. Not that the rods in the pool didn't show them plenty. There were six of us: C. D. and me, a fellow from Vermont staying in a nearby campground, and a friendly family from Quebec City that comes every year. The fish ranged from parr and grilse to great hulking monsters surpassing thirty pounds with the odd migrating lamprey slithering through the streamside boulders to round out the biology exhibit.

Our flies drifted over the salmon, through them, past them, in front of their very noses, and the best anyone got was a semi-curious follow on a Magog Smelt stripped lightning fast.

Just at dusk, the pool turned active with fish boiling everywhere, though still not at flies; just those imaginary stimuli that seem related to the invisible beings in the walls at which cats disturbingly stare.

Finally C. D. , his daily painting drying beneath an umbrella in the soft mist, drifted a White Muddler through the tail-out and briefly connected with a good salmon that tentatively took the fly and unfairly chose to swim toward its would-be captor rather than fleeing in hook-setting terror as the literature implies it ought.

Though the fish was lost, or more accurately never gathered, the event was seen for what it was: a major success on a day that promised everything but delivered nothing—except allowing us to spend daylight to dark doing something beautiful in a pleasant spot with people who shared common interests, goals, and philosophical acceptances of defeat.

And that's how the rest of the week went, pretty much. C. D. caught another six or eight fish in the St-Jean and the Grande, and I caught one—a bright twelve-pounder that ate a riffle-hitched Silver Doctor in Wild Rose Pool on the icy St-Jean—and hooked and lost another at Lady Mary in the St-Jean and one in the intimidating rapids above the falls on the Dartmouth.

In the evenings we sat around the dinner table or the fireplace at Malbaie sharing our interests and goals, our philosophical acceptances of defeat, and our occasional modest victories.

It was peaceful and exciting, restful and exhausting, frustrating and invigorating, and very occasionally triumphant. It was, above all else, beautiful, because it was Atlantic salmon fishing.

10. *Senatorial Salmon*

THE SENATOR ISN'T A REAL SENATOR—NEITHER the American variety, which are electorally replaceable, nor the Canadian variety, which the Governor General appoints provided they know somebody who knows somebody and own four thousand dollars worth of real estate in their home province.

New Brunswick isn't The Senator's home province, but it might as well be, because as soon as the salmon swim home from Greenland, The Senator leaves his home in Toronto and heads for his camp on a tributary of the Miramichi. There he stays until salmon fishing fades into woodcock and grouse hunting, then he stays for that, too.

Which makes The Senator a sort of hero for those of us who, through an injudicious choice of parents or a lack of entrepreneurial fervor, cannot aspire to a life of sporting leisure in the grand manner of, say, a Senator.

I've had only passing interactions with senators—hand-shaking politicians trolling for votes, hotdogs and Cokes and free-form Maine recollections with Senator Edmund Muskie at Dulles Airport some years ago when he joined a friend and I, who addressed him not as Senator but as Governor Muskie, which at one time in Maine he was.

Still, I feel I know the senatorial genus. Who doesn't? We see them every day on TV earnestly seeking someone else's parade to lead, thwart, or divert in the hopes of elevating themselves and eradicating their opponents.

This flexibility of opinions isn't a modern innovation. From their earliest days in ancient Rome, senators were ever thus. If on Monday you announce that children are our future and we must make their world a better place and on Wednesday you vote to cut education subsidies and permit coal-mining conglomerates to dump mountaintops into trout streams that feed those children's drinking water, you need opinion-flexibility by the truckload.

So I'm not saying The Senator couldn't be a senator. I'm just saying that so far he's kept his flexible opinions off the public stage and, for better or worse, saved them up for his friends. Which I had somehow become after we fished together at Helens Falls one summer and had fished with here on the Miramichi a few summers later on my way home from the Gaspé.

And so after a wintertime exchange of e-mails, I collected fellow fish-writer John Gierach on a sunny June morning at the Bangor airport, and we headed north to acquaint ourselves with The Senator's most recent opinions—not to mention borrow his beds, fish his water, eat his food, and generally sponge off him as much as the fish-writer market would bear.

After driving half the length of Maine and three-quarters the length of New Brunswick, we wandered off onto a skein of unmarked dirt roads, and a few hours before sundown we were met by The Senator and Frenchy—his longtime guide, camp manager, major domo, grill chef, spiritual adviser, facilitator, enabler, all-around bad influence, and originator of The Senator's *nom de guerre*. We were also met with a tableful of iced Prince Edward Island oysters and lobster sushi and Ginjō-shu Sake served in little wooden boxes, and the welcome news that fresh salmon were wandering up from the sea.

John, as he always does, wanted to wander around in waders privately to get the feel of a new-to-him river, so Frenchy and I hit the camp pool in his canoe. On the second drop I hooked a small grilse that leapt and tail-walked its merry way back and forth across the river.

Had it been a biologically identical Maine landlocked salmon and not a Miramichi grilse, his size and acrobatic antics would have triggered a high-fiving celebration followed by a much-photographed release. As a five-pound first-timer fresh in from the sea, a Roman thumbs-down from The Senator shunted him to supper.

During supper we learned much from The Senator, including his theory that the United States had adopted intolerant views at sharp variance with those of our founding fathers and the 6.494 billion planetary residents who don't live in the States (no comment), his prediction that the United States would never elect a center-left black man as president (which proved to be incorrect), and that our supercharged economy was a flammable vapor one spark away from engulfing the world (which became correct in spades a year later). Frenchy, having a more retail vision of international politics and economics, noted that at his wintertime home in the Philippines he'd hired an attractive new umbrella girl to walk about the golf course and shade him from the rays.

After a night of tossing, turning, and attempting to banish the image of Frenchy being followed around a Philippines golf course by whatever an umbrella girl might be, we geared up for fishing and wondered whether The Senator was coming, but Frenchy said No because the river was high and it looked like rain. And so John and I drove off to Sunny Corner to meet First Nations guide Betty Ward, then we headed over to the Mi'kmaq tribal water on the Little Southwest within drumming distance of the Metepenagiag Lodge, where Betty works and where, a few years before, I'd had dinner with not just an actual Senator but a couple of actual tribal Chiefs and the Governor of New Brunswick. Wading tight against a brushy bank in very high water, I lost a nice one and John landed one around ten pounds and lost another, which wasn't too shabby considering the high water. With the hypnotic rhythm of spey-casting teaming with the lodge's hypnotic drumming and Betty's friendly ways, the cool drizzly day glowed warm and softly spiritual.

But as we dined that night in The Senator's screened porch overlooking the river, the soft spiritual rain flogged itself into a peevish Old Testament patriarch disappointed with his offspring. And so the next morning, with bleary eyes all around and wading off the table, we trailered Frenchy's big Sharpe canoe downriver and met his friend Buddy Silliker and his big Sharpe. We motored upriver in a downpour with the river rising an inch an hour and bringing all sorts of forensically entertaining flotsam, from leaves and twigs to logs and lawn furniture to a flotilla of bright yellow balloons forlornly lettered *Happy Birthday*. Still, I managed a six-pound grilse and hung two good salmon on the dangle and rolled two more. John, fishing with Frenchy, did, if I remember correctly, a little better or perhaps a little worse.

The next day brought tropical downpours that bulged the river far beyond its banks, and we bagged the scheduled float trip and declared a camp day, with reading and talking and eating and drinking, and learning more of The Senator's opinions and growing a bit uncomfortable.

If you've traveled abroad much over the past decade or so, you'll know what I mean. It isn't that we Americans don't all know that daddy has gambled away the family fortune and taken to secret drinking, busting up the furniture, and trodding over the neighbors' petunias, or that mama is addicted to credit cards, painkillers, and unfortunate stretch pants or that little sister is being entrepreneurial on street corners in ways we wish she wouldn't. It's just that we don't especially enjoy hearing about these things from outside the family. Thus confronted, we can only nod and painfully smile and wish we were elsewhere.

But the next day brought sun and warmth and a new light, with the river still in legitimate spate yet a full foot and a half down since supper. And so we hit the Sharpes again and saw not another soul along the entire Northwest Miramichi despite it being Canada Day, which used to be called Dominion Day before a houseful of pressured senators deemed it excessively confrontational. This time I fished with Frenchy, and I found another facet of my opinions being challenged—not by politics or religion or pseudo-retro-Puritanism versus continental/Canadian amorality but by that most divisive of all faiths: What Fly?

On the fly front, I'm a presentationist. Experience has convinced me that with Atlantic salmon the drift is all-important, and it rarely matters what fly you use so long as it's a Green Machine between size eight and ten with a tail made of six short strands of Pearl Flashabou and five small wisps of white calf tail, not too crinkly.

Frenchy indulged my faith just long enough to point out that I was fishing prime water and not raising a fish, and with the river so high I might want to adapt my beliefs to his reality. I nodded, so from the depths of his contrarian fly box came a Buck Bug the size of a ten-dollar cigar and a Butterfly the size of a chickadee.

I told Frenchy I hadn't realized bluefin tuna came this far upriver, but he said that outrageously violating public opinions is the only way to toll up salmon in a river so determined to flood, so I tied on the giant Butterfly and cast it out. The creature *whop-whopped* through the air like a boomerang and hit the water with a great *sploink*, and on its second Mothra-meets-Rodan swing a nice salmon charged from the swirling black water and ate it like a lobster puff. The rest of the week John and I swapped off with Frenchy and Buddy and, continuing to fish these heathen monster flies, caught a fair number of salmon in roiling water no one else was even bothering to fish.

That The Senator wasn't bothering to fish was a trifle disturbing—I mean, how can you let one of the world's great salmon rivers run through your front yard without fishing it every waking minute? But the nice thing about living on a river is that you don't *have* to fish it every waking minute, and if the weather is ugly or the fishing slow or the floods bring flotillas of lawn furniture and birthday balloons, you can simply sit on your porch and pour another platinum-plated sake, read the *Globe and Mail*, and conclude that the proper course through life is all things in moderation—even fishing.

And when the day dawns bright and the fish are jumping and the warblers are warbling, you can pick up your rod and go out for a while to fish a reasonable fly in a reasonable way to reasonable fish and find life never better.

At least that's what The Senator did the day we left. When we got home, an e-mail from Frenchy read, "Four big grilse and a large salmon from the camp pool between lunch and supper." I'll bet it was a really splendid supper, too.

11. *My Life as a Dog*

Aᴠᴛᴇʀ ᴛʜᴇ ᴜsᴜᴀʟ ᴜɴᴇᴠᴇɴᴛғᴜʟ Fɪʀsᴛ Aɪʀ flight from Montreal in a spic-and-span 727 half full of passengers and half full of freight, we left Kuujjuaq, Nunavik, in a low-flying Air Inuit Twin Otter containing the usual assortment of middle-aged humanity serenely observing the scenery and three young bird dogs frantic to hang their heads out the windows and inhale it.

An hour later, the plane whomped onto the gravel landing strip at Diana Lake Lodge some forty miles northwest of town, and we humans wandered around with our hands in our pockets while the dogs hit the tundra in a dead run. By the time we had reasserted individual ownership of our identical green duffels, the dogs had sniffed, licked, tasted, and peed on every inch of ground as far as the eye could see. Drifting downwind came the sound of tinkling bells and the unmistakable *whutter* of wings. If you replace Buck with pointers and Brittany spaniels and the beckoning wolf pack with ptarmigan, it was just like *The Call of the Wild*.

The wild called me north to fish, of course. The wild is forever calling me north to fish. To misappropriate a phrase from Henry David Thoreau, "I am confined to this theme by the narrowness of my experience." But when my friend Danny Legere said he was bringing his shotgun, I didn't fully appreciate what this might mean.

I should have. Our driver's licenses say I'm senior by two years, but a decade or so earlier we had strapped kick boats and waders and gear to our backs and climbed a Maine mountain, where a glaciological miscalculation left behind a very nice brook trout pond, and when we arrived at the top he was younger than me by at least seven years. At the time I hadn't understood what this meant, either.

But enlightenment comes to he who waits, or something like that, and it was while trudging across the tundra with rod in hand and pack on back while returning from a stretch of river that lodge owner, bush pilot, and raconteur Joe Stefanski called Seven Mile Falls—by which he meant it was seven miles long and a seven-mile walk there and back—that I began to wonder if that seven-year difference in apparent age might owe less to genes or conditioning than to a domesticated form of lycanthropy.

Because on the way back—after fishing downstream through a brilliant series of stair-step falls and swirling pools and picture-perfect pocket water from which the members of our motley party caught psychedelic-bright brook trout measured in pounds, fiercely fanged lake trout measured in feet, and a few Arctic char anxious to show us that ninety feet of fly line and three hundred feet of backing isn't quite enough—I heard a clucking and shucking and saw movement in the tufted, berry-laden tundra. Feeling my nostrils twitching in an unexpected way, I swiveled my head around to see a pair of ptarmigan bumbling into view almost beneath my feet. As they lit out for the territories down a musk-ox trail, I howled upwind at Danny, but by the time he unlimbered the double-barrel .410 stuffed into his daypack they were long gone. Even after catching all those splendid fish, I felt as though I'd failed at something or other.

A few days of impressive fishing later, a southerly storm fire-hosed the cabins all through a long sleepless night, and the next morning, anticipating a lift in the river and a push of char up from Ungava Bay, Joe fired up his Cessna and flew Danny and me some thirty miles downriver to a spot where Diana Lake narrows and drops through a series of quick S-bends and long lovely stretches of riffles and pools.

At Joe's behest we'd packed sleeping bags and food for several days in case the weather worsened and he couldn't come and collect us—frankly, given the screaming northwesterlies, fierce chop, and horizontal rain squalls, I'm surprised he could successfully deposit us anywhere other than as scattered tundra debris. But flying a floatplane in the Arctic is unforgivably Darwinian: either you quickly become very good at it or you don't. Joe's been at it for many years.

Our shelter was an old trapper's cabin set in a compact green meadow aflame with carmine cranberries and Creamsicle-orange cloudberries, and our entrance was a hole ripped through the cabin's wall by a bear that left substantial evidence of being disappointed in its quest for dietary fiber. But humble as were our surroundings, we were grateful to be surrounded, because the huge high-pressure system busily shoving out the huge low-pressure system spun off forty-knot gusts and intermittent rain-squalls all day.

We crossed the river at the lake's lip to get the wind and the willows at our backs, but the casting remained difficult and the fishing episodic—slow here, fast there, slow again. All in all we got one small stale char from this run, three gaudy brook trout from those pockets, and two wolfish lake trout from that pool.

Even without the constant wind, the going was tough. The river was high, cloudy, and rising. The rocks were slippery with algae and the depositions of hundreds of thousands of Canada geese who'd come here to manufacture more Canada geese to crap on all the golf courses in New Jersey. Off the river, there were none of those convenient caribou trails that serve as tundra highways all across the north; only an occasional thin line of musk-ox tracks shouldered through the willows. It was along one of these, bypassing a slow and un-fly-fishably deep river oxbow, that my nostrils twitched again. I went on point, Danny came up with his .410, and the ptarmigan blasted off in all directions with Danny leaping after them through the willows like Peter Pan in chest waders. He got a double on that flush, and although I'd merely indicated their presence and done some elementary retrieving, I felt pride in having played my part. And more than a little disappointed I hadn't got a biscuit.

Finally the river resumed being a lake at the second spot we'd seen where sane people might consider wading across, so we felt our way back to the east bank and were eyeing the long upwind walk to the cabin. By walk I mean leaping from big slippery rock to big slippery rock for a full two miles, as there were, for obscure hydro-geological reasons, precious few small rocks to pad the gaps on this side of the river.

We sat down to lighten our packs by eating all our food and drinking all our coffee, and while snarfling lake-trout sandwiches, Danny thought he saw a fish porpoise just off the current tongue. So he cast, stripped once, and then for the next ten minutes we listened to his reel complain of its treatment by a beautiful silver char fresh from the sea. Then it was my turn to catch its twin and then Danny's turn and then my turn again and then Danny's until we'd each caught four or five dashing, swirling, bulldogging char in the eight- to twelve-pound range.

Under orders to bring back char for the lodge's ever-hungry table, we killed three and slipped them head-down into my daypack, then we set off for the cabin.

The gusty headwind and my daypack's cargo of three char, one flopping over my head like the crested headdress of a Hawaiian king and the other two flapping in aerodynamically unhelpful arcs like penguin wings, made it difficult to calculate the necessary liftoff velocity to propel me onto but not over the next rock. A miss here would have resulted in, at worst, a broken leg and at best in what a former girlfriend who danced ballet once called a flying episiotomy.

It was the toughest wading either of us had ever seen, but the past hour had also been one of the best afternoons of fishing we'd ever seen. Adversity balanced the success and made it sublime— because of, not despite, its imperfections.

Thus ran my weighty thoughts when I should have been calculating coefficients of friction and plotting wind vectors and angles of attack. Because when I leapt to the next rock I overpowered my takeoff. It was sheer instinct that allowed me to hydroplane off the target rock and onto its neighbor—like a memory bred in the bone or perhaps from all those years of watching Bart Simpson vault pedestrians with his skateboard—and I survived with only a twist and not a break.

To gild the day, I flushed another flock of ptarmigans on the way back, Danny got another double, and I made it back to the cabin with thirty pounds of char in my pack and no more physical damage to my knees and hips than a few months of rest, ice, elevation, and cortisone could cure.

And then Joe came after us in the Cessna right on time, and we flew back to the lodge through a golden sky. Along the way we orbited a dozen musk ox formed into a defensive circle around their calves, with the herd bull off to one side radiating defiance at Joe's floatplane and my nose twitching in answer out the open window.

It was a long flight against a sharp headwind, and only my careful Southern upbringing prevented me from doing something very naughty on Danny's leg.

I had been such a very good dog all day, you see, but I still hadn't got a biscuit.

12. *And So It Goes*

IN THE INTEREST OF ANONYMITY, LET'S CALL IT Tralfamadore Lodge, a small place within a very large space somewhere between the tree line and the Arctic Circle.

There's the usual central cabin housing a kitchen, a dining room, a philosophical cook, an avuncular owner, and a quietly indispensable man-of-all-work. There's the usual be-couched and be-fireplaced lounge with a rudimentary bar, stacks of old huntin' and fishin' magazines, and a satellite TV tuned occasionally to the CBC weather but never to the news.

Bee-lining across the usual gooey peat and scratchy knee-high willows, the usual mossy boardwalks connect the usual slummy suburb of plywood huts and canvas wall tents, a storeroom with a droning generator, and a gnarly landing strip bordered by a line of ATVs awaiting the luggage, the lazy, and the lame. Down on the windswept gray lake, a wobbly dock leads to a shiny floatplane and the usual fleet of battered aluminum boats with temperamental outboards.

Beyond, tundra and lakes and rivers and mountains ripple endlessly beneath the sun and the moon and the stars and the humbling psychedelia of the aurora borealis. From time to time an inquisitive bear or a lumbering musk ox breaks the horizon. Ptarmigan cluck in the hills, arctic foxes probe the perimeter, distant wolves soundtrack the night, and on rare days Serengetian shoals of caribou flow past in a click-clacking cacophony.

Absent the caribou, the generator, and the late-night wolves, the predominant sound is silence. Tralfamadore, in other words, is exactly the kind of place we go to become unstuck in time, even if we've never read Kurt Vonnegut or our name isn't Billy Pilgrim.

The guests are the usual north-country habitués: two grizzled seen-it-all retirees and their grizzled seen-it-all dogs who are here to hunt birds by day and reminisce over whiskeys by night. Also after birds is an eager young Wall Street bond trader with an eager young pup, both bounding around with stars in their eyes, amazed to be out of Manhattan, and anxious to accumulate their own reminiscences.

Here for the fish, a couple of hardworking fly-fishing guides vacationing by going fly-fishing, a cheerful septuagenarian on what may be his last trip to his spiritual home, a retired dairy farmer and his wife who are old north-country hands fly-fishing together since the Kennedy administration, and two early-middle-age brothers who are both new to fly-fishing and the north. Missing from the mix are the usual phalanx of camo-clad caribou hunters, last seen headed southwest following the great migration.

Even without the caribou hunters, remote sporting lodges like Tralfamadore are prime spots for observing *la comédie humaine*. Guests chart the middle-class breadth from doctors and lawyers to teachers and truck drivers—a few almost young, a few undeniably old, most pretty much median, and all living together in a week of petri-dish isolation.

Usually these human stews simmer along just fine, the ingredients having self-assembled, after all, for identical reasons: to taste the wild, to pursue passions with rod and gun, to escape the drear workaday existence, and to rough it in an outfitter-smoothed fashion. Given this transitory commonality, people are mostly on their best behavior. We get along in these lodges because we determine to get along. A complainer, a drunk, a braggart, a boor—any of these pervasive human aberrations can sabotage a week at a wilderness camp faster than amoebic dysentery or swine flu. For the most part, we strive not to become the fly in everyone else's ointment.

Except for the brothers. By midweek, we all know the brothers are cultured sophisticates who had lived abroad, gone to the best schools, enjoyed the best of things, and know which wines we don't have go with which meals we're not having. We know these things because they buzz about them incessantly. What we don't know is why they're here at a modest lodge on a modest lake formed on a modest river in a modest corner of near-arctic Canada.

But after a few days of eyebrow-elevating telepathy, our little society knows one thing for certain: the brothers are the most obnoxious lodge guests ever.

They lecture the chef on how to cook. They complain about the provisions—flown, like the guests, a thousand miles north of civilization's last outpost at great expense. They complain about the showers, which are tepid only for them, and about the blackflies and mosquitoes, which bite only them. They explain bird hunting to men who were one with their shotguns when the brothers were still filling their diapers. They coach lifelong anglers about techniques and tactics and the inner Tao of fly-fishing despite being neophyte circle casters who can flop out maybe thirty feet of line with a tailwind and nothing to entangle their back casts. They expound on the science of selecting flies whose names they don't know and which they don't know how to tie on. They brag about angling successes in an innocent, wild place where success mostly means showing up. Most unforgivably, in this land of limitless elbow room, they're as invasive as kudzu.

One day we all boated to a distant river running from a high lake. Near the base of a waterfall, Avuncular Outfitter began to assign the different beats, leaving the soft water between the boats and the rapids for the septuagenarian and the next stretch upriver for the retired farmers, who were only a few years his junior and only slightly less battered by time, arthritis, and arteriosclerosis.

The furthermost spot was a distant lake said to contain many large trout, though it was a steep climb and a challenge to fish, and the brothers immediately claimed it as their own. One of the vacationing guides said he guessed he'd hike above the canyon and fish his way up to the lake; the other vacationing guide and I decided we'd scramble over the falls and fish our way up through the canyon.

Thus we all had our private water sorted by physical capacities, more or less. A cooperative venture. A pleasant day in the wilds with exactly the right ratio of solitude to society.

Except that, en route to their lake, the brothers alternately fished and waded through the septuagenarian's water while he was still wheezing his way upriver from the boats, then they invaded the farmers' water while the farmers looked on in dismay, and then they dropped in on the guide and me as we started through the canyon. They waded into the center of the sweet swirling run we were fishing and cast to the bank we were fishing from, which had no cover and could hold no fish and was rushing past like a runaway train. And then, having slogged and flogged through the best parts of everyone else's water, they finally reached the lake that had been designated their water, where they couldn't cast in the wind and couldn't fathom where the fish might be in the lake's featureless silver expanse. So they got bored, headed back down-river, and befouled everyone else's water once again.

After several days of similar behavior, we all agreed that some-one must do something and soon. The mainstream promoted a full-on confrontation somewhere between a shape-up-or-ship-out meeting with Human Resources and *Lord of the Flies*. A splinter faction suggested that after a few weeks of providing protein for the hungry north, the RCMP could never be sure precisely what happened to the brothers before their conversion to bear turds. Unwilling to become flies in the RCMP's ointment, however, we finally voted the senior vacationing guide Conciliator in Chief and left matters in his hands.

We never learned the full details of the intervention. All we know is, the conciliator invited the brothers out to admire the stars one night, and the next morning they were changed men. At breakfast they inquired after our health and our plans for the day, and for the first time they seemed actually interested in what we said. They divided the pieces of bacon by the people expecting bacon, and for once they took only their share. They didn't loudly measure Chef's communal pot of scrambled eggs against the feathery omelets from a Michelin-starred bistro in Provence. They offered to refill coffee cups, said please and thank you, and began to actually manifest the impeccable manners they never stopped claiming to have. Out on the water, they respected the space of other anglers, stopped bragging about their superhuman skill at catching big brook trout in waters that see fewer than three dozen anglers per year—acted, in fact, like reasonable people who had come to the north for all those reasons that keep people coming to the north.

They had, in other words, encountered a guide doing what guides do best. If they're lucky, they'll remember their week at Tralfamadore as a teachable moment. With guides—at least *good* guides—all moments are teachable. Guides have always needed to be boatman, woodsmen, cooks, anglers, hunters, tackle repairmen, gunsmiths, paramedics, and teachers. But in these days of lifelong adolescence and overfunded entitlement, guides have also had to become psychologists, family counselors, and above all diplomats.

Either that or they become serial killers.

PART TWO

Life in Miniature

Oh, for boyhood's painless play,
Sleep that wakes in laughing day,
Health that mocks the doctor's rules,
Knowledge never learned of schools
— John Greenleaf Whittier

13. *Hooking Bottom*

IMAGINE A SMALL WOODLAND STREAM WHERE dewey-eyed navel gazers turn every seven-inch trout into a poem and a day filled with seven-inch trout into epic opera pregnant with scenery, symbolism, and the meaning of life.

Our hearts rise alongside every jeweled trout. Hooking one, we smile. Losing one, we smile as well, for how can we lose what we never had? There is no place for greed on these miniature waterways because seven-inch trout wait around every bend, in every pocket and riffle and slough, and in the opaque depths of a wide, slow pool just coming into view. Lose a trout, catch a trout. *Que sera sera*, as the song goes.

We drift our small elegant flies through the riffly tail-out down the pool's transparent amber edges. Nothing. We drift through the smooth swirls over the deep green center. Nothing. We cast to the plunge above and watch our flies tumble beneath the froth. Nothing.

Twin furrows deepen our brow as our jaw tightens. We clip off our parachute-hackled dry fly and our trusty draggled wet fly, add a pair of weighted nymphs, tuck-cast into the foam, and lead our flies through the depths again and again. Nothing and nothing. We curve one cast into the rock garden at the head of the pool and miss our target badly. We curve in another, miss as badly, and with philosophic resignation fish out the drift before heading upstream for easier water.

Abreast a jagged chunk of continent torn free in Devonian days, the line comes tight: *bottom*, we sense—the weighted nymph's mortal enemy. We pull, we toss slack, we twang. Nothing. Then, as we decide between fossicking around shoulder-deep in icy springtime water for a pair of well-chewed flies that took us twenty minutes to tie or simply breaking them off and staying comfortably dry, the bottom begins to move—first upstream and then across the stream before accelerating downstream. As our leader knifes through the tail-out we see it's attached not to an unfolding tectonic event but to a brook trout half awash and speeding through the riffles like a surfaced submarine, grown fat as a thigh and long as an arm from eating seven-inch brook trout.

We turn, we slip, we slide, we lurch from rock to rock, we thrust our rod high into the sky. But he's already around the bend, and soon our line goes as slack as our jaw. We fume, we stew, we say very bad things. Should Doris Day show up perkily warbling, "Whatever will be, will be," we'd run her through with our wading staff and send her to sleep with the troutses.

Nothing kills poetic philosophy like a big fish. Especially a big fish we didn't expect to hook. Which, for me, means nearly every big fish I've ever caught. Or not caught.

My first was a six-pound carp that ate a dough ball meant for a four-ounce bluegill that left me with delusions of competence and an old cane rod forever parenthesed. My second was a fifteen-pound flathead catfish I couldn't bring home to show my parents because I'd caught him fishing from a boat I wasn't allowed to be fishing in with a disreputable river rat I wasn't allowed to be fishing with in a dangerous place I wasn't supposed to be fishing.

Neither fish was exceptional except in the context of previous experience. Neither felt like a fish. They simply felt like bottom. I tugged, I pulled, and the bottom pulled back.

It's been nearly sixty years since that carp, well over fifty since that flathead, and eight since that brook trout. In between, I've tried to free my hooks from many immovable objects that then began to move. There was the hundred-pound halibut that ate a striper jig left bouncing along the bottom while I fed spark-plugs to a hungry Mercury. A grouper the size of a chest freezer that ate a billfish popper tossed against Panamanian coral then spat it back with the hook mashed flat as a Calder mobile. A fourteen-foot tiger shark that ate half my circle-hooked baloney sandwich fifteen miles off Midway Island and would have eaten me, too, if one guide hadn't grabbed my belt as I was heading overboard and another hadn't cut the line. An unseen something between the Virginia Capes that melted away three hundred yards of fifty-pound-test line like ice cream in August and might have been a bluefin tuna, a finback whale, or the nuclear submarine *Los Angeles*.

The halibut I might have boated if I'd had a baseball bat and a legal halibut tag. The tiger, the freezer, and the phantom were unlandable by anyone, least of all me.

But I'd have given anything to land them. Who wouldn't? Hooking an enormous fish, we become Santiago in his frail skiff towed night and day through the Gulf Stream by an eighteen-foot marlin. For a big fish, we'll risk our hands, our backs, our tackle, our boat, and our very lives. Big fish turn even the most pastoral Waltonians into Wall Street sharks slashing through rush-hour traffic and widows' pensions. We strive for purity and poetry and end up in a Hemingway novel remade for network TV.

My first truly big fish, at least by my modest standards, was an eighty-pound blue shark caught twenty miles off the Maine Coast followed an hour later by an honest hundred-pounder.

No one will ever rank the blue shark among the world's great game species. Their charm lies in their size, their availability, and their willingness to eat anything remotely edible, such as a chunk of the chopped herring we ladled over the side to attract them. Thus the Chum Fly, a pink-and-gray nightmare in marabou that is to a full-dress Grey Ghost streamer what *The Monster Mash* is to *The Ring of the Nibelung*. Casting an imitation of dead meat into a chum slick may be the least elegant form of fly fishing and a blue shark a game fish only in our minds. Still, if we hook one, their sheer yet manageable size puts us very much in a Santiago state of mind.

And when something unmanageable pulls back, like the twelve-hundred-pound mako that ate my friend A. J. Campbell's Chum Fly and peeled six hundred yards of backing from his Fin-Nor without ever realizing it was hooked, the whole boat gets that shaky-knee feeling that comes only with the unexpected.

Inside the reef on Midway Island, I knew what to expect: giant trevally—GTs—in my limited experience the meanest game fish that swims. Through the week I'd inflated with false competence, landing several demi-GTs in the thirty-pound range and many more of their smaller thick-lipped cousins, the butaguchi.

When the big one hit, I thought I knew what I was in for. But I hadn't a clue. An hour and a half later, I finally did. My 70.3-pound GT—which beat the sixteen-pound IGFA fly-rod record by twenty pounds, or would have if the GT had actually eaten my popper instead of the five-pound rudderfish that ate my popper a microsecond before the GT ate both—made my hundred-pound blue shark from the previous year feel like one of those four-ounce bluegills from nearly sixty years ago. I couldn't sleep for a week and couldn't use my hands in the way they'd been designed for a month. I can't stop smiling all these years later.

Then there was the Costa Rican sailfish. It had been a tough week. Day after day beneath a hot copper sky towing teasers across a breathless painted ocean so aboil with bait that the sailfish refused to be infuriated by our pink plastic squid meant to tease them within fly-casting range. A dozen had hit—idly, indolently plucking the big pink popper from the prop-wash and swimming for the far horizon then tossing the fly with one of those jumps so often immortalized in oil paintings hung on corporate walls. Then, untouched and unconcerned, they resumed their anchovy banquet.

And then it came onto blow, the bait dispersed, and the sailfish got hungry. The slop of wind and wave concealed the slop of a four-weight small-stream trout fisherman trying to cast a fourteen-weight cargo derrick. A hundred-pounder, an eighty-pounder: blistering runs, NBA jumps, high-fives, heroic photos. Confidence, self-regard, delusions of competence. Then the big one came.

It hit like an eighteen-wheeler hooked from an interstate overpass. Instead of tiring itself with hundred-yard runs and theatrical leaps, it headed straight for the bottom. Pump and grind, pump and grind; the fly line almost in view then straight back to the bottom. On the third round trip, the rod's fighting butt broke off just below the reel. On the next three round trips, raw titanium gnawed through meat into bones. That night in the shower I looked like a crime scene on *Law & Order*—a sketchy mugging victim who deserved what he got.

Because back in the boat, with the monster sailfish alongside, the guide reached down for the fly, and the captain readied his intrusive camera for yet another heroic marketing shot for their website. "No," I said, all noble and self-sacrificing. "Just let him go."

"¿Qué?" The guide turned and the sail swung its bill, severing the shock tippet, and the biggest fish I'd ever caught released itself.

I yelled, I fumed, I said very bad things to very good people for doing exactly what I wanted them to do. I thought of Doris Day and her noxious "*Que Sera, Sera*," and I said, as many another philosophical fisherman has done before and will do long after I'm gone, "Screw you and your friggin' whatever will be will be."

14. *The Persistence of Memory*

OF THE MANY WAYS HER FISHING-CRAZY FAMily irritated my non-fishing mother, the worst was our inability to let fish quietly become food. No matter how long they'd been in the freezer or how they were prepared, fish hit our table seasoned with the smallest details of where they were caught, on what, and by whom.

"Can't we just eat?" my mother would finally say, glaring at a forkful of trout she'd just learned had taken a Female Adams in a foamy eddy on Sycamore Creek. "I don't need to know their life histories."

My father, brother, and I would hang our heads and chew with silent contrition. Then the platter would make the rounds again, and we'd serve forth another helping of collective memories.

"Little native?"

"Yup."

"Up on Rough Ridge Creek?"

"Bald River, likely."

"Caught these the day you lost them two browns up under that hemlock wad."

"Boys that was something. First'n took that big Tellico Nymph, and the other'n ate that little Speck on the dropper."

"What a mess, two fish up under them roots."

"I might could have landed one, but not two."

"Big?"

"Eighteen, maybe nineteen, both."

"Been some big'ns come from that stretch."

"Yup."

"This here's that big rainbow from Bishop's Bend's, ain't it?"

"Yup."

"We was up on the road; watched him come right up from the bottom after your Specks."

"Prettiest thing I ever saw."

By then my mother's veins were vibrating like tuning forks and her freckles had merged into a monolithically threatening splotch, and I still don't know whether it was from our insistence on memorializing the life that now was food or our inability to remember homework or chores or thank-you notes to distant relatives while never forgetting anything about any fish we'd ever caught or tried to catch.

Here it is fifty-something years later, and I haven't really changed. Nowadays I have to write detailed lists of all the things that need doing or I won't remember to do them. It makes no matter whether it's taking out the rubbish or buying four bags of chicken feed or dropping by the town office to pick up an absentee ballot so I won't have to remember that the first Tuesday in November is election day. But I don't need notes to keep track of the fish. I remember them all. Especially the biggest trout I ever hooked.

I ran across him on the Madison a few years back, and our first encounter came close to being my first heart attack. Our second encounter came close to being my first stroke.

And my third encounter? Well, God willing and the creek don't rise, that'll come before one of us croaks.

I can almost hear my mother, "You really expect that same fish to be waiting right there for you to come along and catch him?"

Yup.

And if not him then one just like him, for that brown had chosen, lucked into, or fought for the best lie I've ever seen in any

river anywhere. Fishing upstream, as most of us do, you couldn't
see it at all. Fishing downstream, most people wouldn't see it if
they stared in its direction until their eyeballs stood out on stalks.
I didn't see it. I just kind of stumbled into it.

Jim Schollmeyer and I had started fishing early that morning
and divided up the river according to our abilities and tempera-
ments. Jim is a big boy—you'd need two of me standing on a
minnow bucket to make one of him—so I took the bank and Jim
fished the deep pocket water in the middle, breasting current and
depths that would have drowned me. Plus Jim is one of those
maddeningly methodical anglers who rerigs for every rock—
removing weight or adding weight, lengthening leader or short-
ening leader, and changing flies and then changing flies again.
For. Every. Rock.

I mostly trout fish the way I learned on the small mountain
streams where I grew up: three or four casts at every likely spot,
and if the fish in this hole don't want my big dry fly towing a little
nymph then the fish in the next hole might. Fishing together over
the course of an average day, Jim and I might catch about the same
number of fish, but I'd need three times as much river to do it. I
set off rock hopping along the bank at my customary speed and
had dropped Schollmeyer hull-down before the sun cleared the
blue Montana mountains.

When the sun hit its zenith I turned back for the car and lunch.
It had been a pretty good morning—better than a dozen rainbows
in the twelve- to sixteen-inch range and a fat snappy brown about
eighteen—and I strolled back downriver while idly flicking my
flies ahead and looking for Jim and a good spot to scramble up the
bank and onto the road.

At the elbow of a bend a waist-deep riffle ran from bank to
bank, and the current split around a small island shaped like one
of Salvador Dali's droopy pocket watches. Shallow undercuts scal-
loped its riverside edge, and small pines leaned over for shade and
shelter. On the way upriver I'd taken a small brown in its downriver eddy, but I didn't get a touch along its tempting outboard
undercuts.

I'd scouted the side channel that separated the island from the mainland, but an arm's width of ankle-deep pea gravel didn't look very promising, so I passed it by. On the way back downriver, though, I figured the side channel would be way easier wading than the riffle's heavy current and iffy footing, and I could also circle around the island and fish its outside edge again just in case. So I splashed down through the shallow water truckin' like the do-dah man and casually flipping my flies toward the island because, well, you never know.

And you don't. The instant the flies touched, the skinny water exploded in a beaver-alarm ker-*sploosh*, my rod bent double, the line rifled toward the riffle and then snapped back in my face like a bullwhip crack from Lash LaRue, and I found myself somehow sitting in the river with my pulse racing and that certain tingly tightness in my upper left quadrant that folks of a certain age never want to feel.

I sat there a long while trying to figure out what had happened—and what I hoped hadn't. And while I sat there, I saw a long dark shape move slowly in from the riffle and disappear beneath the island not ten feet away.

A week or so later, bound from Ennis for the airport in Idaho Falls and the long flight home to Maine, I pulled over and made my way back to the little island for one last try.

I can't imagine a more difficult lie. Approaching from downriver along the island's outboard edge, you couldn't see the big brown's spider hole at all, and if you cast to the head of the island from the river's side, the fierce current instantly wrecked your drift no matter how far upstream you reached.

There was no approach from the side channel, either. The bank was too steep and overgrown to be negotiated by anything taller and less flexible than a rattlesnake, and even the most cautious footfall in the ankle-deep pea gravel would quickly telegraph a predatory presence.

That left upriver, and where the water shoaled thirty feet up from the island I dropped to my knees to inch along like an Apache scout from a 1950s western. I could just pick out a small patch of black between the blue of the riffle and the amber of the side channel, and a foot upstream I dropped my BFF—our crowd's generic acronym for a dry fly where the adjectives Big and Foam modify a very naughty noun—with just enough slack in the tippet to drift into the Kraken's cave.

And ker-*sploosh*.

This time I was mentally and physically prepared with an osprey's intensity and a brand-new 3X leader instead of the shopworn 5X from our first encounter. And it didn't make a bit of difference, except that I saw those scimitar jaws close down on the BFF, saw those big amber eyes the size of silver dollars, saw that broad bitter-chocolate back and the wide umber flank dotted with black, saw him power into the current, saw the leader coil back like a bungee cord, saw spots before my eyes and a gray haze, and then saw nothing at all. If I hadn't been kneeling in ankle-deep water when the world turned upside down, I might not be writing this today.

Weeks later, my doctor said I might have had what he calls a ministroke or, in Blue-Cross-billable terms, a transient ischemic attack. Hauling out his prescription pad and beginning to scribble, he explained these sorts of things aren't uncommon in folks of a certain age when things get too tense or stressful and that I should remember my mother also suffered from problems like this and maybe now that I'm of a certain age I should dial-down a bit and take life easy.

As he tore a page off the prescription pad and began scribbling on another, I asked, "You mean mellow-down easy with a restful hobby? Like fishing?"

"Yup," he said. "Fishing'll do just fine."

15. *Simple Gifts*

Ⅰt pleased the gods of weather—Aeolus and Anemi and Anemoi and the Harpyiae and all those other Greeks who have precisely as much to do with whether it rains or shines or snows or blows as the fashion-challenged TV weatherperson taking abuse from the unamusing TV anchorperson—to end eight years of drought here in Maine with four years of not-drought.

And in 2008 it amused whoever they are to present us with a not-summer. We didn't equal our April high temperature until mid August. As if the onset of the Great Recession and a nasty political campaign weren't enough, we had the coldest and wettest May, June, and July ever recorded. Weather-dependents like clam diggers, tourist trappers, and farmers beseeched every conceivable deity, TV weatherperson, and government agency for relief. Instead they got paralytic shellfish poisoning, blinking vacancy signs, and the same damp-induced potato-and-tomato blight that triggered the Irish diaspora in 1845.

But life goes on. Or, as the fashion-challenged TV weatherperson said to the unamusing TV anchorperson, "When life gives you lemons . . ."

She didn't have to finish. Those of discerning tastes know that when life gives you lemons, you buy a nice bottle of vodka and make limoncello, and pretty soon you forget all about life singling you out for persecution.

Or you can simply adapt your behavior to what has pleased life to tip your way. Take, for example, the matter of fishing.

The constant rain and cold may have blown out my customary rivers and befouled my customary bay with toxic runoff and that poisonous algae bloom known as red tide, but it brought small-stream trout fishing like I haven't enjoyed locally in ages.

During those eight long years of drought, Maine's small run-off streams were mostly too low and warm to fish by early June, when the fishing should be at its peak, and the autumn rains came neither soon enough nor convincingly enough to provide a week or two of compensatory fishing before the small-stream season closes in September.

Then, when the drought finally ended, the powers that be tried to compensate with the kinds of wrathful weather events that lure fashion-challenged TV weatherpersons out into the elements looking for telegenic disasters to describe. They didn't have to look far, as demure little trout brooks busily gathered cargoes of trees and bridges and double-wide house trailers and roared toward the sea.

But 2008 brought no telegenic disasters. Just nonstop cold drizzle with the occasional cold downpour. Day after day. Week after week. To the small streams, it was the first week of May for three long months.

So when life gives you lemons . . .

During seventeen years as *Gray's Sporting Journal*'s angling columnist, I wrote 128 articles, but only eight were specifically about my obsession with small-stream trout fishing, which probably qualifies me as an advocate but stops short of being an evangelist.

I can't decide, when I visit a jewel of a mountain creek and see no one fishing it, whether I'm disappointed or relieved that my evangelism—excuse me, advocacy—wins so few converts.

Solitude, after all, is a big part of the charm of small streams—their intimate settings and their overgrown paths guarded by sun-fired cobwebs that serve both as a time-line bestiary of stream-born life and irrefutable evidence that no one of my height and breadth has recently passed this way.

Combine that solitude with the other simple gifts from small streams: the toy-like miniature fly tackle and inventive casts and stealthy stalks and the never-heard-of-a-hatchery fish with their coloring, their caution, their furious strikes, and their purely elemental flight from fatality—a heron, an otter, an unknown force clamped to a jaw. This is worlds apart from the famous rivers where drift boats bearing guides and fee-paying anglers commute past in metered intervals, where jaded brown trout take your nymph with dull recognition—*fooled again, dammit; coulda swore that was a real bug*—and now must tolerate an embarrassing tow to shore and a hulking presence flashing a camera in its face before being released to do it all over again.

To have to oneself these small wild places and their small wild fish is a true gift, viewed purely in the short term. But long term it can be a curse—we protect what we love, but we can't love what we barely know exists.

Should a power company decide a new dam across the Madison or a deep-drilled natural-gas fracking operation on the Beaverkill are crackerjack ideas, armies of anglers would descend upon their headquarters with pitchforks and torches and lawyers aplenty. But should a coal conglomerate decide to dump a mountaintop into little Panther Branch or a golf course irrigate its emerald artificiality with most of the flow of modest Mill Brook, hardly anyone squawks. Politically speaking, these small secret places have no constituency and thus no influence.

Maybe small-stream preaching gains so few converts because folks think it's a scam by cynical fish-writers flushing innocent anglers from famous pools on famous rivers and sending them view-hallooing up the mountainside after trout the size of sardines while we devious fish-writers catch trout the size of tuna in smug self-generated solitude.

And there's a reason to suspect us. Some years ago, noted small-stream advocate John Gierach and I were fishing a small Colorado creek many low-range rock-hopping miles past pavement. We fished up there a couple of days, caught a lot of wild pretty trout, and saw no more evidence of humanity than contrails thirty thousand feet overhead.

Then one day we decided to fish a well-known creek in Rocky Mountain National Park near the highway, complete with picnic tables, outhouses, and uniformed rangers superintending its officially protected existence. As we arrived, we saw two anglers in the crowded parking lot stripping off their waders and putting away their gear. This is never a good sign when you're heading off to fish a small stream, especially when the unknown anglers appear to know what they're doing—an assessment based not on their well-worn equipment or philosophical demeanor but on how the stream fishes in their aftermath.

Following in their boot prints, I caught maybe a dozen trout over a mile of water and then only in the unlikeliest spots. But when I nosed up a narrow side channel so overgrown even the craziest small-stream specialist would pass it by, I caught a trout from every pocket—maybe two dozen in fifty yards of gymnastic fly-dapping. Back in the main channel, the fishing returned to normal: a fish now and then and only from the unlikeliest places.

We drove home conflicted—glad to know a couple of other dedicated small-stream fishermen were around but hoping it hadn't been something either of us wrote that brought them to this particular spot on this particular day.

* * *

Fast forward a few years back home in Maine. I was knee-deep into a three-month May with my striper rod dust-covered over the office door, the salmon rod down from its pegs for only one trip, and the big-river trout rods hardly even uncased. I was casting a favorite little split-cane four-weight my brother made, swapping back and forth as the water dictated between a pair of stout caddis larvae and a biggish March Brown parachute trailing a tiny Pheasant Tail nymph.

My brain was aswirl with the familiar sights and smells from these intimate waters, some I hadn't fished in a dozen years thanks to meteorological intervention and some I will never fish again thanks to human intervention—the new house, the new gas station, the new "No Trespassing" signs, and the impenetrable tangle of downed trees courtesy the great ice storm of 1998. But most are just as they were when I last visited, which was the last time the gods of weather opened them to visitors beyond the two-week flush of expert wormers in the high roil of spring.

I had fished for a few hours almost every day and hadn't seen another angler in a month. Releasing my umpteenth bright little brook trout of the afternoon, my brain began to swim with an old Shaker song about how it's a gift to be simple and a gift to be free, and I remembered the right line, the appropriate line, "'Tis the gift to come down where we ought to be."

And then sprang forth a bit from Sarah Orne Jewett's *The Country of the Pointed Firs*, the single best book ever written about Maine, and in one small passage the single best thing ever written about the lure of small-stream trout fishing:

"If there is one way above another of getting so close to nature that one simply is a piece of nature, following a primeval instinct with perfect self-forgetfulness and forgetting everything except the dreamy consciousness of pleasant freedom, it is to take the course of a shady trout brook. The dark pools and the sunny shallows beckon one on; the wedge of sky between the trees on either bank, the speaking, companioning noise of the water, the amazing importance of what one is doing, and the constant sense of life and beauty make a strange transformation of the quick hours."

I don't know what to add to that, except maybe *Amen*. And a great big thanks, to whomever or whatever, for giving us three months of May in that year of the Great Recession, the Great Blight, and the summer that never was—even if we paid for it with the destruction of our retirement portfolios and a whole year of eating store-bought potatoes and tomatoes.

16. *Blackberry Winter*

Every time I buy a Tennessee fishing license and the lady behind the counter asks resident or nonresident, I always say resident followed quickly by wait, no, I mean nonresident. This even though I left East Tennessee behind at the age of seventeen and haven't been back more than a dozen times in the intervening fifty years.

But how can you think of yourself as a nonresident where your family has lived for nearly two-and-a-third centuries, leaving its name on creeks and roads and mills and old houses and historical placards? How can you feel anywhere but at home standing in the high-mountain clearing where you first camped in a tent and slept beneath the stars even though a seventy-foot yellow poplar now reaches skyward from the ghost of the fire ring where you toasted marshmallows and fried trout? How can you not feel at home catching an acrobatic rainbow from beneath the very boulder where you caught your first trout on a fly?

For various reasons I had wanted to show all this hometown trout fishing stuff to my friend John Gierach, and finally we'd gotten around to it. The plan was, we'd stay with my brother Walter at his cabin on Tellico River for an uninterrupted week of fishing little streams for little mountain trout with little cane rods, a three-step addiction for all three of us.

Driving down from the Knoxville airport, we detoured past our old house in Lenoir City and, a block away, the old house of John's aunt Francis, who married my father's cousin Jack Babb, both of whom graduated with my father and his sister from Lenoir City High School in 1932. It was, as John wrote later, "a left-handed family reunion" when we stopped in Sweetwater to collect my brother and his gear and headed up for those rolling old mountains I still think of as home.

The fishing started out good but not spectacular on a favorite distant creek—forgive me if I don't name names—with a lot of tunnel fishing and difficult casting and eager rainbows that were much quicker taking a dry fly than I was at taking them. I counted somewhere shy of two dozen, mostly rainbows in the sardine range and one brilliantly colored brown trout just entering his sardine-eating years.

And the weather started out unusually for one of my trips, by which I mean not that hot and not that cold but pretty much just right—seventies days, fifties nights. The water was a bit thin for early May, but the slow-moving, cautious angler (is there any other kind at our age?) could catch fish.

After supper we went to a favorite nearby river, which was low and clear and the fish scarce, although we all managed a few while swapping off rods—a Walt Carpenter John had brought along and rods my brother made adapted from F.E. Thomas and Paul Young tapers. It was a restful evening of messing around after a stiff four-mile hike in the hot sun, a day that pretty much set the pattern for the week: a lot of walking, a lot of small trout and a few bigger ones, a lot of mountain scenery, and very few people besides us.

But we weren't entirely alone. One day we went over the mountain to another drainage and found footprints that seemed to say someone was up the left fork, so we went up the right fork, which, as it turned out, was a strategic error because Walter saw the guys we thought had gone left up ahead of us playing a fish. Turns out they'd gone up the left fork first and thought it looked too skinny—and where they turned around it is, but it isn't a few miles uphill—so we'd outsmarted ourselves out of miles of un-fished water. Un-fished water is important on thin mountain streams and crucial when the water is low and clear. There are far more dangerous two-legged trout predators running wild in those mountains than catch-and-release fly guys, and the trout in those perfectly transparent waters are spookier than I've ever found them anywhere. Which is, of course, why fishing for them is such fun.

That evening, as compensation for an unproductive though enjoyable forced march, we headed back to our familiar nearby river for a good Sulphur hatch that turned on half an hour before legal quitting time. We all caught surprising numbers of surprisingly large fish in the brief spell between supper and sundown, but the evening was simply too pretty and the fishing too splendid to bother with something so trivial as mathematics, so please forgive me if I don't quantify the experience.

The next day was a little easier to measure. It dawned with a warm front and intermittent light drizzle overspreading the mountains. We decided to take a break from the old standard East Tennessee diet and fry something for supper that didn't divideth its hoof but yet cheweth not its cud, so we bought daily permits for the main river and went off to fish pocket water using our old standard East Tennessee nymphing method—something like high-sticking and something like Czech nymphing but not quite like either, a technique our father learned third-hand about midway through the Truman administration and taught us during Eisenhower's.

With the familiar modern nymphing technique practically everyone uses, you tie a nymph to a length of tippet then tie this to the bend of another fly—a different nymph, say, or a dry fly. With two nymphs, you'll typically rig a high-floating, brightly colored strike indicator. This works wonderfully well, as everyone knows, but so does our old-fashioned way—better, in my experience, in thin, nervous water. We tie a length of tippet to the leader with a blood knot, leaving about six inches of tag-end free, and tie a wet fly—sometimes a dry—to that tag and a weighted nymph to the tippet. Rather than the standard dead drift, we lead the flies downstream just a tad faster than the current, which makes strikes easier to see and animates the wet fly most enticingly. Or so goes the theory.

It was one of those rare days when the fish were feeding and, thanks to the overcast sky, weren't particularly skittish. Every pocket produced a strike and—if I was fast enough and my eyesight good enough to see it without a strike indicator—a fish.

We fished from mid-morning until mid-afternoon with a lingering lunch break, and I lost count somewhere around forty—a mix of native and stocked rainbows, one fat brown whose circumference roughly equaled his fifteen-inch length, and a rainbow around eighteen inches that considerately unhooked herself at my feet.

Of course Walter, the family fish-hawk, did way better, and cousin John, who was playing catch-up in new country with an entirely new technique and trout of a whole different level of fast and jittery, was finally into his stride.

That was probably the best day of pure trout fishing I can remember in a place you didn't need a floatplane or a helicopter to reach. That it came on the river where I learned to fish was a nice bonus. And so were the trout we ate that night.

At lunch my brother told John, "I've fished all over the west and the Catskills and have had some great fishing for some big fish, but when people ask me where my favorite place to fish is, I tell them right here. And the thing is, nobody believes me."

I've given up trying to convince anyone. But John didn't need convincing. That we'd seen so few other fishermen over the week seemed almost miraculous in an area so near the great eastern population centers and in country so striking—the ancient rounded mountains, thickly forested and garnished with pink and white mountain laurel just then being superseded by budding rhododendrons, the flame azaleas so bright against the deep green that wandering botanist and paleo-hippy William Bartram, visiting here in 1776, wrote that he was "alarmed with the apprehension of the hill being set on fire." Sometimes, when fishing surrounded by the largest concentrations of wildflowers in North America, you find your eyes watering for no good manly reason.

Toward the end of the trip the weather turned against us—cold and sunny: exactly what mountain trail walkers want and mountain trout fishermen don't. It was a Blackberry Winter, in local parlance: a cold snap after a warm spell that comes when the blackberries bloom. Although we didn't know it then, this was the onset of the worst drought to ever hit the southeast. We caught fish the rest of the trip—and some good ones—but the barometer guides fish in the mountains as it does everywhere, and we had to work hard for them.

But we seldom value what comes easy. As Robert Penn Warren wrote in the famous coming-of-age story from which I stole this chapter's title, "When you are nine, you know that there are things that you don't know but you know that when you know something you know it."

And when you revisit the place where you began learning to truly fly-fish at nine and found that what you left behind is still pretty much the way you left it, you know that is something to know.

17. *Tangled Up and Blue*

Picture the perfect fly-fishing scene: a bouncing freestone creek high in the Colorado Rockies. A sparkling early autumn afternoon. Golden light carving rugged red sandstone. Lodgepole pines clinging to cantilevered cliffs. The season's last plump raspberries overripe-red against holly-green foliage. A scattering of Flavs—*Drunella flavilinea*, the lesser Green Drake—emerging from icy transparent water. Brilliantly colored trout rising with growing enthusiasm—brooks, browns, cutthroats, and the occasional rainbow. Two good friends—hip-boots, tattered vests, well-seasoned hats, scraggly gray beards, fine old cane rods, and eighty-some years of fly-fishing experience between them—leapfrogging up the mountainside pool by pool and close enough to share the day but not too close to spoil it.

In the perfect scene, the grizzled guy wearing the battered packer hat would be carefully releasing a trout in the back eddy of a foamy plunge pool just as the grizzled guy in the battered duckbill cap hooks one in the glassy tail-out of the next pool upstream: a Trout Unlimited calendar, an artist's holiday greeting card, or the opening scene of a fly-fishing movie about the meaning of life.

But this is a real scene from fly-fishing, and packer's classic cane rod teeters in the bushes while he hops about like Elmer Fudd chasing a wabbit and twying to wescue his flies and weader from a distant pine limb bolo-hitched by a mistimed strike. Duckbill is slumped on a rock with his glasses pushed up and his eyeballs inches from the cat's cradle that a hyperactive little trout has made of his dry fly and nymph and eight feet of leader as he tonelessly sing-songs the misremembered lyrics of a Bob Dylan tune and decides between an intricate unweaving or simply whacking it all off and starting fresh.

This isn't the first such scene today, and it won't be the last. Packer and duckbill, like most fly fishers, especially small-stream fly fishers, spend nearly as much time untangling tangles as they do unhooking fish. But just try publishing that image as a calendar, an artist's greeting card, or a thoughtful fly-fishing movie. Reality doesn't sell fly rods or waders or other profitable paraphernalia of the fly-fishing lifestyle and has no place in its idealized image. "Reality," to steal a line from Flaubert, "does not conform to the ideal, but confirms it."

Reality is also pretty funny, which is why it's such a popular topic of conversation among reality-based fly fishers. The folks I enjoy fishing with rarely sit around talking about all the great fish we've caught, the great trips we've had, or the improbably athletic casts we've sometimes made. But we do talk a lot about how bad fishing can suck and still be fun.

Take, for example, the hoary image of landlocked salmon fishing in Maine. Think brawling rivers, dripping spruce forests, moose peering from the shadows, bear cubs shinnying up spindly birches, and ruffed grouse exploding from the alders. Conjure visions of Grey Ghosts, Nine-Threes, Barnes Specials, wood-and-canvas canoes, checked wool shirts, felt fedoras, and a bent brier pipe laying down a smoke screen against no-see-ums, mosquitoes, and blackflies. Imagine yourself a thoughtful fly fisher casting a delicate mayfly emerger into a current seam on High Bank Pool, bouncing a nymph below Middle Dam, or swinging a feather-wing streamer through Big Eddy as the ghosts of Henry Thoreau, Carrie Stevens, Hiram Leonard, F.E. Thomas, and Cornelia "Fly Rod" Crosby look on from the mists of time. Imagine the Atlantic salmon's slightly smaller but far more kinetic cousin rocketing into the air, a silver meteor jumping, jumping, around the bend and out of sight.

Reality? Sometimes. But far more often you'll catch a foot-long salmonette that, unrestrained by the demands gravity places on an adult body, spins two nymphs, a strike indicator, and twelve feet of leader into a solid ball of yarn the size of your thumb that cannot be unraveled and can barely be cut. Not to mention you stopped smoking twenty years ago on your doctor's orders, your bug dope stopped working an hour ago, and with rivulets of mingled blood and sweat trickling into your eyes, you don't notice as you struggle to nail-knot a fresh leader to your line that just to your right a pair of bumptious young moose calves have slipped into the river for a drink while just to your left their mother spies a fumbling, muttering, crouching apparition separating her from her maternal responsibilities. As you begin your third attempt to tighten the knot without crossing turns, she begins to swell with indignation . . .

Avert your eyes and instead imagine a restful English chalk stream where an angler studies to be quiet. He wears a tattersall shirt, a snap-brim cap, tweed breeks, and Le Chameau boots. His rod, his reel, his line, and his flies all come from Hardy's of Alnwick, where his name and preferences are well known by attentive clerks. Swans drift by in the distance and ripple the reflection of a ruined castle. Ancient water burbles along in sinuous curves. The Mayfly has just passed and with it the end of Duffer's Fortnight and the dilettantes down from London. Small olives are popping off, and very large browns are beginning to dimple the meniscus. Just beyond a comfortable cast, he sees a monster trout nosing through a gap in the jungle of ranunculus, for this is a wild stream and not a manicured pitch-and-putt course like those famous names on every angler's lips.

Easing forward through the osiers, our angler begins to lengthen line just outside the big brown's field of view and casts sidearm and flat to the water. Then his fly snags behind him, and as he turns to contemplate his next move, loops of slack braid themselves into the most pernicious entangler of line and leader known to humanity: the hemlock water dropwort, cousin to carrots and parsnips and parsley, and the most poisonous plant in Britain. Our angler curses, fumes, contemplates chewing its roots in a suitably Socratic end. But a quiet splash just upstream tells him the big brown is still feeding, and he patiently begins the interminable process of untangling. Just as he clears his line and resumes his stalk, a trio of doe-eyed Guernseys galumph into this river that waters well the verdant plains of the Vale of the Great Dairies, spreading mud and panic in their wake. Fun? Maybe not at the time. But later, over a pint of scrumpy in the pub . . .

Back in the mountains of Colorado, packer and duckbill sit leaning against a cottonwood and watch the creek ripple the sunset while sharing the last of the coffee. It's been a good day, they figure; around two dozen trout each, most on dries and some on dropper nymphs, all the fish highly colored and full-bodied, some in the expected six- to nine-inch range and some real lunkers for a creek this size at this elevation—twelve-, thirteen-, one or two maybe even crowding fourteen inches. By any measure a good day just as yesterday had been a good day and the day before that and very likely tomorrow and the day after and the day after once again.

Along with the coffee they're sharing observations—inconspicuous little pockets that held good fish and beautiful classic pools that held no fish, small fish, or simply unwilling and thus unseen fish. They discuss the mechanics of a modified bow-and-arrow cast that duckbill learned as a small boy, the sidearm roll cast that packer figures is simply a miniature version of a single spey, and the utter uselessness on water like this of the classic flycasts taught in books and classes. They figure all their really good trout came from spots that were hard to fish, and that learning to fish these difficult spots is the key to success on small streams and large. They decide that most anglers pass these spots by because they're afraid they'll get all tangled up and blue. They laugh at how angry some anglers get when their lines and leaders tangle. They figure that's a bit like getting angry because the sun sets, summers end, or politicians betray our trust.

They laugh at all the times they've gotten tangled—on small streams, on big rivers, with indecision casts on bonefish flats, and during the counterintuitive movements of spey casting—all the spectacular failures balancing all the modest successes in an eccentric sport where success is measured less by how much you accomplish than by how much you've enjoyed the journey.

Finally, packer says that no matter where they fish or how they fish or how long they've fished, fly fishers who can't accept that they'll spend much of each day untangling leaders and lines and unhooking flies from trees and rocks really ought to take up golf. And duckbill leaves off mangling Bob Dylan and tries to remember a line from Emerson—something about the reality being more excellent than the report.

Which is true of life in general, and of fly-fishing in particular.

18. *Subjective Fish*

In her deliciously depressing book *The Mill on the Floss*, George Eliot wrote that the doomed Maggie Tulliver's dimwitted but well-meaning mother, in trying to prevent the humiliating bankruptcy auction of the Tullivers's mill by convincing the vengeful lawyer Wakem not to buy it, brought about an outcome exactly contrary to her intentions. She had "undertaken to act persuasively and had failed; a fact which may receive some illustration from the remark of a great philosopher, that fly-fishers fail in preparing their bait so as to make it alluring in the right quarter, for want of a due acquaintance with the subjectivity of fishes."

A thorough reading of fly-fishing's copious literature shines scarcely a guttering candle upon the subjectivity of fishes—by which I and Ms. Eliot's great philosopher mean an individual fish's individual take on the matter or meal at hand or fin based entirely on whim, taste, inclination, or sheer contrariness of the moment. But upon the objectivity of the great generic mass of fishes—the tendency of whole species to do what is expected of them based on past behavior observed in similar conditions—the literature of fly-fishing brings great banks of Klieg lights to bear, with data-rich hatch guides for every pond, lake, brook, stream, river, and drainage ditch from one end of trout country to the other.

According to the literature, if it's mid-June on the West Branch of the Penobscot and the weather is neither unseasonably cool nor warm nor the water unreasonably high nor low, the chocolate caddis are sure to be hatching, and the landlocked salmon and brook trout will surely be eating them. At this time and in these conditions, the most objective of anglers will tie on a pair of chocolate-bodied caddis imitations with mottled wings in about size fourteen—a floating fly and a sunken pupa to hedge our objective bets with the adult and emergent stages—and then clear the decks for action.

Fortunately—or unfortunately, depending on how you feel about these things—the expected action comes often enough to become dogma except in those rare times when the chocolate caddis are hatching but the fish aren't so much eating them as nipping at them like Epicurus at the end of an orgy. Then we launch a frantic exploration of our fly boxes and try everything and anything before finally giving up in disgust, surrounded in the pale evening by fish that rise but rise not for us.

And then there are those times when the fish that rise not for us rise not in desultory silence but with the sound of large angry dogs being tossed from helicopters. We find ourselves changing flies even more frantically as big fish chase something they can see but we cannot until, surrendering to the unrewarding dark, we trek back to the truck. En route we shine our headlamp upon a ticklish sensation creeping up our elbow, and we see a slate-winged chocolate-cherry-bodied mayfly dun of considerable size and personality and realize that the fishes have been subjectively ignoring the chocolate caddis that reams of objective literature and the evidence of our own eyes and ears say they ought to be eating and instead have been scarfing *Isonychia* mayfly nymphs. And that the editorial "we" and his companions, Tom Fuller and Will Ryan, both frequent illuminators of the literature of angling, have conspired to miss our one great opportunity to catch fish on those claret-colored nymphs we've been carrying around un-fished in our fly boxes for most of our optimistic lives—missed, in fact, the year's one great opportunity to take the biggest landlocked salmon in the river, brought to the surface by those swimming, darting, apparently delicious nymphs that in these northern waters appear in the dark of night as infrequently as the citizens of Brigadoon, the magical Scottish village that comes to life only one day every century.

The thing is, we *knew* those salmon out there making all that noise were eating chocolate caddis. And because we knew it, we didn't cast our figurative nets quite far enough while searching for reasons why the fishes weren't doing what we knew they were doing.

And this other time at band camp, John Gierach and I had been messing around in the small streams near his Colorado mountain home, and on a subjective whim we decided to upgrade our pounds-per-bite a bit beyond what small high-altitude streams typically supply. We drove over the mountain to a couple of small spring-fed ponds where John shares a lease and the ranch owner dumps in rainbows from time to time for the entertainment—and retainment—of his lessees.

Swallows were swooping low over the pond taking flies we couldn't see, and occasional swirls along the shoreline showed us that trout—some of them very big trout—were on the hunt. But for us the hunting was interesting but tough, because the bank was thick with waist-high buffalo grass and, where scattered springs gushed cool clear water, it bristled with that back cast entangling native sunflower called Jerusalem artichokes. The wayward wind contrived to wander toward contrary no matter which side of the pond we fished, and the trout were easily spooked in the hyper-clear water and seemingly super-selective as well. But just what they were super-selective about remained a mystery.

We flushed several large trout feeding tight against the bank in shallow water, their backs awash like breaching whales, and finally John spotted, stalked, and caught a nice eighteen-incher on a smallish black beetle—always a useful choice when it's clear the trout are eating something but it's unclear just what. Beetles are to trout, goes the collective wisdom, what a cube of interesting cheese skewered on a toothpick is to people at a party:

a reflexive choice—to see one is to eat one provided you can metabolize lactose.

Freshly armed with black beetles, we fished the pond with new optimism that went sadly unrequited, so we walked down to the next pond to see if its inhabitants might be less discriminating. Unfortunately, they proved even more so: ten or so trout were stacked in front of the overflow pipe draining from the pond above while indifferently snacking on something we couldn't see, but conveying the general impression of Romans at *cena* leaning on one elbow and occasionally plucking a roasted rabbit fetus from a passing tray. We tried everything logical and some things illogical, and sometimes we'd get a look but never a take.

Eventually we gave up and walked the shoreline to make deprived puppy-dog eyes at the trout rising here and there, and then John got the bright idea of seining the water and hauled from his vest a small folded piece of fine mesh.

Finding large numbers of tiny cinnamon ants, we immediately rerigged with very close imitations and tried them on the outlet strainers, and although this time we got a response from the trout, moving aside to let our ants drift past wasn't quite the response we were looking for. So we headed back to the upper pond, where the swallows were still swirling and so were the trout. Though not, as we proved with innumerable casts, for ants.

Finally I stretched out on a teetering catwalk leading to the inlet pipe and squeezed my eyes tight to the water. I saw one small rusty mayfly spinner orbiting a tiny eddy, and I was sure we'd found the key until I realized that if the spinner fall was still on, the spinners should be visible in the air and that trout are more likely to rise to falling spinners by sipping than by swirling.

So I squeezed my face even closer to the water and began to see them: tiny weird shucks, discarded exoskeletons, thousands upon thousands that were like nothing I'd ever seen: little greenish-black threads with two big googly white eyes. Of course John knew just what they were—a kind of locally prominent largish midge that hatches erratically and infrequently—and he quickly produced a pair of pupae. The temperamental weather chose just then to turn in our favor, and with the stiff wind no longer at our sides but at our backs, we could roll-cast to the swirls far out in the center without knitting our back casts into the artichoke jungle.

Before the weather notched up from bracing to frightening, the clouds bruising greenish-black and more than a little reminiscent of what swept Dorothy Gale to Oz, I finally blew my skunk with a fat sixteen-incher that had John's weird little midge notched firmly into one corner of its jaw and a slow trickle of midge pupae oozing from the other like a hungry college student who'd vowed to bankrupt an all-you-can-eat oyster bar and very nearly succeeded.

And then John hooked up, and I hooked up again, and everything was right with the world, because the trout had been an interesting mystery but not one so interesting we couldn't solve it.

19. *The Sot-Weed Factor*

Going on forty years ago, not long after my father died of lung cancer from a lifetime of puffing Chesterfields, I quit smoking. This was a big step because I was no dabbler.

I smoked unfiltered Camels—two packs a day. When on a health kick I smoked filtered Marlboros. When I had a cold and cigarettes rasped my throat like barbed wire, I switched to menthol Kool Regulars, as I was convinced their cough-drop taste made them therapeutic. Mornings, I scouted for my eyeglasses by the glowing cigarette I lit the instant my head cleared the pillow.

I was an addict and an idiot, and I needed the tangible evidence that smoking abbreviates life to get me to quit. Which is too bad in a way, because since I quit smoking I don't catch as many fish.

It isn't that I smell different—tobacco smokers' stinky orange fingers befoul everything they touch, so by rights flies that smell of mere human ought to be less repellent than flies that smell of a human smoked like bacon in the chimney of an insecticide factory. It's just that without tobacco I think different, and not in an ungrammatical Apple-computer-ad sort of way but in the way I portion time.

Among the most important factors in successful fly-fishing is patience, especially the patience to rest a pool roiled by haste. And this is where smokers win out. Raise a good fish that doesn't quite take, and most nonsmoking anglers will fidget a minute then put a fly right back over it. If our angler's especially experienced or has absorbed the advice of others who are, he'll change to a smaller fly or a bigger fly or a different fly and try again, perhaps a bit upstream or downstream or perhaps with a bit more slack in the tippet or a slight upstream curve or whatever else he can retrieve from memories of past success. Often nothing happens, perhaps because the fish hasn't quite resumed its feeding rhythm or it's been caught and released one too many times and is still congratulating itself on its most recent escape.

But when a smoker raises a good fish that doesn't quite take, he finds a comfortable rock, lights up, and sits there staring at the spot to watch what happens and think things over. True, he's abbreviating his life by an average of eight minutes, but he's also contemplating the matters at hand in the most calming yet focused fashion humanity has discovered short of prayer, illegal medication, or short-circuited synapses. Finally, when the coal nears his fingers, our addict snuffs out his smoke, pockets the residue, wades into the stream at a completely different spot that provides the pool's one sure angle for a drag-free drift, and catches the fish on his first try.

Of course anglers who are naturally philosophical, meditative, and analytical can think through confusing situations without tobacco. But in sixty-something years of fishing, I remember only a handful of nonsmokers who could sit for ten minutes staring at a spot where they'd just missed a big fish, mulling through all the possible scenarios before crafting a successful assault. Of smokers who routinely did this I remember dozens and dozens, including, at one time, me.

In fishing as in life, the first and most obvious answer to a question is rarely the right one. Often it isn't even the right question.

When a trout in moving water doesn't take our fly, our first question is why did he miss it? But in a river's competitive environment, an opportunistic feeder with faulty targeting skills is a designated loser in evolution's unforgiving race. A trout smart enough to eat enough to grow big enough for us to care that he "missed it" didn't. He simply decided that what he'd thought was food wasn't.

Except for spawning season's brief diversion, a fish's sole role in life is eating. If the fish lives in moving water, it spends its days sorting the endless objects that drift past its lie into the edible and the inedible while struggling to maintain its lie against the force of the ever-busy current or the pressure of other fish seeking their own little lebensraum. They plot vectors toward each potential meal with the fast-moving mathematical uncertainties of a naval gunner's mate training his twin Oerlikons on a zooming Zero.

The longer you sit there watching the water, the more likely you'll notice why your big trout "missed it," which is a less precise way of saying that he spurned it. Although obsessive tiers of flies take a different view, a good trout is far more likely to have refused your fly because it was the wrong shape than the wrong color and the wrong size than the wrong shape. And far more likely than any of these is because your fly did something unexpected.

Proper food drifts naturally with the current, but then so do twigs, leaves, and cigarette butts. To stream-born fish, proper food is alive—though Alaskan rainbows eating drifting chunks of spawned-out salmon will disagree—and if it moves on its own within the drift, it does so in small and predictable ways. Proper food doesn't skitter across the current, cutting a V-wake like a water skier—at least not very often; a stonefly nymph lumbering ashore to hatch comes to mind, as do darting *isonychias* nymphs and scattered species of water-skiing caddis.

What proper food mostly does do is go with the flow, and in the moving water of a trout stream there is no such thing as a uni-fied flow to go with. The uneven nature of the bottom, the banks, the rocks and logs and bends and riffles that characterize the kind of water most trout fishers like to fish means that every foot of stream is different in its movements: eddies, swirls, thin threads of slow current sneaking between fat threads of fast current, and slow current rolling along the bottom like tumbleweeds while the meniscus above slides downhill in a featureless laminar sheen.

Our seemingly idle smoker, sitting there dragging his way into a hairless future of chemotherapy, radiation treatments, and an oxygen bottle wheeling in his wake, sees what our hasty non-smoker doesn't: the minute, almost imperceptible change of current that pooched his drift. He sees, after ten minutes of staring, thinking, and French-inhaling his life away, how to defeat the almost invisible micro-drag that turned his fly from food into not food. And he goes out there and does it.

I don't advocate taking up—or worse, taking back up—what King James I described as a "custome lothsome to the eye, hatefull to the Nose, harmefull to the braine, dangerous to the Lungs, and in the blacke stinking fume thereof, neerest resembling the horrible Stigian smoke of the pit that is bottomelesse" simply to improve your fishing.

But I'm suggesting that if you would be a better angler for those big tough trout that so often "miss it," you must find some way to become a better dawdler, to learn to be patient in a focused sort of way, and to pass your time in a more productive fashion than by turning admiring eyes on your marvelous surroundings—and it's far easier for me to suggest this than to actually bring myself to look away from the chirping birds and chittering squirrels and buzz-bombing dragonflies that surround anglers in any place worth fishing.

To get those big tough trout you must become, as Darwin said of himself, "a sort of machine for observing facts and grinding out conclusions." You must put in the time to patiently and meticulously analyze what military commanders call the situation on the ground. Or, in our case, the water. And you must not let yourself be diverted by endlessly humming Deep Purple's "Smoke on the Water."

PART THREE

Enabling Devices

One cannot think well, love well, sleep well, if one has not dined well.
—Virginia Woolf

20. *Misty Water-Colored Memories*

As YEARS GO, 1975 WAS PRETTY GRIM. THE aftermath of a stock market crash, the Arab oil embargo, runaway inflation, a bitter recession, the disco crisis. "The Way We Were" the treacly song of the year. *Gunsmoke* gone from TV after a twenty-year run.

The communists took Saigon, the Khmer Rouge took Phnom Penh, and the Pathet Lao took Laos. Britain and Iceland declared war over codfish. Dutch elm disease declared victory over elm-shaded New England. There were massive layoffs in Detroit, gas prices a dizzying fifty-nine cents a gallon, and the Federal debt a shocking $542 billion.

President Ford made it official: "I must say to you that the state of the union is not good. Millions of Americans are out of work; recession and inflation are eroding the money of millions more. Prices are too high, and sales are too slow."

But life wasn't all gloom and doom. Because in 1975 the last Japanese soldier from World War II finally surrendered in Indonesia. Because Basil Fawlty televised his Towers in Torquay. Because Patty Hearst heard the burst of Roland's Thompson gun, and she bought it.

Because after paying my fuel and lobster-bait bills and finding a few spare dollars in my pocket one stormy autumn day, I stopped by the bookstore for something to read and bought my first copy of *Gray's Sporting Journal*. Finally, a huntin' and fishin' magazine for English majors, meant to be read purely for pleasure and not just for tips on whacking that big ol' buck or matching that hatch or surviving the dangerous and unfamiliar wild.

That first copy of *Gray's* proved tremendously influential if you measure influence by its many imitators. It might even have influenced me a bit—not that I'd have recognized it back then.

Because this was a full seven years before a lifetime of avidly reading accidentally made me a writer; twelve years before it even more accidentally made me an editor; twenty years before I became, a little less accidentally, *Gray's* first angling columnist; twenty-two before I became *Gray's* editor; twenty-three before I first heard *fly-fishing* and *monetize* used unironically in the same sentence.

Because way back then fishing was still a . . . hobby? sport? pastime? obsession? An aesthetically pleasing way of acquiring the evening's entrée? Whatever fishing was in 1975, it wasn't yet an industry or a competitive sport just waiting to be monetized. It was simply what folks had been doing as long as we'd been folks.

In our family, fishing was all those things with an extra serving of obsession. So when I came to Midcoast Maine in 1972, at the dawn of a global recession, and looked for a job in a state that had been in recession since the demise of wooden shipbuilding, it seemed in character to skirt popular local career paths—stitching shoes, packing sardines, eviscerating poultry, or inquiring if there'll be fries with that clam roll—and, after some false starts working in a camera store, go fish for my living. In a way, I still am.

We fished in a different world back then. Our rods and reels, lines and leaders, and flies and tactics were nowhere near as refined as those of today, yet somehow we managed to catch a lot of fish. Too many by most measures. And so by 1975, visionary messages, such as Lee Wulff's 1939 decree that "gamefish are too valuable to be caught only once," finally penetrated our lizard brains, and ever more fishermen began releasing ever more fish.

Until fishing in the Gulf of Maine began to slide into crisis in this new millennium, I froze flounder and hake and haddock against the long hungry winter just as I still freeze broccoli and corn and peas, but I'm pretty sure 1975 was the last year I froze trout. That I ever did now seems barbarous.

By today's sartorial standards, we looked pretty barbarous back then. Fishing clothes were simply regular clothes that had become too tattered and threadbare for anything else. Had I appeared on a Maine salmon river in 1975 decked out in the color-coordinated engineering edifices we fly fishers wear today, I'd have been laughed straight into the puckerbrush. Had I gone home to East Tennessee in 1975 and zoomed onto our hometown bass lake driving a neon-purple metal-flake bathtub toy with an outboard motor the size of a refrigerator while wearing a matching jumpsuit placarded with advertisements for sparkplugs and crank baits, I'd have been shot.

That contrast between packaging and contents was the most interesting thing about *Gray's*. I opened the stark white cover with its tasteful type and dreamy painting and found not the expected pinkies-up snoot-fest of tweedy self-congratulation but real writing by real people doing real things—carefully crafted fiction, essays, and poetry you might have seen in *The New Yorker* or *The Atlantic* if not for all those trees and mountains and fish and birds and deer and antelope, some of them decidedly dead and often by the writer's own hand. And, of course, *Gray's* had all those decidedly un-tweedy writers like Charley Waterman, who popped bluegills from dustbowl tank ponds back during the Depression, or John Hewitt, who discovered that catfish stink bait crimped his teenaged love life, or Annie Proulx, who passed through *Gray's* with fine short fiction on her way to a Pulitzer after an early career writing grind-your-own-apple-cider features in hippie homesteader magazines.

Our tackle in 1975 was just beginning to accelerate into its technological rush toward damn-the-expenses excellence. But with few exceptions—navigating and fish finding with gee-whizz electronics instead of a compass, chart, and cunning—today's tackle isn't startlingly different from its predecessors. I can cast about seventy-five feet with my eight-weight fiberglass Fenwick Feralite, bought in 1972 for $35. I can cast about ninety feet with my eight-weight nanotechnology Orvis Helios, $795 in 2009. Sometimes that extra fifteen feet means the difference between catching a fish and not. But only sometimes.

Reels are way better these days, but I can't remember ever losing a trout on a click-drag 1950s JW Young Beaudex that I wouldn't have also lost on a $600 computer-machined abstract aluminum sculpture equipped with carbon-fiber brakes whose design and composition were literally lifted from a Le Mans Porsche by a man who drove one. Of course it's a different story at sea. Today's corrosion-proof sealed-drag reels are so much better in saltwater that I have permanently walled off all memories of soaking my rusty Pflueger 1498 with WD-40, trying to make it spin.

Not many fly-fished in saltwater back then. Joe Brooks wrote a good book about saltwater fly-fishing in 1950, Lefty Kreh wrote another in 1974, and Frank Forester was writing about it way back in 1849. Still, saltwater fly-fishing was mostly a bonefish and tarpon enterprise in the 1970s, so when anxious Maine birds urged I take a break from monetizing lobsters to haul the Fenwick out from under the *Lucy B's* washboards and toss bright yellow bucktails into schools of mackerel and harbor pollock, I was seen as peculiar and not just by the birds.

What wasn't peculiar was my choice of footwear. Like most folks in my line of work, I wore hip-boots—all day on the boat and in the bait shed and folded down at the knees in the market, bookstore, or neighborhood bar. To supplement the rubber-cleated Red Balls I wore at the office, I had felt-soled hip-boots for spring and early summer recreation, when lobsters were scarce but trout weren't, and I had some full-bore chest waders for the big northern salmon rivers. And this brings me to the one thing about the 1970s as irremediably evil as the down-sucking economy and the leisure suit and Barbra's misty mem'ries: those heavy, leaky, stinky, galumphing, naughty-verbing waders.

It's fashionable in some circles to source the beginnings of fly-fishing's modern popularity to Robert Redford's 1992 movie from Norman Maclean's 1976 novella, but if anglers in the 1990s had still been slogging upstream in those old rubberized canvas monstrosities or slowly cooking *sous-vide* inside those impermeable PVCs we all wore in the 1970s, I doubt all those riverside fly-casting classrooms would ever have filled with stockbrokers and English professors and cardiologists learning to double-haul no matter how cool the Movie made us futsy old river-haunters seem.

Today, most of us flailing away on the rivers and streams, if not looking cool then at least being cool, in a temperature-and-relative-humidity-measurable sort of way, can thank not Robert Redford and Norman Maclean but Wilbert Gore, Robert Gore, and Rowena Taylor, the inventors of Gore-Tex. And for the folks at Simms for saying, "Geeze, this here Gore-Tex'd make cracker-jack waders."

In the past forty years, lots of things have changed in the world around us, though at its core not much has changed at all: may-flies still hatch, trout still eat them, prices still rise, salaries still stagnate, and politicians still parrot implausible excuses why it isn't their fault.

But at least after all these years we can still go huntin' and fishin' pretty much undisturbed, though there are fewer places to fish these days and even fewer places to hunt, with 102 million more Americans now looking for our own rocks to stand on. And at least, in this relentlessly monetizing world, the tiny slice of hunters and anglers who avidly read still have something to read with *Gray's*—as long as they don't entirely ignore all the intrusive advertising that makes it possible.

21. *Ultimate Innovation*

THE ENTERTAINING THING ABOUT MIDDLE AGE is how you become utterly invisible—at least to those who aren't middle aged. Given the reproductive underpinnings of mating rituals, the almost-elderly expect to be invisible to attractive young members of the opposite sex. But a while back I was surprised to find myself invisible to a group of eager young fly fishermen discussing the most important angling innovations of the past century.

The discussion morphed into an argument, as these things do, and the group divided into factions, as groups will. One faction passionately promoted the graphite fly rod as the most important development, and over time they pretty much shouted down the various smaller factions singing the virtues of floating fly lines that actually float, knotless tapered leaders, Gore-Tex waders and jackets, wading boots built like comfortable running shoes instead of Li'l Abner's galumphing leather brogans, rustproof reels equipped with real instead of hypothetical drags, polarized sunglasses that reveal the hidden depths like portable X-ray machines, vests of many pockets, rotary fly-tying vises, genetically marvelous dry-fly hackle, sparkly yarns, tungsten beads, and, of course, that viral disseminator of information and misinformation on all known topics, the Internet.

I nearly ha-hemmed and volunteered my own pick, but then I remembered what I was like at their age, and I didn't fancy a dozen twenty-somethings jointly advising the briefly visible old goober in the corner to attempt an anatomical improbability with himself.

And so I spared them my unrequested wisdom, and when the plagues-of-Egypt storm that had driven us individually to shelter collectively inside a designer-rustic destination fly shop finally huffed and puffed and blew itself out, I watched them dissolve their temporary tribal bonds and head in small groups back for the rivers inside the most important angling innovation since the fish hook: the automobile.

Automobiles remade the landscape, remade society, remade humanity into its virtual support system. Ninety-five percent of Americans own one. We feed each one more than a thousand gallons of gasoline annually. We spend an hour and a half a day in them commuting to work or ferrying children or shopping for things we need, or think we need. We spend more of our hard-earned money on our cars than on anything but our homes, our children's education, and our end of life health care.

Transportation—trucks, buses, airplanes, automobiles—constitutes North America's largest single source of air pollution, even though today's automobiles fart forth 90 percent less pollution than they did only thirty years ago and use less than half the fuel. Evolving technological innovations promise to throttle back tailpipe nastiness another 90 percent within fifteen years—sooner if our short-sighted Congress will stiffen its stones and accelerate the mandate.

But to set aside these larger societal questions, about which I know little, in favor of a topic I thoroughly understand: where would we anglers be without our cars? And the answer is fishing much closer to home or perhaps not fishing at all.

Sport fishing as we know it arrived in the nineteenth century along with the railroads. Before railroads, average people fished within a short walk or horseback ride of home. But when the cars

130 FISH WON'T LET ME SLEEP

arrived, adventurous tourists like Henry David Thoreau could be whisked upon whims and iron rails from urban areas into the wilds. Soon, fishing lodges and a sport-fishing industry—often built by and certainly promoted by the railroads—blossomed in the wilderness, and our great-great-grandparents began to do pretty much what we do today: travel into the silent beyond to catch fish purely for pleasure. These days, thanks to the SUV in the driveway, we rarely go fishing via train or steamboats, not to mention buckboards and stagecoaches. But even an airline trip halfway around the world to fish New Zealand or Chile begins and ends in a car.

In 1912, when my father was born, the Model-T Ford had just begun redefining automobiles beyond the expensive playthings of the very rich. A dozen years later, he was heading up into the East Tennessee mountains on Boy Scout troop trout-fishing expeditions in a Chevrolet touring car belonging to his father, a not-particularly-well-off master mason.

In 1919, a young army colonel named Eisenhower commanded a military truck convoy making North America's first ever sea-to-shining-sea trophy dash. It took them sixty-two days from East Coast to West Coast over a patchwork of virtually nonexistent roads. Fifty years later, zooming along on the interstate highway system built when that very same Eisenhower was president, the average driver made it in five. Back when my brother and his friend Rick Blackburn were fishing Montana every summer, they figured three days from East Tennessee towing the aluminum capsules where they and their families would live for the next month or so.

Today, cars are essential fishing tackle, and I remember them all as clearly as my favorite fly rods.

There was my father's 1939 Chevrolet, a black business coupe with a sample-case platform behind the single bench seat where my brother and I wobbled atop little wooden folding chairs. My mother said the car knew the way to the mountains so well it could almost drive itself. One day, returning from a trout-fishing expedition, it came to a stop sign and obediently did so and never ran again. A farmer towed it home, and my mother paid him with a jar of homemade pickles.

Its temporary replacement was an army-surplus jeep called Penelope, on loan from a fly-fishing friend who'd just bought a behemoth Buick convertible. I remember riding to the mountains in Penelope's front seat with my leg stuck out the open door and resting on the fender as I scanned the passing river for trout. I would never ever feel so cool again, and I was only eight.

Next came a wheezy '53 Plymouth sedan, egret-egg green with an art-deco hood ornament resembling a three-masted schooner being melted by a solar wind—or, if you held your head just right, a self-satisfied sailfish preparing to leap. My father took that car up two-tracks I would hesitate to drive my big-tired four-wheel-drive Toyota pickup today, and we never got stuck, at least not irrevocably.

My uncle Jimmy drove a Nash Rambler, robin-egg blue and utterly without charm except for its cavernous trunk, which held all of us and our camping gear: a big wall tent, kitchen tent, boxes of food, Dutch ovens, iron skillets, crates of fishing tackle, lawn chairs—everything. I found the stodgy Nash socially embarrassing and would not appreciate the possibilities of its famous reclining seats until my hormones arrived five years after the Rambler had been replaced with something less versatile.

My own early autos were meant more for hormonal gratification than for fishing, but when I moved to Maine and became a lobster fisherman I acquired something only a fisherman could love: a 1954 Chevrolet pickup with a homemade stake body forever permeated by the tons of lobster bait hauled by its original owner and by me. On recreational days, when I'd slide my rubber and canvas waders from its deeply marinated body and slog off into the upper Penobscot, I wondered if I was violating the laws against chumming for salmon.

When I accidentally fell into writing for part of my living, I acquired a bright red 1966 Jeepster that was sporty, fleet, sure-footed, and unbelievably unreliable. Close on its temperamental heels came a 1972 VW bus—your basic crunchy granola fish-mobile that was bear-poop brown, had one broken headlight crazily flashing the stars, the middle seat replaced by a sleeping bag and a Coleman stove, and its interior warted with homemade rod holders and a wobbly fly-tying vise. In it I could become invisible quicker than a middle-aged man at a mall full of teenage girls, and many a weekend I spent creeping up remote tote roads, guerrilla camping in abandoned log yards and living on trout and beans and unbridled youth.

Its replacement was the best auto I've ever owned, before or since, a four-wheel drive Toyota pickup long bed with a slide-in pop-up camper providing all the comforts of home. In its residential half I slept and ate and slowly learned the difference between typing and writing. In its operational half I saw as much of the east as was piscatorially interesting, including a memorable month-long circumnavigation of Quebec's Gaspé Peninsula. One day, after many rode-hard-and-put-away-wet years together, I stood on its brakes to avoid destroying half the world's remaining Stanley Steamers, hooting and pooting from a Maine motel where their owners were conventioneering, and the rusty frame cracked like a breadstick. When I heard that, I wept. A week later I bought another just like it only fifteen years newer—a short bed, alas, as Toyota no longer made long beds in the States. Goodbye to the slide-in camper, and hello to worrisome searches for a dry spot to pitch a tent.

I ought to have explained all this to those glossy young fishermen, heading off in their glossy new SUVs to fish with glossy new graphite fly rods that to them were the most important fly-fishing innovation in recent memory. But without those cars, without those individual conveyances to wherever from wherever, we would scarcely need these fly rods at all. We'd be home dangling worms in a ditch instead of spreading out across the planet with rods in the trunk, spreading out across the planet for better and for worse, to be absolutely clear about the ecological and sociological damage of automobiles, including all those roads that scar and pollute and make accessible the once-secret feeder streams of once-great rivers.

I'm not smart enough to know if the tradeoff was worth it in the grand scheme of things. But I'm smart enough to own my share of the guilt. And I accept this, turn the key, and head off toward a distant river as often as I can.

22. *The Right Stuff*

Mark Twain wrote that the difference between the right word and the wrong word is the difference between lightning and a lightning bug. This is just as true in fishing tackle as in writing, as I found out one April in New Brunswick while fishing the Miramichi's spring run of black salmon—kelts that have wintered beneath the river ice and are heading for the sea with spring breakup.

Unlike sea-run Atlantic salmon, which eat flies for reasons no one can fully explain though not for want of trying, black salmon eat flies because they're hungry, especially for smelts, which are beginning their spawning run upriver from the sea precisely when the salmon are heading downriver toward the sea and its ample larder. This fortuitous collision of ravenous predator with bounteous prey gives winter-lean salmon a chance to quickly pork up and anglers a unique opportunity to catch an Atlantic salmon—the fish that famously doesn't feed in fresh water—for reasons we can actually understand.

At least most years it does. But that particular year the weather was as tortured as a politician's logic, and its unintended consequences just as damaging. One week it was March with snow and ice and screaming northeasters and electricity-deprived homeowners shivering in the dark, and the next week it was July with temperatures in the 80s, a blistering southwest wind, and acres of wan Yankee flesh crisping in the sun.

Upriver above Boiestown, the Miramichi was all Nanook-of-the-North ice floes when I drove past. Fifty miles downriver at Blackville, the ice was all but gone—a month-long process squeezed into twenty-four hours. The river was high and rising and filled with debris, and the fishing, which I was told started out pretty good last week—maybe eight or ten salmon per rod per day—was now down to two or three at best, and I don't mean per rod.

I sat on a riverside bench in front of Byron "Byzie" Coughlan's Country Haven Lodge in Gray Rapids watching ice floes ranging in size from bread loaf to bread truck bombing by as Byzie and I clucked our tongues and shook our heads. "Never seen nothing like it," said Byzie, a lifelong river resident. "The fishing's just shut right off."

In one of those amusing coincidences that litter real life, Byzie and I found we knew each other from previous careers cranking up with forty-weight coffee and red-snapper hot dogs at Buzzy Hanscomb's truck stop in Portsmouth, New Hampshire. And there we were twenty-five years later, two old truck drivers sitting alongside North America's most productive Atlantic salmon river and talking about tomorrow's angling prospects for the king of fish and the fish of kings during the weirdest spring weather anyone's ever seen.

It's a strange world.

And it was a strange company of anglers assembled at Country Haven, too: a gaggle of fish-writers from Europe had flown in to admire this magnificent river and its unique spring fishery. I was the token North American—a homeboy, so to speak, from across the border in Maine, where the most noticeable differences between Maine and New Brunswick, besides fishable populations of Atlantic salmon, are gas pumps and speed limits that believe in the metric system.

So in theory I should have had home-court advantage against this European invasion. But theories, like a politician's promises, are made to be broken.

Not the next day, however, for with the river a roiling bouilla-baisse of ice and trees and weeds, the fishing was at best Quixotic, though this didn't stop us from dodging disasters with our guides in a motley collection of watercraft ranging from repurposed run-abouts to an indigenous breed of flat-iron plywood skiff that skips across the waves like a stone going ducks and drakes. At day's end I was the undisputed highliner with an easy bushel and a half of weeds brought to the boat. I could have taken twice that had I set my mind to it and used a wider-gapped hook. I lost the main trophies, though: a pair of *Titanic*-worthy icebergs that took me into my backing and broke me off when I couldn't convince my guide to follow them downstream until they melted to a manage-able size.

But my glory was fleeting, for on succeeding days the stew began to thin, and although the river remained frightfully high and roaring, it became far more fishable—at least for those with the right stuff.

That I didn't have it was apparent even before the reel on my favorite little summer-weight spey rod imploded and left me with a backup single-hander of a different line weight rigged with either of two inappropriate choices of line: a floater or a slow-sinker. That Riccard Bakken of Norway had the right stuff was painfully evident, as he quickly hauled in several good salmon with his grown-up-sized spey rod and the fastest-sinking fly line I've ever seen.

And then David Profumo of the UK cadged a spare line off Riccard and began catching fish, too. As the river continued to drop, John Bailey, Keith Elliott, Pierre Affre, and Phillipe Boisson, with their European fast-sinking lines and heavy brass-weighted tube flies and long, long casts, were all catching fish. Finally I broke my skunk with a grilse of around twenty-seven inches that skittered across the surface in dramatic fashion but looked like a small-scale model of the corpulent forty-incher that Bailey was photographically releasing into a nearby backwater as I brought my adolescent to heel.

"Still ain't what it ought to be," said Byzie that evening as the Euros attempted to quantify success. "Lots of times with black salmon y'has to stand behind a tree to tie on your fly."

Finally the river dropped another foot and my lazy-sinking fly line could dawdle down to where the fish swam. I also shelved my trusted box of prissy summertime salmon flies in favor of something more seasonally suitable borrowed from Axel Lerche, a large and immensely friendly German businessman who vacationed on the Miramichi a few years ago, fell in love with the area, and went native by acquiring a bankside house, a tin skiff, and an ear-lapper hat, and starting a property management firm called Salar Enterprises with Neil Freeman, the English sporting-tackle auctioneer and hyperactive involuntary channeler of every Monty Python episode ever aired. Their firm, which as near as I could tell from my habit of nodding and smiling and not really listening as people talk about business, was meant to ease the way for well-off people also wishing to go native along the Miramichi without the bother of actually having to go native, if you take my meaning—folks who might want to come here from Europe or across America to fish and shoot birds and ski and golf and do all those other things people with the right stuff tend to do with their time without having to learn which day the town of Gray Rapids picks up rubbish, or who can be found on short notice to acquire a new cylinder of propane, or evict from their shiny new cottage a squatter who weighs 375 pounds and thinks your grandmother's needlework throw pillows are just as tasty as the contents of the refrigerator that she and her two cubs toppled onto the kitchen floor and opened like a tin of tuna.

But to avert our eyes from the business of business to the business at hand, newly-natived Axel claimed to have *the* fly and gave me one, a fat bright wad of red and yellow marabou and Krystal Flash that, to a fly fisher from Maine, where streamers are as svelte as a smelt, seems more suited for sharks or pike than the noblest of all fish.

And that's just how the noblest of all fish attacked it: like pike after innocent ducklings or sharks after the struggling survivors of what airline flight attendants call a water landing. When I finally gave Axel back his fly, it had thinned down significantly and its shank was bent in three places. I had taken four salmon, one just over forty inches, plus three grilse and a grilsette of around eighteen inches. The fish were feeding up fast and had grown as thick and active as sea-runs, dashing around and shaking their heads and exposing your backing and jumping and re-jumping and doing all those Atlantic salmon things that make otherwise rational people perform such fiscally irrational acts as fishing for them in the first place—or, worse, buying riverfront property on a distant continent and devoting your life to their pursuit.

23. *The Righteous Stuff*

TRENDS IN FLY-FISHING EBB AND FLOOD LIKE the tides and are just about as unstoppable and far less predictable. Given the relentless industry emphasis on hyperlight, hyperfast, and hyperexpensive, I figured not even King Cnut could have turned back that particular flow, but a quiet trickle of fishing rods that began quietly a few years ago recently and surprisingly turned into a gusher.

By fishing rods I mean rods meant for dull normals like you and me, fishing mostly in unheralded trout waters far off the hero-shot paths, mostly at casting distances between ten and forty feet with a searching dry fly that might suspend a probing nymph for the sizes of fish most of us actually catch.

Of course these are the kinds of fly rods most of us long ago exiled to the closet's dark corners alongside our canvas waders and flared trousers and high-school letter jackets and composting piles of *Ramparts* and *Evergreen Review*. But thanks to advances in fabrics, resins, and tapers trickling down from the relentless quest for ultimate line speed, this new breed of pure fishing rods feels better than any of the artifacts in the back of my angling closet not made of split-bamboo by master craftsmen. Perhaps this heralds a new trend emphasizing the act of fly-fishing over the consumption of fly-fishing, if you take my meaning. Because—surprise,

surprise—some of the best-feeling new fishing rods these days are also the cheapest.

When I wrote the angling column at *Gray's*, I looked forward each year to triaging my way through the shiny new toys with mixed feelings. Sure, there'd be shiny and new, but along the way I wouldn't get to play with my favorites, some of which were recent award winners for Gray's Best and some of them personal bests since the Eisenhower administration.

Among these is old-fashioned red-tin Mucilin, a waterproofing goo I prefer to the new breed of wonder-whips for floating fly lines and big hairy dry flies. You can still find très passé Mucilin with a bit of Googling, although it now comes in a modern plastic "tin" that won't stay closed and lacks that marvelous applicator made of sheep's wool and soft red leather.

Given my fondness for red-tin Mucilin, you'd probably figure me for a silk-line nut, but I'm not quite that far over the rainbow. I do love Cortland Sylk lines, though. They're completely synthetic, sturdy, skinny, slinky, and just stiff enough to form proper loops and turn over bushy dry flies on very short casts. They do feel almost made from silk, and when I'm fishing small streams and not testing new fly lines fresh from the laboratory, I'm probably casting a Sylk.

When teetering about in those small streams, or on big rivers or long trails or sometimes just out to the woodshed when it's icy, I stay vertical with a Folstaf. There's a virtual forest of new high-tech wading staffs, but none has proven as handy and trouble-free for me as the old reliable. After years of constant use, my Folstaff, like my body, finally began having issues, but a few winters ago its maker refurbished it good as new with fresh cork and a double-strength internal shock cord while carefully preserving its badge-of-honor patina.

I'm not sure patina is the right word for my W.C. Russell wading shoes. Scarred and battered after twenty years of constant wear and on their seventh set of felt soles, these rugged Cordura and leather boondockers still bust through underbrush and rocks like a D6 Cat—with more comfort and less noise. And nothing without studs sticks to slick surfaces quite like those real wool felt soles. Sooner or later, I expect that the growing call for a ban on felt soles, thanks to their efficiency in transporting unwanted organisms from watershed to watershed, will shunt my Russells to the back of the closet, though they may enjoy a limited afterlife in the local trout brooks, where they won't spread any bacilli not already present.

Fortunately, felt footwear regulations won't impact another old favorite: Bean boots from L.L. Bean. These rubber-bottom, leather-top reliables are virtually unchanged since 1912, and for wet climates like mine there's nothing better for negotiating the littoral mud and crud around camp or on long sloggy explorations up the topo map's thin blue lines. Now in their forty-fifth year, fifth set of bottoms, and second set of tops, my moccasin-comfortable Bean boots will never see the back of my closet as long as I'm ambulatory.

Nor will my Crocs, which are mostly what's on my feet whenever Bean boots or waders aren't. Made of nonabsorbent, nonmarking, nonskid plastic resin, these squeezably soft little-Dutchboy clogs may be international emblems of dorkhood and, lately, incarceration, but they're also cheap, light, and durable—not to mention the most comfortable footwear you'll find for slouching around the house, town, camp, or working in such slippery environments as commercial kitchens, operating rooms, portage trails, canoe bottoms, boat decks, and airport security screenings.

Speaking of which, flying fishermen will always need carry-on insurance, and for this I've found nothing better than the Orvis Frequent Flyer rods. I first fished one when my checked luggage was chasing me around the minor chalk streams of southwestern England almost two decades ago. By the time my favorite spring creek rod finally ran me to earth, I'd already decided the emergency seven-piece, eight-and-a-half-foot five-weight from my carry-on was its equal, if not its superior. With truly fishable multipiece rods becoming the norm and not the exception, packing a spare rod—or the sole rod if you're going carry-on only—is a no-brainer everywhere from the Rockies to Los Roques.

I've tried many gear-lugging systems over the years, but Patagonia's Pack Vest works best for my needs. It's a vertical-pocket vest logically arranged to hold enough fly boxes and accessories to satisfy any reasonable angler; it clips to a three-compartment backpack that effortlessly totes a fleece, a rain jacket (walled off from your nice dry sweater in its own scuppered apartment), a thermos, a water bottle, a decent lunch, spare reels and spools, a camera, and more. Sans vest, the pack becomes my favorite airline carry-on.

For light-carry days or in hot weather, a conventional double-pocket mesh vest back replaces the backpack. But my pack usually stays attached because I enjoy the comforts of Stuff, especially a Zip Stove, a double-wall steel firepot with a battery-powered fan that turns twigs and pine cones and dried moose poo into an 18,000-BTU blast furnace.

As the clown tells Lafeu in *All's Well That Ends Well*, "I am a woodland fellow, sir, that always loved a great fire." But here in Maine, building a fire for an impromptu mug-up or trout fry requires a premeditated fire permit. The Zip Stove doesn't—and it does its job in less time using less fuel with far less chance of spreading your great fire into one expensively memorable Great Fire. It weighs only two pounds, complete with kettle, lid, and batteries for the fan, and is the best packable solution I've found for campers and backpackers doing their part to inconvenience the white-gas and propane industry.

Around front, in the vest's business district, is a motley collection of new plastic fly boxes and favorite old metal ones from Wheatley and Perrine housing an equally motley collection of flies, mostly gathered as regional specialties when traveling or as wild-eyed experiments from friends on the fly-tying edge. But unless I've recently suffered through a war of attrition, I'm always well-stocked with my personal essentials: Parachute Hare's Ears, beadhead Pheasant Tails, generic stoneflies of various sizes and colors, Specks, and Green Rock Worms.

Doubtless someone could have tied a better searching dry fly than a Parachute Hare's Ear, but of all the ones I've tried outside of western hopper season, only a Klinkhamer comes close. Like most of my favorite flies, Hare's Ears imitate nothing specifically and so represent everything generally. They're shaggy and buggy and durable and work as well for searching booming pocket water as glassy spring creeks. If tied with a wing post and tail snipped from a snowshoe hare's feet, they float like corks.

Trailing behind on eighteen inches of 5X tippet will almost always be a small beadhead Pheasant Tail tied scoliosis style with the body curving down the bend of a short-shank caddis hook and beads of gold, copper, or black. Over the past twenty years and on three continents, I've caught maybe three-quarters of my really big trout and landlocked salmon on size-eighteen beadhead PTs.

If the fish aren't looking up, I go down. In small streams I'll fish old school with a generic stonefly nymph in gold, black, or brown bumping the bottom. About eighteen inches up, tied to a dropper spurred off the tippet knot, will usually be a Speck, an old Southern Appalachian wet fly with a clipped spun-deer-hair body and brown-and-grizzly hackle and tail that radiates edibility.

In bigger, faster water I'll go depth-charging with a Green Rock Worm ballasted by two tungsten beads, a lead underbody, and a body of Rhyacophila-green aluminum-fiber dubbing spun directly onto waxed copper wire. Reinforced by a trailing bead-head Pheasant Tail, this is my go-to deep water nymphing rig suspended beneath a Thingamabobber, the brightly colored soft plastic balloons that have become so ubiquitous with the strike indicator set that they've entered the language like Kleenex.

The accessory pockets house a collection of tippet materials of no consistent brand except for, when Atlantic salmon fishing, old reliable and just-the-right-degree-of-stiff Maxima. And of course there's the customary assortment of nippers, hemostats, hook-sharpening files, dry-shake fly restorer, a good compass, and the same green candle stub that's been waxing my ferrules since 1972.

Missing but not missed is the big leaky bottle of plastic-eating 100 percent DEET bug dope thanks to the various flavors of per-methrin-impregnated clothing, such as Buzz Off Insect Shield, Simms' No Fly Zone, etc., that emerged around 2006 from the military-uniform complex. I can't think of a single product that has brought more smiles of relief to us folks here in the heart of mosquito, blackfly, and Lyme disease country than Buzz Off. I still carry a small bottle of a picaridin-based bug dope to treat bare skin, but for me, DEET is pretty much an unpleasant artifact of the past.

For which my righteous old plastic fly lines, waders, jackets, fly rods, and sunglasses are eternally grateful.

24. *Extreme Makeover*

JUST AS THERE HAVE BEEN FEW HUMAN TRANS-
portation devices that didn't eventually sprout the generational
equivalent of Baby Moon hubcaps and a pair of four-barreled car-
buretors the size of lard pails, or a human habitation that didn't
eventually sprout Corinthian columns and epoch-appropriate yard
art, so, too, have the totems of anglers been subject to relentless
makeover campaigns—to make them better, to make them different, or to make them above all personal.

Who among us hasn't looked at an Adams, the perfect dry fly,
and imagined it even better with a sheen of silver tinsel underly-
ing the muskrat-gray dubbing? Who hasn't seen in a time-hon-
ored Rapala an opportunity to repaint its drab factory colors with
baby brook trout greens and creams, rearm it with razor-red circle
hooks, and lightly weight its stern so it goes all bobble-head with
a twitch? Who hasn't taken file and sandpaper to a favorite fly
rod's corks and inadvertently reinvented South Bend's 1940s-era
Comficient Grip, the ergonomic thumb cozy modernly found on
Winston's wonderful Joan Wulff Favorite fly rods?

Not all of us have the time, skills, or inclination to fiddle around
with sandpaper and files and paints and silver tinsel, not to mention drywall and crown moldings and click-lock bamboo floor-
ing. Yet as a spin through the aisles of Home Depot or the how-to

offerings on basic cable quickly reveals, few among us can resist the urge to re-create. We imagine a result, and if we can't ourselves pitch in and realize that dream, we can at least pay someone to do it for us.

Almost any good cane rod builder will make you a bespoke rod, tweaking a trusted taper to suit your stroke or preferences or purposes and decorating it, within reason, to suit your particular fetishes for seat, grip, guides, wraps, and ferrules. Winston had a program a while back that did this with their highest-end graphite rods, complete with reconfiguring the blanks to your specific requirements, but it seems to have suffered logistical problems and gone quietly away. Scott had a similar program that felt slightly more ambitious where you could virtually build your rod online, but I'm not sure it survived, either. And of course anyone can buy a rod blank from the likes of Winston, Scott, or St. Croix and wrap it and guide it and grip it and seat it to your heart's content—providing you have the time and the skills and the necessary equipment. Or know someone who does.

But it isn't really necessary to buy a new fly rod to have a new fly rod—or a whole rack full of new fly rods, as I discovered entirely by accident.

I found the rod, a 1950s-vintage Heddon, at a yard sale, though I can't remember where or when. But it must have been a yard sale because those of us with a taste for old bamboo simply cannot drive past a fishing-country yard sale, where we find just enough of what we're looking for to keep our repeated visits from meeting the popular definition of insanity. Over the years, I can't say that I've found any sparkling IF diamonds hidden in the rough of polyester leisure suits and Slim Whitman LPs, but I have found at least one genuine tourmaline along with a couple of jaspers, agates, and the usual clutch of rhinestone poodle pins.

Were I soullessly assessing monetary value, I'd probably rank my Heddon No.8—Heddon was among the best of the production-cane rod builders, but this was its lowest-level rod—as not far above the poodle-pin category of pedestrian Montagues and

Horrocks-Ibbotsons. A quick search of used rods lists turns up prices in the two hundred dollar range for the No.8 depending on length and condition. But the tapers were the same throughout the Heddon line, and at eight-and-a-half feet with a Standard Trout No.2 ferrule, the No.8 is a desirable and effective everyday trout fishing rod.

Of course the varnish was scaly, the wraps were frayed, and it was missing a guide, a sack, and one of its tips. But it was mine for a twenty dollar bill, so I took it home and tubed it up and mailed it to my rod-building brother and forgot all about it until it appeared at the post office one snowy winter day an undetermined number of years later.

The old rainbow-variegated thread was no longer available, but after varnishing, the tan-and-black jasper my brother chose nicely matches the rod's glowing caramel finish, and if you didn't know better—and if the previous owner hadn't shared my bad habit of spearing flies into the cork grip—you'd think it had just emerged from the rod shops at Dowagiac, Michigan, where James Heddon virtually invented factory-made fishing lures and produced some of the best factory-made cane fly rods ever known.

And so the old rod was made new, or somewheres near, as we say in Maine, but the project didn't become a makeover until I took it out to the pond after a spring thaw, mounted a reel, and began to cast.

Bamboo is a living thing and is thus subject to a living thing's whims, so you never know just which line will suit a cane rod until you try. Older bamboo predates the plastic-era concept of standardizing fly lines by grain weight rather than diameter, and all cane rods cast out their hearts with use, which means that while a mint-condition rod marked HDH might cast a six-weight brilliantly, the exact same rod that had been fished hard for half a century might feel better with a five-weight, four-weight, or even, in extreme examples, a three-weight.

The No.8 was labeled for an HDH double taper, the modern equivalent being a six-weight DT. After a dozen different tries, I found the resurrected Heddon a bit logy with a six-weight DT, overly brisk with a five-weight DT, and a brilliant performer with a weight-forward six-weight—specifically the venerable peach-colored Cortland 444. For reasons I can't explain, that particular WF6F brought the rod to life in ways a half-dozen different brands and permutations of WF6Fs did not.

And so, with twenty dollars, an accommodating bamboo rodmaker for a brother, and an hour of experimental casting in the backyard pond, I had a pleasant trout rod—and the growing sense that, if this particular rod cast so differently with theoretically identical lines, how might my stable of modern graphite trout rods transform?

The answer: they'd change character with every change of line as well, and reimagine themselves as quickly as I could mount a new reel and line.

A favorite Winston LT five-weight liked the peach-colored Cortland WF6F as much as the Heddon did but seemed depressed by the five-weight double-taper Cortland Sylk and too frantic with a WF5F, while a Sage five-weight I had never especially liked folded up and whimpered with the peach but jumped up and shouted howdy with the Sylk. A six-weight Loomis IMX that had always felt under-gunned with a trout line metamorphosed into a corker bass-bug rod when a WF7F RIO bug line replaced the WF6Fs and DTs that had tried but never quite managed to truly flex its ferrules.

Oncoming darkness and the evening shift change from blackflies to mosquitoes ended my makeover campaign before I'd gotten through every possible combination—twenty-four trout rods, twenty-eight reels spooled with trout lines from delicate DTs to long-belly steelhead tapers to Royal Wulff's brutal short-headed truncheon of a fly line appropriately called Ambush. Every rod had its specific loves and hates, and typically only one or two lines truly made each sing, which goes a long way toward explaining why some days we find our casting spot-on and other days inexplicably off.

All up, it was cheap and useful fun. As is explaining the rationale behind the marker scribblings all over my rod tubes. *Loves Sylk, Hates Peaches.* I can pass this off as poetic claptrap to other fly fishermen, but I don't think I'll be taking my rod tube labeled *For Ambush Only* through airport security anytime soon.

25. *The Big Switch*

Like bonds, stocks, and hemlines, fly rod lengths go up and down—first long, then short, then somewhere in between. Depending on where you fall on the long-short curve, you're either broke or rich on the finance side and a fashion plate or a total skank on the hemline side. Fly rods are easier because unlike Wall Street or the runway, you can go long or short or somewhere in between without risking either your reputation or your financial solvency. The popular choice will never be entirely wrong. The corollary is that it will seldom be entirely right.

When I was learning to fly-fish back in the 1950s, the most popular fly rods were nine feet long. My first rod was a hand-me-down Montague bamboo that cast, by modern measure, a six-weight line and weighed more than a modern twelve-weight. I cast it two-handed because at four feet tall I couldn't swing it one-handed. And I mostly deployed what the charitable might describe as a flying roll cast—constant tension, sideways and back, then a circling overhead *fling*—because the bouncy, canopy-sheltered little trout water we fished was an unkind place for the lovely brand of overhead fly-casting we saw in *Field & Stream* and endlessly practiced in our backyard. Forty years later, battling a fifteen-foot ten-weight while salmon fishing in the Aberdeenshire Dee,

I realized that my boyhood adaptation was simply a bastardized spey cast.

Meanwhile, influential fish-writers, such as A.J. McClane, Lee Wulff, and Arnold Gingrich, began to champion ever-shorter fly rods—Flea Rods, McClane called them—and rod-makers began churning them out both in cane and the newfangled fiberglass.

But the flea rods weren't new, either. Way back in the 1880s, the average fly rod was more than ten feet long and weighed a half-pound, about the weight of the average trout—a mismatch between tool and quarry that led pioneering Maine rod-maker Hiram Leonard to build the Fairy Catskill: ". . . a 3-Piece Fly . . . length, 8 $^{1/6}$ feet, Weight, 2 ounces. . . . The lightest Rod ever successfully made."

Then as now, little fly rods make little trout feel like big trout, but as A.J. McClane wrote in *Field & Stream* in the 1960s, "The real purpose of a light fly rod is to make it possible to cast a light line, long, fine leaders, and small flies . . ." to a "1-pound trout poised on nervous fins not 40 feet away." Which makes you wonder why so many of us these days choose trout rods designed to throw monstrous weighted sculpins to ten-pound brown trout living in the next county.

Hairy-chested turn-of-the-century trout men called the new fairy wands "effete toys," to which Charles F. Orvis replied that his eight-footer was "not a toy but a practical rod with which to fish." Not to be outdone, an august English tackle-maker called J. J. Hardy used his new seven-foot, two-and-three-quarter-ounce Casting Club de France to cast "twenty-five yards, which is much further than the average cast of an expert fisherman using a rod three times this weight."

And the fairies kept emerging. Under his own label, Leonard's nephew Hiram Hawes offered a rod called Fairy: a two-weight six-footer said to weigh only one ounce. Divine's 1920 catalog showed a seven-and-a-half-foot, two-and-a-half-ounce Fairy-Fly. Heddon had its Featherweights—"a 'fairy wand' of a rod . . . for those who wish to get the most sport out of their fishing." Maine's Fred Thomas built a seven-foot, two-and-a-half-ounce three-weight, although he didn't give it a spritely name, nor did Jim Payne with his No. 96, a six-foot, one-and-a-half-ounce splinter.

When he was at Cross in the 1920s, Wes Jordan built his famous Sylph, a two-piece, two-ounce seven-footer, along with a six-and-a-half-foot Fairy. After joining Orvis, Jordan turned out such fun toys as the six-foot, one-piece Superfine and the six-and-a-half-foot, two-ounce Deluxe—although, like Paul Young's famous six-foot, three-inch Midge, these were more wrist-rockets than fairy wands, which balanced with five- to six-weight lines not three-weights. True light-line rods appeared at Orvis in the early 1960s with the seven-foot, three-weight Seven/Three and the four-weight Flea, all in Orvis' trademark impregnated cane.

Around 1960, the new fashion finally visited the family Babb in the form of seven-foot Shakespeare Wonderods. Our flying roll casts were harder to execute with the shorter rods, but we could now sidearm proper picture-book loops far back beneath the rhododendrons. Their dramatically lighter weight made our fishing days feel effortless and our ten-inch trout like the monsters we read about in magazines.

Soon everyone who was anyone was fishing short rods. The late 1960s and early '70s saw the high-water years of hemlines, which defied both the laws of physics and decency. Anglers, not to be outdone, crowded the physical limits of light and short. A rod's casting ease and line-mending abilities became forgotten artifacts of history.

The mid 1970s saw the introduction of light, crisp graphite rods, and as hemlines began lengthening to non-gynecological levels, so, too, did fly rods. By 1980, the default trout rod was once again a nine-footer, usually a five-weight, and thanks to the new composites it weighed less than Arnold Gingrich's six-foot, three-inch Paul Young Midge. For most of us today, the nine for five is the trout rod of choice. But it isn't the only choice.

My favorite trout streams are all freestone and forested and between ten and thirty feet wide. Here, I reach for something between seven-and-a-half and eight feet—short enough to sidearm a dropper and a dry up under the mountain laurel but long enough to lob a pair of nymphs straight upstream with a flying roll cast . . . excuse my unfashionable terminology: a single-handed spey cast. Fishing this kind of water, a nine-foot rod is a liability, or at least it is for me.

On big trout rivers, where nine-footers rule, my go-to rods seem to be stabilizing at around eleven feet, give or take. Trout-weight rods of this class are modernly known as switch rods—presumably because an angler can switch easily between single-handed casting and two-handed casting. Though I can't imagine why someone would want to.

Popular for three hundred years and reintroduced some quarter-century ago by Oregon's R.B. Meiser, two-handed trout rods have especially benefited from today's lighter, stronger, stiffer composites. An eleven-foot five-weight of today weighs about the same as a nine-foot five-weight from the 1980s. Perhaps this is why it's tempting to try casting them single-handed. Or perhaps it's because two-handed casting is seen as wimpy or cheating or too hard to learn after a lifetime of hardwiring single-handed muscle memories. But the physics of the cast doesn't care whether you're using two hands or one. Your muscles and cartilage, however, do.

My own hardwired muscle memories make me at best a fair-to-middling caster, single- or two-handed. But with a two-handed trout rod I can fire seventy-foot casts all day. With a single-hander, a dozen of these hero casts starts me studying the overdose warnings on the naproxen bottle. A switch rod's big bonus, however, isn't really lengthening the cast while halving the effort; it's minimizing the back cast and maximizing line control.

If more than 20 percent of a cast involves shooting line rather than casting it, my accuracy goes from dinner-plate diameter to Hollywood hot tub. To hit a particular current seam at seventy feet, I need fifty clear feet behind me. Because most big trout rivers come factory-equipped with back-cast-eating obstacles, this means either wading way out into the neutral-buoyancy zone or going to work with a chainsaw. Spey-style, that seventy-foot cast needs only about ten feet of stern clearance. At more reasonable trout fishing distances, a water-hauled back cast needs only a few feet.

Once you've hurtled your pair of big nymphs and your mooring-buoy strike indicator way out into drift boat country, you've still got to manage the drift. Compared with a nine-footer, a reach cast with an eleven-foot rod gives me at least eight more feet of drag-free drift. Fishing at normal trout fishing distances, thirty or forty feet, drag ceases to be an issue. Most of the line is off the water and away from inconvenient currents except when actually casting. When swinging wet flies, the long rod means you can adjust the angle of drift easier and more accurately, and when waking wet flies or sparrow-sized dry flies across the current, you can create mayhem in distant seams otherwise unfishable from shore.

Like most fashion extremes, switch rods aren't the answer to all life's problems. The long flexible rod provides an effective built-in shock absorber when fighting fish, but at close quarters that length is a liability. The end game usually becomes a primitive and decidedly inelegant improvisation on a hand-lining theme.

Trekking through the woods with an eleven-foot rod is recommended only for compulsive puzzle solvers with no family history of hypertension. The rest of us had best break down the rod into two pieces, which is easy to do if you first reel in line until the fly hooks in the tip-top then carry the rod with the tip-top next to the reel seat. It's even easier if you burgle a friendly fashion plate's elastic hair bands and cinch together the leading and trailing ferrules.

Lining and leadering a switch rod can be an unintuitive and hypertensive adventure. Mount your favorite five-weight reel and line and nine-foot trout leader on your shiny new eleven-foot five-weight, and by the end of the day you'll have determined that all those people championing switch rods in the fly-fishing press fish only in Internet chat rooms.

This is because with switch rods there truly is a bit of bait and switch at work. Your WF5F trout line weighs about 140 grains for the working end—just right for your nine for five but way underlined for your eleven for "five." Mount a seven-weight Rio salmon taper—190 grains for the first 30 feet and 350 for the whole 110-foot head—an eight-weight Wulff Ambush, an Airflo 40+ seven-weight, or a purpose-built switch line such as the Beulah Elixer 5/6 or the Rio 5/6 Switch, which all weigh somewhere between 280 and 350 grains, and your eleven-foot five-weight comes alive and casts across the river.

For overhead casting, lighten the line by stripping part of the head inside the tip-top, and experiment with loading until it feels right. For spey casting, you'll want most of the head outside the guides.

Leaders ought to equal the rod's length, and mono-core tapered, coated leaders are the elegant way to go. A ten-foot floating tapered leader, such as Airflo's Polyleader or Rio's Spey VersiLeader, looped with two to six feet of the proper tippet, is all you need most of the time. If you want to get deeper, replace the floating leader with a sinker coated with powdered tungsten—it will plummet up to seven inches per second.

Of course, you'll need to learn to make a proper flying roll cast. I mean spey cast. If you're not the class-attending type—I'm not— you can go autodidact with a good video. I like Lani Waller's *The Art of Spey Casting* and Scientific Anglers' *Spey to Z*. Or teach yourself the old-fashioned way from books, preferably written by anyone named Simon Gawesworth.

Fishing with Simon in Colorado a few years ago, I watched him using an eight-foot four-weight to rifle single-handed spey casts I can barely make using both hands on my fourteen-foot, nine-weight skagit cannon armed with a 575-grain tugboat hawser.

This told me that long isn't always better than short, and two hands aren't always better than one. Unless you, like me and unlike Simon Gawesworth, are a mere human.

26. *Enchanted Dragonfly*

O<small>F THE MANY ADVANTAGES OF LIVING AND</small> working 247 paces from a fair-to-middlin' trout brook, the best is being able to fill unexpected fragments of unallocated time by merely donning hip-boots, pocketing a fly box, and lifting the ready-rigged fly rod from its permanent perch above the office door. Instead of squandering .00000631 percent of my three-score and ten while clicking through the World Wide Web's constant flow of woe or calculating how much deeper into my years the Great Recession has flushed my retirement, I can sneak off and spend a therapeutic hour or so fishing while awaiting the 3:45 conference call.

If more than an hour or so should wriggle free from the daily schedule—a cancelled conference call, a bulging inbox of new *Gray's* manuscripts that didn't bear reading past the first awkward page, or a five-thousand-word story for *Gray's* so well-written it needed only a few hours of easy editing instead of the anticipated eight or nine—I can head for one of several brooks and streams within a half-hour's drive and fish away an entire afternoon the way afternoons are meant to be fished away.

This is provided, of course, there's fishable water in the neighborhood brooks and streams—all of them freestone, all of them fueled by inconstant rainfall, and all of them bony by mid-July and mostly unfishable by mid-August, at least if you measure fishability by the probability of a fish surviving even the most tenderhearted catch-and-release.

All isn't theoretically lost, because Maine's lakes and ponds hold both water and fish year-round. There's a small trout pond a mere 114 paces from my office door and dozens of way better trout and bass and perch and pickerel ponds within a half-hour's drive and a five-minute paddle.

But for reasons I have given up trying to understand, unmoving water doesn't thrill me at all. I get my kicks from riffles and rapids and runs, from falls and back-eddies and chutes, from the constant ebb and flow of the sea, from tide-races and rips and surf—interesting water defined as moving water: animated, energetic, vivacious. Placid water does not invite; it just lies there looking bored, and boredom is contagious.

So rather than fill an empty hour or two by fishing uninterested water or pestering heat-stressed freestone fish better left unpestered, I fritter away late-season time nuggets by indulging the fly fisher's other great passion: entomology. Or, more accurately, bug watching.

True believer fly fishers sometimes seem more obsessed with the bugs than with the fish that eat those bugs. If trout ate only angleworms, would there be $650 rotary fly-tying vises, $125 rooster necks, or more published fly patterns than visible stars in the sky? Would the ardent angler's bookshelves groan beneath the weight of so much painstaking scholarship, windy Latin, and derivative theories?

We are bug watchers all. But in the low, warm water of late summer and early autumn, active bug watching can be as environmentally intrusive as fishing for heat-stressed trout. Once upon a time I left no rock unturned and no riffle unseined to gratify my curiosity, but these days I regret each little life whose summer's play my thoughtless hand has brush'd away.

But that's why they make binoculars. Few non-fishing fishing activities are more harmlessly fulfilling than sitting beneath a tree with a pair of close-focusing binoculars and watching bugs be bugs. And while mayflies are the fly fisher's traditional bug-crush, with endless scholarship exhausting every aspect of their ancestry, behavior, and genetic permutations, I find their sole surviving fellows of the infraclass *Paleoptera*—to dredge up some decorative Latin that means, more or less literally, older than the hills—far more interesting to watch and more accommodating, too. A mayfly hatch is by definition an ephemeral thing. But from early summer through freeze-up, dragonflies, also more or less literally, are forever.

Like our familiar Ephemeropteran friends, the dragonflies and damselflies of the *Odonata* date to the Carboniferous era—354 to 290 million years ago, way back when nature was busily fabricating today's coal mines and trying out improbable new species to see how they'd go, as inventive and trend-tragic as a teenager dressing for the mall.

But with the *Odonata*, nature nailed it. The same green darners and riffle snaketails we watch today watched the Appalachians lift from the sea, the glaciers ebb and grow, the dinosaurs come and go, and the evolution of *H. sapiens piscipiddler* who now watches them while wondering what's going on behind those enigmatic compound eyes, what they'll next pluck from the air to eat, and what might leap from the water to eat them.

That's what it's all about, of course. Fly fishers may find bugs fascinating, but for most of us that fascination begins and ends with the bugs fish eat. You won't find us sitting in the garden admiring tarnished plant bugs and striped cucumber beetles. We'll be down by the water spying on mayflies and stoneflies and caddis flies and, of course, damselflies and dragonflies. Who can see a trout pluck a delicate Northern Bluet from the air or a bucketmouth bass smash a hovering Twelve-Spotted Skimmer without running to the vise and feverishly inventing something floating, fluttery, precisely imitative, and utterly un-castable?

Yet it's the underwater forms of these entertaining aerialists that most interest fish. Anglers all know this, whether we know we know it or not. To pluck a theory from the air as fecklessly as a Common Whitetail plucks a mosquito or an acrobatic brook trout plucks a Common Whitetail, most of the fish taken on a skinny tan or olive Woolly Bugger twitched slowly and steadily toward shore in a pond, lake, or back-eddy of a large river thought they were eating a damselfly nymph. And most of the fish—trout, bass, bluegills, whatever—that ate a fat olive or brown Woolly Bugger thought they were eating a dragonfly nymph: in a pond, a river, or a freestone mountain stream.

The nymphs—*naiads*, to skid past Latin and straight into Greek, the daughters of Zeus who ruled over brooks, streams, and springs—are there for the eating all year round while crawling about the bottom, swimming along in quick jet-propelled darts, preying like crazy on anything that moves, and being preyed upon with equal craziness by anything ambitious enough to gulp them down.

There are probably more patterns for damsel- and dragonfly nymphs than there are species of damsel- and dragonflies, but I've never found one that works so much better than a Woolly Bugger that I bothered tying it twice, no matter how artistic the act of imitative model-making. For damselflies, a few long fronds of marabou for the tail, a gaunt body in olive or tan, the sparsest possible wrap of soft webby hackle, perhaps a nice brass bead for a head, and you're done. Twitch slowly toward shore, where the delicate damsels seek a reed to climb and unfurl filmy wings. "To glimpse a Naiad's reedy head," if I may invert a line from Rupert Brooke, you truly feel "the Classics were not dead."

Stillwater dragonfly nymphs tend toward the Hobbesian: nasty, brutish, and short. A scruffy mottled olive or brown Woolly Bugger with a short tail and short soft hackle thickly palmered; unweighted and inched along with a short leader and a sinking line—that's it. A few pond dragonflies resemble the fleeter species found in running water: finger-size, finger-shaped, bottom-colored, jetting along in four-inch bursts, scooping with rapacious articulated jaws whatever they find: caddis pupae, mayfly nymphs, newts, small fish, tadpoles. Over the years I've caught half a dozen dragonfly nymphs while drifting small wet flies in streams, and two or three hovering adults have taken untethered dry flies left blowing in the breeze. If it moves, a dragonfly will eat it.

When I watch dragonflies, I often think of "The Enchanted Dragonfly" ballet in Michael Powell and Emeric Pressburger's peculiar 1951 film made from Jacques Offenbach's peculiar 1881 opera, *The Tales of Hoffmann*. In it, lissome Scottish prima ballerina Moira Shearer, shrink-wrapped in a spandex dragonfly costume, emerges onto a lily pad, dries her wings, flutters fetchingly about, and then enjoys a *pas de deux* with a dragonfly suitor. It's an ill-fated interspecies relationship, as these things go, because she—as near as I can tell—is an Emperor, or at the very least an Azure Hawker, while he's merely a lumpen Common Darter, and suffering a bit from spandex-unfriendly muffin-top to boot. So after she's had her way with him, so to speak, she very properly bites off his head and sends him to the depths.

The scene ends with her fluttering off across the lily pads and into the rising moon while looking as elegant and ethereal and purely murderous as this most ancient of species can possibly be. It's clear the choreographer was no fisherman, though. Because a fisherman would have had Ms. Shearer performing her final *grand jeté* straight into the mouth of an immense brown trout.

27. *The Several Stages of Obsession*

My SMALL CIRCLE OF NEW ENGLAND BROTHERS of the angle fish together corporeally when we can during our short season and vicariously via e-mail once the closure of open-water fishing leaves us few angling options beyond traveling somewhere warmer, jigging through holes in the ice, or tying flies. What we mostly do in the off-season is tie flies and tell each other about it.

Here's an example from Marcel Rocheleau, who was suffering the first pangs of late-November withdrawal over in Vermont with a long season in his wake and next season in the distance:

> "Tied my first flies yesterday, going from pitiful to acceptable in three, and I suspect (if my last tying excursion is any indication) I should hit 'not bad' by 12, 'good' by 18; 'very good' by two dozen, and when I hit three dozen I'll be having delusions of expertise unsupportable by empirical evidence. But I'll at least have convinced myself that I'm being productive, technically accomplished, moderately artistic, and exceedingly predatory. The illusion will likely fall apart about the first hour of the first trip, but I'll enjoy it in the interim."

This, as Will Ryan pointed out in a reply-all from Massachusetts, is a textbook example of "self-actualization through fly tying"

—nurtured, like so many -ations prefaced by self, in the incubator of obsession.

All obsessions—fly-fishing and fly tying certainly fall under the dictionary definition of "an irrational fixation, mania, preoccupation"—progress through stages. Fly-fishing itself, as famously mapped by pioneering American nymph-meister Edward R. Hewitt, begins with wanting to catch any fish, wanting more fish, wanting bigger fish, and finally wanting harder fish. Fly tying, too, progresses through its own version of the Kübler-Ross cycle.

Upon inventorying our boxes and realizing how many flies we burned through last season and how many we must tie before next season, we feel *shock*. There, we say to ourselves while looking at vast stretches of unpopulated fly-box foam, is where three-dozen tiny Pheasant Tails used to live. Over here is the forlorn survivor of a once-immense armada of Parachute Hare's Ears, its wing post ragged and its hackle spiraling outward into nothingness like the Milky Way. Tucked in a dusty corner, behind the rows of semicolon-sized midge pupae we expectantly tied and never used, is the sole surviving Speck, its spun deer-hair body chewed raw and what's left of its brown-and-grizzly hackle matted with fish slime. Of the regimental rows of crisp new Clousers, Deceivers, Surf Candies, and Dahlberg Divers that once filled the battered saltwater box, nothing remains but a rusty blunted hook trailing a blood-stained strand of chartreuse bucktail and the archaeological curiosity of a thimbleful of saltine crumbs, half a mummified sardine, and a chartreuse crust of wasabi paste.

We dutifully list all the fly-box slots that want filling and prioritize the replacements by season, and when we finally sit down to refill all these voids we feel *denial* that after six months of obsessive fishing our reflexes could have so completely forgotten the minutely intricate movements of fly tying or that our brains could have lost the thread of recipes that decades of repetition should have indelibly engraved or that our fingers could ever have been sufficiently dexterous to maneuver a two-millimeter brass bead onto a size-twenty hook—never mind maneuver dozens of two-millimeter brass beads onto dozens of size-twenty hooks.

We feel *anger* as those beads shoot across the tying desk and dive into the cracks between the floorboards. There's more anger as threads break under too much tension or tails and wings skew under not enough. And still more anger when our shiny new magnifiers insufficiently magnify the vision we deny we're losing, and the special color-compensated light bulb we recently bought to enhance the color-matching of natural mayfly bodies goes supernova in a Fourth of July *pffffft*. But this is nothing compared with our righteous wrath upon discovering that the moths have out-evolved the protective halo of their eponymous balls and have turned a box of prime rooster necks and saddles for which we can't quite admit we paid a hundred bucks each into a wasteland of naked quills and pepper-like poo.

We *bargain* with the fishing gods for the return of our eyesight, manual dexterity, muscle memories, and ravaged chicken necks, and we pore over the fly-fishing catalogs that have just begun arriving along with the snow plows and the flu and the merciless Christmas jingles. We seek new and more devious ways to conceal from our fiduciary selves and our semi-tolerant loved ones that we paid hundreds of dollars for dried chicken necks and then fed them to moths and are scheming to do so again.

We order endless airdrops of things we need and things we didn't know we needed and things we'll never really need, and we wait impatiently at the door for the UPS driver, wondering whether she's carrying something useful—a box of new chicken necks that cost more per ounce than platinum or boxes of tiny brass beads or strangely repurposed industrial materials that sparkle and shimmer and wiggle in the waves or a rainbow assortment of spooled thread to replace the current inventory that, like us, has deteriorated with age—or whether she's merely freighting something as uninteresting as a box of manuscript submissions or book galleys or the tiny back-ordered doodad that has kept the fancy foreign toilet from flushing properly ever since that unfortunate conjunction of leftover Halloween candy and cassoulet.

Depression settles unexpectedly on our shoulders when we audit our production and learn how many flies we've tied that we thought we might need some day and how few we've tied that we know are as indispensable to our fishing success as fresh leader material and polarized sunglasses. We wonder at our inability to apply ourselves with the unrelenting industry needed to repopulate a season-ravaged suite of fly boxes, and deplore our tendency to wander off on tangents chasing some sparkly new apparition from *Fly Tyer* or *American Angler* or *Fly Rod & Reel* or *Fly Fisherman* or any of the other magazines we receive, expending our precious time on experimental fly-box ornaments when there are legions of bread-and-butter Pheasant Tails and Specks and Clousers to fabricate.

Finally we achieve the happy equilibrium of *acceptance*, and on good days we sit at the bench like automatons as we mindlessly manufacture copy after copy of the old standard patterns without which next season will be pointless, or at the very least fishless, which is pretty much the same thing.

As the empty slots fill we look once more at the tattered survivors of last season. The ruthless profligates among us send these quickly to the trash. The tight-fisted cheese-parers shave off the remnants of thread and fur and feather, sharpen the hooks, and slot them back into the assembly line. But the mush-headed sentimentalists see far more than simply chewed up Pheasant Tails and Hare's Ears and Clousers, and we could no more toss or repurpose their remnants than we could euthanize a favorite bird dog merely because he farts like a mule and no longer bounds like a puppy.

I look at that Speck and see not ragged deer hair and matted hackle but my brother tying it at the kitchen table of his teetering hillside cabin down in East Tennessee and the wild little rainbows that chewed it raw beneath the bright bloom of mountain laurel. I see in the ragged Hare's Ears the bouncing St. Vrain in Colorado and the fierce wild browns that rose beneath blue Rocky Mountain skies. I see in the Clousers and Deceivers the bluefish and striped bass of the Maine Coast that methodically dismantled a winter's work and left laughter and racing pulses in their wake. I see Pheasant Tails being eaten one by one by the Penobscot's rocky bottom and, just often enough to justify their loss, by landlocked salmon that shoot from the depths like Trident missiles. I see the one remaining Mad Dog and remember Shawn Gregoire, the first of our small circle of angling brothers to check out in that most corporeal of senses. Here's to you, Shawn. May your impressionistic March Brown imitation catch as many salmon for you wherever you've gone as it did on the West Branch of the Penobscot.

I see *anticipation* in all these flies for another fishing season soon to be arriving, for times spent on streams, rivers, ponds, and oceans alone or with the small circle of people that a shared obsession has drawn together as fellow travelers on this all-too brief journey.

Here's to us all, who have become who we are through the charming hobbyhorse of this most harmless of obsessions: the winding of feathers and threads and furs and tinsels around hooks that catch far more than just fish.

PART FOUR

Here Be Dragons

We may guess that in dreams life, matter, and vitality, as the earth knows such things, are not necessarily constant; and that time and space do not exist as our waking selves comprehend them. Sometimes I believe that this less material life is our truer life, and that our vain presence on the terraqueous globe is itself the secondary or merely virtual phenomenon.

— H.P. Lovecraft

28. *Snide and Prejudice*

As YOU WOULD EXPECT OF THREE DAYS SPENT
bass fishing on Maine's Moosehead Lake with a college fresh-
man and two professors, one of them an eminent economist and
one a writing department cochair and the author of an authori-
tative book on fly-fishing for smallmouth bass—and all three a
mere *Micropterus* tattoo away from bass fishing's lunatic fringe—
the conversation didn't suffer from a shortage of opinions. Nor
did the opinions suffer from drear unanimity since the fishing
was, like Huck Finn's analysis of *Pilgrim's Progress*, "interesting,
but tough."

Not that we'd been entirely unsuccessful. We had simply
achieved our modest successes through such different paths that
no one opinion could prevail. By sheer weight of boated bass,
synthetic mucous clots—excuse me, soft plastic tube jigs in a
Halloween-candy color called melon-copper—were the clear winners, in part because with no concentrated schools of baitfish to
rally them 'round, the bass were scouting for scattered crayfish on
rocky shoals twenty feet down, and melon-copper tube jigs loosely
resemble scattered crayfish. And also in part because melon-copper tube jigs were mostly what Stan and Brody fished, and their
collective paths to success were signposted by past successes in

similar circumstances and smoothed by the tattletale fish finder in Stan's big comfy-chair bass boat.

Will Ryan and I were far more Spartan in his Gheenoe, a square-stern canoe-like watercraft that Will is passionately proud of and which I view with the bemusement peculiar to saltier-than-thou wooden boat snots. Still, one must keep an open mind, and in its defense the Gheenoe hadn't drowned us—it had, in fact, kept us relatively comfortable and stand-to-castable in what was proving to be a typical Will Ryan and Jim Babb fishing trip, by which I mean wind and rain and thunder and much nervous monitoring of the horizon.

Without a sounding machine, we couldn't pickpocket the shoals with Stan and Brody's digital precision, so Will and I chose our own divergent paths toward theoretical success. Will fished a sinking fly line and a monstrous kerwhacking construct of marabou feathers and fake fur of the Vegas showgirl variety and angry red-lead eyes of the Vegas barfly variety that he'd tied to be an exact imitation of a melon-copper tube jig, because it was obvious that melon-copper was the color and tube jigs the form and because there's something about un-fly-castable wind that makes Will want to cast an un-castable fly. I fished a light spinning rod because I'm either too wise or too lazy or too skeered, depending on whose opinions you're following, to cast heavy flies on a sinking line in a gusty wind, so I tipped my four-pound mono with a tiny silver Shad Rap crank bait because it caught my eye in the dollar bin at Hamilton's Marine and because I giggle a la Beavis and Butthead every time I say crank bait.

When the crackling storm front and stiffening southwesterlies finally chased us ashore, Stan and Brody had boated three or four smallmouth between two and four pounds, Will had one around the same size and lost another, and I lost one in the same neighborhood at a point in the encounter where *losing* might in some circles be reinterpreted as *missing*. As compensation, I caught an active and well-fed fourteen-inch brook trout, which blushed with embarrassment at getting caught swallowing a bargain-basement crank bait—snicker, snicker—in public.

There was no difference of opinion about the brook trout's fate, which was to receive the tender, self-consciously ceremonial release reserved for noble salmonids. The bass's fate, however, spawned the next difference of opinion, with Will a proponent of the git-'er-done approach of his native St. Lawrence River Valley and me advocating the more precise and elegant method evolved over centuries along the New England coast.

Will, an educator and the offspring of educators, likens this particular difference of opinion to one commonly confronted in academia. My way, he claims, is like writing the whole sentence on the blackboard one hundred times. His is like writing columns of *I*, then columns of *must*, then columns of *not*, then columns of *talk*, then columns of *in*, then columns of *class*.

So we compromised. He filleted half the bass his way—cutting down behind the gills and then sawing along the backbone on both sides to, but not through, the tail, which leaves the fillets attached, and then using the tail as a handle for the amalgamated process of skinning and hacking off the ribcages.

My method, learned from generations of professional fish cutters wearing white smocks and hairnets and tall rubber boots, slices the fillet free in one piece with the rib bones left on the zoologically intact skeleton and the fillets surgically skinned with one smooth swipe of a long, flexible, and shockingly sharp filleting knife.

Will's method is quick and brutal and to-the-point. Mine is precise and beautiful and a trifle prissy. But the thing is, once dipped in buttermilk; rolled in a mixture of cornstarch, flour, lemon zest, and Old Bay Seasoning; and fried in fresh peanut oil in my grandmother's cast-iron Griswold skillet, they looked and tasted exactly the same.

"Wait a minute," I hear you saying. "You caught a brook trout? While bass fishing? And then you caught some nice smallmouth and you killed and ATE them?"

Why yes we did. Because we had assembled at Maine's largest lake not merely to catch bass and argue. We, like the Blues Brothers, were on a mission—in our case to help right a wrong by fulfilling a biological imperative.

Because brook trout, those gaudy emblems of eastern American wilderness, are under pressure—from pollution, from deforestation, from warming waters, from rampant development, and from hungry alien species armored with spines and scales and defensive parenting and other survival-of-the-fittest adaptations that our poor primitive brook trout have yet to evolve.

Maine is America's brook trout bastion—pretty much the last place south of Canada where anglers can realistically expect to catch wild brook trout measured in pounds and not inches. And Moosehead Lake, "forty miles long by ten wide, like a gleaming silver platter," as proto-spruce-smoocher Henry David Thoreau wrote on his first wide-eyed trip here back in 1853, is at the brook trout's very epicenter.

You'd think anglers would look out across Moosehead's vast silver platter surrounded by Thoreau's "solemn bear-haunted mountains" with its shoals of brook trout that averaged four pounds in the 1890s and still occasionally reach five, and think, "Nature done good. Let's leave 'er be."

But you'd be wrong. Because back in the 1980s, when bass fishing began morphing from sport to televised reality show to multibillion-dollar industry and bass began to surpass trout and landlocked salmon as Maine's favorite fish, a few enterprising bass men looked out upon Maine's almost endless smallmouth fishing in lakes and rivers too warm for trout—smallmouth fishing that dates back to a well-considered and legal introduction by credentialed biologists back in the 1860s and which a host of knowledgeable luminaries such as baseball legend Ted Williams have long called the world's best—and they felt shortchanged. And so, armed with buckets of illicit bass, they set off into the wilds to sow the seeds of redress.

Indian Pond, a recipient of Moosehead Lake's twin outlets and the headwaters of the Kennebec River, got its first charge of bass around 1980. Now it's almost entirely a bass fishery—and a good one, too. Moosehead got its first taste of bass around 1987—drop-downs, as near as anyone can tell, through the feeder stream from Prong Pond, once an excellent producer of wild brook trout and now the domain of smallmouth bass and yellow and white perch—all illegally introduced by bucket biologists who saw evolutionary perfection as needing improvement.

That we don't see brook trout fetishists sneaking onto bass lakes with a bucket of *fontinalis* in each hand isn't because trout fishers are principled and high-minded and environmentally concerned people who would never consider such an indefensible act of ichthyological sabotage. It's because brook trout can't survive in the warmer waters bass enjoy. Bass, on the other hand, adapt to cooler waters just fine.

I can think of many adjectives worth pasting onto bucket biologists, but *principled*, *high-minded*, and *environmentally concerned* aren't among them. Of course that's just my opinion.

Well, not just mine. Maine's conservation department is attempting to contain the spread of illegal introductions that "threaten one of our nation's premier wild brook trout populations," but in immense waters like Moosehead and Umbagog Lake, part of the upper Androscoggin River drainage that includes the famous Rapid River, little can realistically be done about metastasizing smallmouth bass.

Except, perhaps, some old-fashioned American vigilantism. According to the Moosehead Lake Fisheries Coalition, a consortium of area conservationists and anglers dedicated to preserving Moosehead's traditional fisheries, 80 percent of its membership supports a MLFC-supported spring and summer "bass catch and cook, a concentrated effort to catch and kill bass in Moosehead Lake."

Anglers can argue endlessly about whether this will have any measurable effect, just as we argue endlessly about the merits of frog poppers versus silver sliders, Dahlberg Divers versus wacky worms, and tube jigs versus, uh, crank baits.

But it's difficult to argue that what America's imperiled brook trout need are more hungry bass. What they need are more hungry bass fishermen.

29. *Invisible River*

W<small>E MUSCLED THE DRIFT BOAT DOWN THE</small> bank through dripping spruce and maple and into the river as the sun burned through the morning mist and painted the snow-capped mountains a pantsuit shade of pink.

A quick scout revealed caddis larvae, stoneflies, and crayfish by the bucketful. A mink patrolled the shoreline. A bald eagle drifted overhead. A beaver splashed an alarm as guide Sandy MacGregor bent to the oars and levered us into an eddy. A quick cast toward a bankside dimple stuck a fourteen-inch rainbow—a madcap acrobat despite a lard-bucket belly.

We drifted downriver for seven uninterrupted miles, never seeing another angler. Now and then we glimpsed a fragment of road or a house on a distant hill, but mostly we saw high mountains and thick forest morphing from green to red and orange. Broad graveled riffles and deep rocky pools held slashing rainbows and savage browns. A wiener-length smallmouth ate my fly, and as he ricocheted across the water a twenty-inch brown trout ate him.

It was a perfect day on a perfect river flowing through a perfect autumn landscape. We might have been deep in the Rocky Mountain west or in the Cascades or the Adirondacks or the Laurentides a hundred miles from civilization. But no. We were drifting through settled and civilized southwestern Maine a hundred yards from busy Route 2, northern New England's major east-west artery gone autumnal-sclerotic with leaf-peeping RVs and Jake-braking log trucks.

We could hear them growling over there behind the trees, but we couldn't see them nor they us, a boatload of happy laughing fly fishers drifting down an invisible river, the infamous Androscoggin, once one of America's ten most polluted, right up there with Ohio's famously flammable Cuyahoga.

Thanks to the Clean Water Act of 1972, by Maine's Senator Edmund Muskie, who grew up a few miles downriver in the reeking mill-town of Rumford, I was catching trout in a river I've avoided since I first saw it back in the early 1980s. I was hauling a load of lobsters to Montreal and stopped alongside the road to pee, heard a river running in the distance, hiked in to investigate, and found a thick stew of bark and sewage and car-sized clots of brown foam that smelled like Exit 15 on the New Jersey Turnpike.

The Androscoggin didn't begin life this way. Its waters rise in the wildlands along the Maine-New Hampshire border and flow through some of the greatest names in northeastern fly-fishing—Magalloway, Parmachenee, Aziscohos, Kennebago, Rangeley, Oquossuc, Cusuptic, Mooselookmeguntic—before gathering in vast Lake Umbagog to emerge from beneath the dam at Errol, New Hampshire. Here the Andro has long been a famous trout fishery, but after running afoul of the paper mills downriver at Berlin and the seeping Superfund site at Gorham, it became an industrial conveyor of phosphorous-laden suspended organics—not to mention residual PCBs, dioxin, mercury, and other byproducts of the paper this book might well be printed on.

Thanks to the mills' and municipalities' lengthy and expensive and often foot-dragging cleanup efforts, the river below Berlin and Gorham is dramatically cleaner than it was only a few years ago, and trout, like the rainbows and browns we were catching, are growing fast and supporting a blossoming, though still largely invisible, fishery.

The trout here are mostly stocked, both by Maine and New Hampshire, though Sandy says almost every tributary has reproducing rainbows, and there's anecdotal evidence of spawning browns. Upriver near the New Hampshire line, rainbows outnumber browns and the smallmouth are few and far between, and as you near Rumford the proportion shifts toward browns, and the smallmouth begin to grow in size and numbers.

In the warmer waters below Rumford, some enormous browns reportedly show up for late-evening hatches, but the real draw is perhaps the best river fishing for smallmouth bass in all New England. So the next day, with leaden skies threatening an early taste of winter, we went looking for the fish Dr. James A. Henshall enshrined in his 1881 foundational *Book of the Black Bass* as "the gamest fish that swims."

It didn't look promising when we parked alongside the railroad just below the Mead-Westvaco paper mill and dodged the faded Maine Central locomotive switching the yard, but after a five-minute walk down the tracks and a semi-controlled slither down the bank, we emerged onto a magnificent stretch of river that flows through as green and pleasant a land as the upper Andro, albeit with the loom of snow-capped Mount Washington replaced by a dark satanic mill and its columns of sulfurous steam.

It's easy to beat up on the paper companies. For years they treated New England's waterways as toxic-waste dumps and power sources to be dammed and damned. But then so did everyone else. And now that Maine has lost more than fifty thousand manufacturing jobs over the past ten years, most of them in the wood-products industry, beating up on paper companies—especially if you're doing it in print on paper—carries a toxic whiff of hypocrisy.

Everyone knows the mills could do more for the environment. Who among us couldn't do more to help tidy the mess we collectively make of our only planet? But these days the mills finally seem to be trying—at least those few still hanging on in the face of competition from countries where paying attention to river pollution and sustainable forestry are even less important than paying workers a living wage. As a newly laid-off paper-mill worker told me at the corner store last week, "Somebody's gotta do something. We can't all work at friggin' Walmart."

Which, oddly enough, is right across the river from us, Sandy said. I saw only unbroken forest until he pointed out a parking lot security light poking above the trees like a periscopic alien eye from *The War of the Worlds*. In an act of all-American symbology, a bald eagle perched atop a light tower meant to keep watch over row after row of Japanese cars made in America and American cars made in Mexico.

The eagle was fishing, and so were we. But the smallmouth weren't coming fast for either of us thanks to a plunging barometer and intermittent "heavy to moderate rain events," as the early morning TV weatherman said. But over the course of a long, wet day we each had a dozen or so good bass—two-pounders mostly with a few around three—strong, healthy fish that jumped and ripped line and kicked our middle-aged butts up one side of the river and down the other. They were the very personification of Dr. Henshall's "gamest fish that swim."

I told Sandy I would have to come back with this bass-crazy friend of mine. Which, the following July, I did.

As we drifted downriver with Sandy, we needed most of the strategies in Will Ryan's *Smallmouth Strategies for the Fly Rod* to take a few fish on a day that proved tough in a different way—glaring sun, unseasonable heat, and the loom of thunderstorms gathering over the Presidential Range. But as the shadows lengthened the fishing turned on, as it often does, and soon we were hooking up on almost every cast—fat and savage dark bronze smallmouths ranging from a pound and a half up to three pounds, along with a couple of enormous rainbow chubs that actually jumped and stripped line.

During this mini-blitz we saw only one other boat carrying three indolent spin-fishermen, and the next day, when Will and I came back by ourselves and waded the broad riffles and back eddies and deep dark pools we'd fished from Sandy's drift boat, we didn't see anyone—not a house, not a car, not anything at all but trees and eagles and beavers and otters and a feeling of splen-did isolation, though busy Route 108 was just out of sight on the west bank and even busier Route 2 was just out of sight on the east.

By the time the clouds that had been gathering over Mount Washington dumped their load and drove us to the truck for shelter, we'd caught satisfying numbers of smallmouth that aver-aged better than two pounds, including one that taped an honest twenty-two-and-a-half inches and weighed an estimated four-and-a-half pounds, and we both lost fish that in our imaginations ran even bigger. It was the kind of smallmouth fishing that might draw keen anglers from across the country if only they knew this river were here.

On the way home I stopped off in Rumford at the Labonville logging supplies store for a new log chain and some tree-marking paint for my own small contribution of spruce and fir to Maine's paper industry and, very likely, to its river pollution and, not impossibly, to the pages of this book. The nice lady at the counter said I looked dressed to go fishing, and I said I'd been fishing the past few days and had done great—lots of fish from a pound and a half up to better than four.

She wanted to know where, of course, because she'd lived in Rumford all her life and was a keen brook trout fisherman.

And I said I'd been on the Andro right over there across the road, and I'd been catching bass, and the bass fishing was as good as any river I'd ever fished.

"Bass?" She said. "Why nobody fishes for bass around here. And nobody fishes that river."

30. *Treasures of the Sierra Madre*

To twist a pivotal passage from John Huston's 1948 classic *The Treasure of the Sierra Madre*: largemouth bass are a very devilish sort of thing. You start out, you want a twenty-pounder. After days of sweating yourself dizzy, you finally come down to fifteen pounds then ten. Finally you say, Lord, just let me land a couple of eight-pounders and I'll never ask for anything more the rest of my life.

This was pretty much the state Jerry Gibbs and I were in after a week on Lake El Salto, down Mexico way in the Sierra Madres of Sinaloa, about two hours northeast of Mazatlán by car and not far from where mysterious writer B. Traven set his classic tale about the transformative power of greed, which John Huston made into one of the greatest psychological adventure movies of all time.

For us, just getting there was an adventure, with a twelve-hour snow delay at the airport in Maine and an involuntary overnight at the airport in Houston. When we finally arrived the weather was bright and warm with crisp northerly winds—exactly what you'd want for a respite from the vicious New England winter and exactly what you don't want for serious fishing.

And make no mistake, all forty guests at Angler's Inn had come for serious fishing. Most had been there before, many were from Texas, and all were bass fishing fanatics as expert as they come.

We didn't see a Humphrey Bogart, Tim Holt, or Walter Huston in the crowd, but several famous bass tournament guys were there along with two Hank Hills, a Boomhauer, and for better or worse a Dale Gribble. Everyone was varying degrees of bemused that Jerry and I had flown all this way to fish one of the world's best big-bass lakes armed only with fly rods.

It *was* a bit quixotic, fly-rodding this twenty-four-thousand-acre reservoir that produces more ten-pound-plus bass than any other lake in the world. For one thing, the bass eat mostly tilapia, that supermarket ubiquity preferred by fish-eaters who don't like fish, and the tilapia run bigger than the average river smallmouth. For another, we were competing against some of the best bass fishers on the planet.

Not that *we* were competing. Fly fishers tend not to be very competitive—at least not the ones I voluntarily fish with. But modern-day bass fishers are as competitive and intense as commodities traders.

We'd pass them out on the lake and give a friendly wave, as one does, and not once did anyone look up from relentlessly chucking swim baits and fall baits and crank baits and wacky worms to acknowledge our presence. Yet every night in the bar those same cold-eyed anglers, were as friendly as boot-buffing puppies, were genuinely interested in our day and happy to tell us about their own.

I blame big-money bass competitions for this perversion of recreation into occupation. Not that how someone else chooses to enjoy fishing is any of my business. Fly fishers often imagine their choice of terminal tackle bestows moral superiority. But fly-fishing is merely a technological handicap self-imposed purely for pleasure. We are Anglers All, treading different paths to the same goal.

Our goal—everyone's goal at El Salto—was to catch a bass over ten pounds, and in this climatologically challenging week no one had broken that barrier despite heroic efforts. Yet in that hard-charging crowd, where fly-fishing seemed a bit like digging for gold with an atomizer and an oyster fork amidst hydraulic miners wielding water cannons and mammoth excavators, Jerry and I very nearly held our own. Like everyone else we'd averaged around fifty bass a day in the two- to five-pound range with several around six. We hadn't landed any of the nine-pounders reported by a fortunate few, but Jerry caught a freakish looking tadpole of a bass with the head of a nine-pounder and the body of a three-pounder, and I hung an honest nine-pounder but couldn't bulldog him out of the drowned trees that forest this immensely fecund bass factory, impounded on the Rio Elota only twenty years ago and just now coming into its prime.

El Salto reminds me of the twenty-year-old TVA lakes I grew up fishing back home in the East Tennessee hills—not the numbers or size of the fish so much as the amazing array of fish-holding structures left behind when a dam drowns a long-inhabited valley. I can imagine the El Salto locals sitting around the marina talking about big bass caught from the ruins of a childhood home just as East Tennesseans talked about big bass caught from the stump of a cousin's silo. I'll long remember the four-pounder that ate my popper in El Salto's old churchyard right between the stone fleur-de-lis and the Virgin of Guadalupe.

I hope the other anglers found time that week to look up from the serious business of accumulating poundage to drink in their surroundings—the soaring mountains, the flooded Spanish villages built before Plymouth Rock ever saw a Pilgrim, the grebes and coots and red-footed ducks that peppered the shallows and darkened the skies, the overfed ospreys preening in every tree, the white egrets mincing along the banks, the blue herons presiding over the shallows, the clanking copper bells of zebus and burros cropping sparse grass amidst cacti and thornbushes and gnarled sprawling oaks where Mesozoic iguanas toasted in the sun.

One thing no one missed was the lake's treasure-trove of biomass. The shoreline was a virtual spectrum of life. Tight against the bank, a thick stew of larvae and fry swirled against a grazing ribbon of thumb-size tilapia, which flashed in the sun like new dimes. Farther out, a mixed band of hand-sized tilapia and bass darted in for spare change, and the occasional behemoth pushing a supertanker's bow wave exploded through the rainbow like a baleen whale seining krill, and just like that the lake held one less tilapia.

But not for long, because tilapia go forth and multiply beyond belief. It's no accident that this native of the Nile is the fish with which Christ famously fed the multitudes. It's doing that here on El Salto—feeding the bass and feeding the locals—and El Salto's intense commercial gillnet fishery helps feed North America's hungry multitudes.

"It bungs up the fishing," grumble some guests. And while it's difficult to imagine that all those gillnets spiderwebbing everywhere don't in some way impact the bass fishing, government biologists concur with lodge owner Billy Chapman that gillnetting, which is restricted to certain periods, certain areas, and to tilapia only, is the bass's salvation. For every egg the Florida-strain largemouth extrude, ten tilapia hover nearby waiting to eat it. Even though bass grow two pounds per year in this hothouse tropical environment, they simply cannot reproduce quickly enough to keep up with the tilapia competition without help from a two-legged predator.

And the tilapia have other ways of evening the score. One day we found a nine-pound bass floating on its back with a two-pound tilapia, its stiff fins flared like punji sticks, jammed down its throat. The day after, TV bass man Shaw Grigsby found an eight-pounder in the same condition. In both cases, rescue attempts resulted in the bass dying and the tilapia swimming away—a jujitsu warrior exploiting the greed of its oppressor to bring about its downfall.

The downfall for the truly big bass here—an 18.8-pounder was the biggest so far—tends to be giant swim baits, Senkos, or Carolina-rigged plastic worms fished deep against the abundant structure. Although a properly rigged fly rod can plumb the depths, it's much happier fishing shallow water. So am I.

Fortunately, the bouillabaisse of life that bands the El Salto shoreline brings enough big bass inshore early mornings and late afternoons so that top-water fans and fly fishers self-handicap only in theory—and then mostly at midday when sane Sinaloans are enjoying a siesta. Once I found the right fly—a big Dahlberg Diver with its buzz-cut deer-hair head trailed by long grizzly saddle hackles over soft yellow marabou, which swam very tilapialike stripped slowly from the bank toward the boat—I was happy to abandon the unwieldy 350-grain sinking lines and midday doldrums and perhaps a chance at the ultimate fly rod bass in favor of a reliable stream of largemouths exploding on top.

On my last day there, having bargained myself down from twenty pounds to ten and having muffed my chance at a nine, I found it impossible to be anything but happy as a six-pounder blasted my burbling Diver and powered for the lily pads with the line thrumming like a bowstring and my nine-weight flexing into the corks. I released him into the shallows and nodded to the guide: it's time to go.

The greed for more and ever more was the undoing of Midas and of Bogart's Fred C. Dobbs. Only Walter Huston learned to be satisfied with what riches he'd been given in his quest for treasure. In his honor I turned toward the massively purpling Sierra Madres and, as Carlos the guide gunned his big Yamaha, I payed homage to Huston's knee-slapping, elbow-pumping dance, cackling merrily away into the dusk knowing I was surrounded by gold.

31. *Dressing for the Thousand Islands*

I'M NOT SAYING WILL RYAN CREATES HIS OWN weather. All I'm saying is Will Ryan may possibly generate an electromagnetic vortex into which the surrounding weather involuntarily flows.

On the surface this isn't scientifically possible. But the scientific method teaches us to closely observe natural phenomena and draw reasoned conclusions over time, and it's worth remembering that broadcasting moving pictures over long distances to be viewed on flickering glass screens was also once scientifically impossible. Now it's merely annoying.

As a talking head from one of those moving pictures recently reminded me, it pays to keep an open mind. Consider, for example, a trip to Cape Cod one spring a few years back, when former *Fly Rod & Reel* editor Jim Butler and I drove down to Popponesset to fish with former *Fly Rod & Reel* columnist Jack "Grey Ugly" Sayers. The weather was pleasant and warm and serene, and young women wandered about fetchingly underdressed. Old people smiled and ate ice cream unencumbered by their usual futzy sweaters and Eisenhower-era windbreakers, and everyone was happy and carefree and gay, in a manner of speaking.

And then the wind veered sharp and cold from the east, and it began to rain and blow, and the Cape's infamous mung—a breed of indigenous seaweed created in Beelzebub's biolab specifically for the frustration of fly fishers—advanced on the beach in floating windrows no one yet born could cast a fly across. Growing suspicious, I called Will's cellphone, and our friend Marcel Rocheleau answered. I said, "Where are you?"

Marcel said, "Somewhere south of Wusstah on foah-ninety-five and headin' for the Vineyahd; goin' stripah fishin.'" And then I walked back from the beach to Jack's cottage and turned on The Weather Channel. Just south of Worcester, Massachusetts, on Interstate 495, a bright orange and yellow spiral was sucking most of eastern North America's emerald-green troposphere into its maw, and it was headed our way.

Then there was the time Will and I hiked several miles into a secluded cove on the lower reaches of the Kennebec River where immense stripers were alleged to lurk, and it rained harder than I have ever seen it rain anywhere north of the thirtieth parallel. Except for the time we hiked up the shoulder of Mount Katahdin and cowered for several hours deep within the soggy bowels of a low-lying thunderstorm that flashed lightning above, alongside, and below us, and swelled the stream we had intended to fish for wild mountain brook trout so that it rose four feet out of its banks and nearly cut off our escape route back down the mountain to camp.

And so when I packed my truck to drive to Ryan's natal shores in New York's Thousand Islands district for a bit of late-season bass fishing and maybe a shot at a musky, I ignored the calendar that said *August* and packed not one but three complete suits of rain gear plus enough fleece and wool for a month in the arctic. I'm happy to report that it was very nearly enough.

A full day passed before we grew brave enough to try our luck on Chaumont Bay, "the largest freshwater bay in the world," as various chamber of commerce placards proudly proclaim. A week of unrelenting southwest wind had whipped these usually crystalline waters—rendered so transparent by the relentless hoovering of its nutritious planktonic cloud by zillions of zebra and quagga mussels unintentionally imported from Europe in the bilgewater of ocean-going ships—into a froth of whitecapped instability. We bounced around in Stan Warner's boat for four or five hours with some success, if you measure success by not drowning, freezing, or otherwise perishing from the elements. For which I thank Gore-Tex, fleece, and freeboard.

Stan was high rod with a six-inch yellow perch and a two-inch goby, another inadvertently introduced exotic that, unlike the inedible but ruthlessly efficient filter-feeding foreign mussels, actually contributes enough to the Great Lakes' forage base to interest such voracious predators of the unwary as smallmouth bass, walleyes, and molders of Mister Twisters.

Will and I maintain that we each had strikes from good smallmouth, but unavoidable delays in grinding in our lines' protruding wind bellies meant the bass expectorated our tube jigs before we could set the hook. Stan actually boated his two trophies, but as he hadn't exactly hooked them in the mouth but in other, more unintentional portions of their anatomy, Will and I disallowed them on technical and ethical grounds.

On the way north to a musky and bass rendezvous near Massena, we stopped at a rest area along the St. Lawrence River and encountered an intentional foreign import interacting with another intentional foreign import: English anglers lured here by the planeload for The Great American Carp Adventures Tour.

The night before, moving pictures broadcast from the Watertown TV station featured a teenage newsperson rendered inarticulate by the proximity of a teenage English actor named Tom Felton, who apparently played someone called Draco Malfoy in the *Harry Potter* movies and was grand pooh-bah of the Carp Tour the third year running. On the subject of St. Lawrence carp fishing, Mr. Felton said he was "right chuffed," which translates into American English as certifiably, perhaps dangerously, pathological.

So, too, were the contestants lined up along the riverbank in his or her own numbered and precisely delineated spot and equipped according to his or her temperament or pocketbook. We walked about with the bemused air of fly fishermen among spin fishermen or spin fishermen among bait fishermen or bait fishermen among golfers or golfers among the not-yet-retired, and we were very much gratified when two giggling local girls sporting Walmart-level tackle and pink plastic lawn chairs winched a carp the size of a Labrador retriever to the bank while an anoraky Englishman in the adjoining chair—an expensive bespoke carp-fishing chair with stainless-steel rod holders, cup holders, and various scientific apparatuses whose purposes we could not fathom—cast a stonking-great surf rod armed with an aluminum tube whose precise perforations scattered a cloud of bread crumbs across his fishing station like antiradar chaff from a bomber. He seemed more than a bit put out that his teenage neighbors had profited at his expense. Perhaps during the fierce naval battles of the War of 1812 one of his ancestors received similar unseemly treatment in these very waters when the unlettered locals took up positions unsportingly downcurrent from the Quality. And kicked their asses.

Eventually we made it to Massena, and along with Will's son Brody we launched Will's Gheenoe into an oddly shaped body of water known colloquially as The Trench and officially as something long and bureaucratically unmemorable. Lashing rains washed away too much ink from my notebook to read the entries I copied from the sign, but I can just about pick out the capitalized words "Industrial" and "Sanitary."

The wind blew fiercely up and down The Trench, and we thought how wonderful an electric trolling motor might be compared with Will's splintery plastic discount-store paddles. But the fish seemed unconcerned by our careening randomly about, and in the few hours before the weather turned a bit too Biblical even for us, we boated well more than fifty bass, a mixture of smallmouth and largemouth running to maybe three or four pounds, all bright and clean and doggedly determined, not in the least industrial but certainly sanitary enough for recreational purposes.

On the way back to the motel, whose sign enthusiastically welcomed the All-American Carp Tour, we stopped to rescue and retie the Gheenoe, as the storm front hurrying north spawned a tornado that, en route to match-sticking a nearby farm and tin-canning an even closer house trailer, paused to shoplift Will's boat from his roof racks—perhaps as a warning that if he insists on attracting unfortunate weather and carrying a fat plastic canoe on his Subaru's roof, he ought to invest in something stouter than discount-store clothesline and learn to tie some properly nautical knots not named after someone's granny.

Next day's weather, according to the local moving picture station's effervescent forecaster, was great, by which she meant bright sunshine and those bracing northwest winds that always push out a storm. Of course one person's great can be another's grim.

We met Will's friend Tony Zappia and a young blonde Scandinavian giant named Nils Peterson along the banks of a small river I've been asked not to name, which was allegedly a favorite haunt of North America's apex predator of the freshwater unwary, the muskellunge. Nils, a locally legendary hunter of these great striped sharks of the shadows, showed us inspirational photographs of the many giant muskies he'd caught in the area, and then he apologized for the bright sun and stiff northwesterlies that made it unlikely we'd actually get to catch one ourselves. I looked accusingly at Will on the theory that it's always useful to have someone to blame for your problems, and then we pushed off in our canoes into the river.

We cast a lot and, as our friend Marcel always says, acted exceedingly predatory, but except for a few smallmouth and a chance encounter with a musky around thirty pounds that relieved Tony's crank bait of a nice walleye, we didn't catch one.

I'm blaming Will for this, too, while carefully ignoring a recent salmon fishing trip to the Miramichi where it rained in wrath-of-God fashion for a week, and a trip to Belize the following week when hurricane-force wind and rain rendered the bonefish flats un-fishably opaque for the duration.

In the one case Will was six hundred miles away and in the other twenty-two hundred miles, but I'm sure it was somehow his fault.

32. *A Tale of Two Rivers*

I WAS ON THE FINAL LEG OF A MARATHON couch-surfing expedition and sponging off old friends Ted Leeson and Betty Campbell in Oregon after sponging off John Gierach and Susan McCann in Colorado. I was lingering over breakfast and the *Oregonian* and eyeing last night's empty wine bottles and pondering the great questions of our time.

Such as, where can you fish in coastal Oregon on Labor Day weekend without tripping over hordes of other anglers yet have a chance of tripping over a few fish? Ted's answer was to go after sea-run cutthroat on the Siletz, a small coastal river locally known for its salmon and steelhead and literarily known as the locale where an enigmatic fisher-babe called Eddy jumped naked from an overhanging alder and swam off like an otter after a big steelhead. Eddy landed both the steelhead and the heart of one Gus Orviston, the fish-addled hero of David James Duncan's coming-of-age-with-a-fly-rod classic *The River Why*.

So the next morning, after another evening of helping various Oregon vintners to prosper, we headed out from Corvallis in the dark of night and literally hit the river before dawn. By literally I don't mean virtually. Thanks to the long hot summer, the river was as low as Ted had ever seen it. When we levered the drift boat off its trailer at the bottom of the ramp, the echo of fiberglass on basalt resounded through the canyon like a Biblical stoning from the second book of Cecil B. DeMille.

The river's overly evident geology had its advantages, though, for we had it all to ourselves except for two territorial dogs and their apologetic owner hanging out laundry behind a cliff-side house trailer; an old guy with a Zebco sitting on a bucket and asking if we'd seen any salmon—we'd seen four, and good ones, we hailed back; and a small rubber raft crewed by two decidedly un-Eddy-esque teens boom-boxing depressing music and coiffed with what appeared to be giant eggplants. We noted in passing the famous broken alder—if I'm correctly remembering Duncan's scribblings on a long-ago Christmas card—where sky-clad Eddy made her magical emergence, ensuring that naughty old fly fishermen would forevermore eye broken Oregon alders with a certain primitive stirring. This time, no Eddy. And in the low, clear water, no steelhead, either.

But our bumpity-bump drift was fruitful in the way we'd hoped, because when we'd lumber into one of the river's deep holes we'd find bluebacks—sea-run cutthroats home for their own procreative purposes—and they were happy to eat our flies. To my eastern eyes it seemed unlikely anything would happily eat Ted's bristly gold and scarlet horrors. But Ted said that he had invested hours of painstaking research to craft these flies into exact imitations of the sea-run cutthroat's favorite food: a Panther Martin, a flashy painted metal spinner bait billed as "the greatest fish catcher of all time." I couldn't argue with that. Nor could the bluebacks.

Over the course of a long and pleasant day of bumping and grinding down the dehydrated river we caught around twenty blue-and-brass cutthroats to sixteen inches, and we both left flies in considerably larger fish, shin-length shadows darting snake-like from the depths in the coastal cutthroat's peculiar mixture of lightning savagery tempered by extreme timidity.

Connecting with this contradictory species is a matter of accurate casting to shadowy lairs combined with lightning-flash reflexes and perfect timing. Although I can sometimes accomplish the first, I'm well past the age where I have the middle, and thanks to a congenitally wandering mind I've never had the latter. But having spent the previous week high up in the Colorado Rockies fishing small mountain trout streams, where accurate casting to shadowy lairs, lightning-flash reflexes, and perfect timing are as necessary as Parachute Hare's Ears, dry-shake floatant, and high-capacity lungs, I was as close to simultaneously owning all three as I'm ever likely to be.

Which didn't help at all the next day, when we dragged Ted's drift boat down the bank and into the rushing McKenzie River below Leaburg Dam—we being me, Ted, and John Larison, author of *The Complete Steelheader*.

And that was our simple plan: completely fish for steelhead with flies. I won't say that Ted and I were confident. In our experience, "confident" and "anadromous fish" belong in the same sentence only if you quarantine "confident" between "I'm not" and "we'll catch any." But on a quiet misty morning on a river world-famous for its steelhead, accompanied by an experienced steelhead guide fishing for fun instead of profit—Larison having recently traded guiding for a life in academia—we were at least guardedly optimistic.

I had a good take early on, and with my lightning-flash reflexes still wired for Rocky Mountain browns and coastal Oregon cutthroats, I struck like a cobra. Which was exactly the wrong thing to do with a large anadromous fish—I knew that even as I did it. It was a good fish, too, somewhere around fifteen pounds swirling up from the tail-out to eat my slowly swinging wet fly, all pink and purple and black and Gothic to eastern eyes, like a teenage Blue Charm that had taken to wearing an eggplant on its head and listening to The Cure.

As we drifted, we saw plenty of steelhead hugging the river bottom in exactly those places you would expect to see steelhead hugging the river bottom, and we saw one and heard of two caught by an odd creature clad all in forest green who stalked the bank like a spidery frog hunting bugs. His mirrored sunglasses peered from beneath a furious green ball cap as he cast a heavy sinking line and a weighted fly in a furious lightning-flash sort of way, and he set the hook with what seemed to my innocent eastern eyes both excessive frequency and excessive furiousness upon no visible evidence of a strike.

I hesitate to say for sure that he was snagging steelhead, though I don't hesitate to think it. And yet the one steelhead we saw him fight and land, and the two others that a fish-census crew we chatted up had seen him fight and land, were carefully, even lovingly released. So who's to say that drifting a heavily weighted fly through visibly holding fish and setting the hook when it drags across their uninterested faces is less sporting than waiting for a fish to open its mouth and voluntarily eat a fly—or a salmon egg or a crawfish tail?

Over the course of a long and aggressively sunny day we tried everything—traditional swinging wet flies, dead-drifted nymphs on indicators, not-quite-dead-yet-nymphs drifted without indicators, actively manipulated streamers, Atlantic salmon dry flies dead-drifted and skittered, floating and sink-tip lines, and even, to stretch the definition of fly-fishing far past any reasonable interpretation, lead-head jigs suspended from bobbers and cast with a noodly ten-foot spinning rod. And except for the one take ruined by my lightning-flash reflexes, we didn't touch a fish.

The McKenzie was exactly the kind of river where you'd expect to touch whole crowds of fish, with its bouncing riffles and sharp rapids separating deep, dark pools littered with house-sized boulders that split the current and created magnificent holding water. We fished each in turn and thought each spot empty of fish, but when we'd drift down over the hole we'd just flogged we'd flush two or three steelhead from exactly the spots we'd been flogging. As the day progressed and more and more drift boats emerged onto their ancestral river, we didn't see anyone else catching fish, either.

Once we spotted a fish of six or seven pounds holding in a classic lie, and from easy casting distance we tried every technique we could devise. Ted and I became convinced it was one of those oversized fish-shaped potholders planted on the bottom to distract anglers from better water, but when we drifted over it the potholder yawned and swam away.

So the great question of the day became whether we might have been able to swing a heavily weighted fly right into its mouth, or at least across its face, and then set back hard to drive home the barb like the batrachian green Gollum stalking the bank.

Somehow, though, we couldn't bring ourselves to do it, nor could we begin to explain why it was okay to try for steelhead with, say, a ten-foot spinning rod rigged with a jig and a slide-through bobber and not okay to set the hook when a fly swung by a fly rod phrenologically examined a fish's face.

Which brings me to wonder if I'm spending too much time pondering the great questions of our time instead of merely drifting toward the logical conclusion that fishing, as David Duncan wrote in *The River Why*, is "nothing but the pursuit of the elusive." And, provided it's done with respect, whether it really matters how you go about it.

33. *Hall of the Mountain King*

IT THRUMMED THROUGH THE FUSELAGE ON THE turboprop's flight from Vancouver to Bella Coola, British Columbia's Coast Range poking its snow-covered peaks through a sea of clouds, staccato cellos and bassoons poking through the bass clef of a pensive orchestra.

The next day in the helicopter it grew stronger, an oscilloscopic symphony in plate tectonics, jagged teeth of granite and basalt gnawing water from clouds to feed trees and rivers. Specifically the Dean River, crashing through a canyon straight out of Middle Earth.

And in the Dean, nudging upriver toward the falls in a jet-powered dory, wading into the head of a pool and trying to remember how to spey cast, the orchestral cliché became overpowering. High school band? Tweety and Sylvester? Trolls and giants and heroes oh my?

"What is it?" I asked Pat, a retired commercial salmon troller and forty-year steelhead fanatic revisiting the Dean after a fifteen-year absence.

"Grieg, Dude. The Hall of the Mountain King."

Like many first-timers, I arrived on the Dean with great expectations, in part fueled by magazine articles from the 1950s, the pioneering days when the river was stiff with fish and the handful of fishermen who could find their way to this out-of-the-way place were coming home with slack jaws and speaking in tongues. And in part fueled by communiqués from friends: "The closest I get to religion is when I'm on the Dean," Marc Bale wrote. "The chinooks are brutes, bright as a sun ray and just about as fast and powerful. One a day or even one a trip is plenty." And then at the fly-fishing retailer show running into Joan Wulff, who had just returned from British Columbia and was gushing: "You really must fish the Dean."

And there I was, thigh-deep in the Dean and trying to figure out this Left Coast spey-cast aberration called skagit, which, as a deliverer of anadromous payloads, compares to the delicate Atlantic salmon casting I can kind of do as a hellfire missile compares to a peashooter.

Head guide Scott Baker-McGarva watched me cast my prissy eight-weight spey line with its ineffectual interchangeable sinking tips and discreet basic-black fly and then casually replaced it, reel and all, with a 750-grain skagit head as thick as a forefinger, fifteen feet of tungsten-coated T14 sinking tip, and a fly that resembled a palm-sized purple Easter bunny wearing a black feather boa and a fat red clown nose. It was so heavy it cratered the rapids like a mortar shell and stretched the definition of fly beyond plausibility.

"Got to get down where the fish are. Lot of current here."

For countless centuries, the wild current that carved the canyon of the Dean has culled the weak, the floundering, and the foolish from its gene pool. Only the stoutest, strongest, and swiftest steelhead and salmon can make it through the Mountain King's intimidating hall to reach the spawning water beyond.

"Set the drag to stun," Dana Sturn suggested. Dana, like the steelhead and salmon, is an annual returnee to the Dean. The creator and mediator of a website called speypages.com, where speycasting fanatics worldwide go to learn, teach, rant, and preach about everything two-handed, Dana is a wellhead of low-key advice. "These fish are really strong. From the current, from the canyon."

Set the drag to stun? Good thing, because only an hour or so into my first day, halfway through the swing of an accidentally decent cast, the thick line jerked and the long Sage bowed, and I was into my first-ever chinook salmon. It wasn't a leaper like the Atlantics I know—more a roller and a runner and brutishly determined in a whole new way. After much burning of backing and pumping and grinding and rock hopping downriver to a quiet back eddy just above a point of no return, I managed to snub the beast close enough to the bank for Scott to extract the hook, and there it was: twentyish pounds of chinook, to say it in Canadian, or king, to say it in American—thick, powerful, like two Atlantic salmon duct-taped together and enpurpled with indignation. "We," the King's fierce eye implied, "are not amused."

I knew I should go all Roderick Haig-Brown and worshipful and thankful and, dare I say, hopeful, but I also knew how seldom a hero's great expectations find reward until the final act, and sometimes not even then. Still, with the addition of a five-pound Dolly Varden down where the Dean meets the sea, I was high rod thus far—an unnatural state of affairs that lasted until an hour or so after lunch, when long experience took over from beginner's luck, and a good chinook dragged Dana a quarter-mile downriver before he landed it, and then Pat landed a fifteen-pound steelhead that ricocheted across the water like a grasshopper on a hot griddle.

Which was the only thing in that neck of the woods you could describe as hot. The weather cycled between miserable and frightening with forty-knot winds and icy rattles of rain. The experienced looked alternately at the cold clear water and the cold cloudy skies and the tall surrounding mountains all coiffed in white and shook their heads.

But the next day dawned bright and sunny and ever warmer, and the experienced lifted up their eyes unto the hills and nodded with anticipation as the sun began to melt the snow and turn the crevasses into waterfalls. This would be a long-range, not an immediate, cure, however, because the bright sun combined with the low clear water made fishing while waiting for the runoff to arrive even more difficult. Pat had a five-pound steelhead in the morning, and the other Dana, who co-owns a cabin on the lower river, caught a fifteen-pound chinook two casts after stepping into the boot prints of his roommate, Parker, who'd just spent the past hour casting nonstop to the same lie.

Pat, fishing late in the afternoon, hooked and lost a fifteen-pound steelhead. Two casts later, as I sat watching a murder of crows and a cruising eagle reenacting a Sharks-and-Jets scene from *West Side Story*, he spent half an hour slugging it out with a twenty-five-pound slab of chinook. When he knelt for the obligatory hero shot in the low afternoon sun, he looked less like a middle-aged man who had caught more than four thousand steelhead and lord knows how many commercially trolled chinook than like a twelve-year-old 4-H'r hugging his prize-winning pig.

The following day, with the river still low and clear and the thermometer climbing toward triple digits, the fish became—I guess the right word is tentative. Everybody hooked up, as I recall, but nobody stayed hooked up very long. Way out in the middle a pod of four salmon porpoised their way upstream, one of them as long from dorsal to tail as Pat's pig had been in its entirety. All through the day the snow peeled off the mountaintops, and by suppertime the river began to color and rise. That evening, lounging on the porch in shirtsleeves, the experienced nodded and smiled.

In the morning, with the river up two feet and opalescent green, wading entirely lost its visible component and left us tap-tap-tapping along like Blind Pew from *Treasure Island*. But with the rise in the river came a rise in the fishing, and over the next few days everybody was into fish—steelhead here, salmon there, tens and twelves and fifteens and at least one thirty-pounder for the folks on the far bank: fish enough for Mike and Dana's celebratory cigars to overwhelm the persistent sardine-cannery-meets-eighth-grade-locker-room odor of the teenage grizzly bears wrestling around in the willows a few feet in our lee.

At week's end, I can't say that I especially covered myself with glory. I wasn't quite low rod, but it was close: the twentyish-pound chinook, a twelve-pound chinook, a fourteen-pound steelhead, a five-pound dolly. Experienced Pat did that well the last hour of the last day, when, as is characteristic of most fishing trips, the fishing really began to turn on. And kept at it, as I heard from friends who were on the Dean the following week. "Dude, it was awesome. The river was just stiff with fish."

But as Marc said, "One a day or even one a trip is plenty." And it was, really, honestly—more than plenty. Although the image I'll file away under *Dean* won't be my first-day king glowering next to the bank but the last-day steelhead suspended in a sharp beam of sunlight—at least thirty pounds and probably more, just hanging there, defying gravity and physics and me and seventy-five yards of backing and a hundred feet of running line and twenty-five feet of finger-thick fly line and fifteen feet of tungsten-coated T14 and six feet of twenty-pound-test Maxima.

Then he finally bent in half and kicked his tail and reentered his element as seamlessly as an Olympic diver, and all that technology corkscrewed back at me and landed at my feet just like the flailing crescendo of Edvard Grieg's manic music—beginning slowly and building, building, building to a final roar of timpani, a clash of cymbals, and a beaten hero, an aspiring plunderer of the Mountain King, wheezing like a locomotive.

PART FIVE

Once More into the Brine

Yet it is in our idleness, in our dreams, that the submerged truth sometimes comes to the top.

— Virginia Woolf

34. *Fishing the Flats*

Some years ago—never mind how long precisely—having little or nothing worth eating in the fridge and nothing particular to interest me in the freezer, I thought I would cruise about a little and cadge a meal off the watery part of the world. It is a way I have of feeding myself and regulating the digestion. Whenever I find myself growing pinched about the waist, whenever it is a damp, drizzly November in my alimentary canal, whenever I find myself involuntarily pausing before displays of frozen fish sticks and pulling up behind every fish-peddler I meet, and especially whenever my hypos get such an upper hand of me that it requires a strong moral principle to prevent me from deliberately stepping into the street and methodically stopping the Schwan's Food Service truck—then, I account it high time to get a-fishing as soon as I can.

This is my substitute for pistol and ball. With a philosophical flourish, Cato throws himself upon his sword; I quietly take to the water. There is nothing surprising in this. If they but knew it, almost all humans in their degree, at some time or other, cherish very nearly the same feelings. How else to explain all those wharfs and piers and pilings and bridges and boats lined with hopeful patient faces? Their lines a-dangle in the fresh or brine, their eternal optimism, their stoic persistence and unbending belief that the right bait or reel or rod or blessed hat or lucky sunglasses or incanted squirt of Days Work might soon fill expectant coolers.

And so it was that I set forth into a soft mist and gathering tide with what I can't call optimism, because my thoughts kept drifting back to other days more than thirty years ago, when a similar urge led similar expeditions.

We fished every fishable day, David and I, he on a thirty-eight-foot Cape Islander called the *Mary R* and me on a twenty-eight-foot Friendship boat called the *Lucy B*. Every fishable day but one, when the state of Maine decreed it unlawful to haul lobster gear between four o'clock on Saturday afternoon until half an hour before sunrise the following Monday morning—so lobster fishermen might not turn their faces from their Maker, goes one argument. So that gouging one day out of a two-day weekend might inconvenience part-time lobstermen with full-time jobs and union paychecks goes another. Of these I bet on the latter, because the ban applied only between June 1 and August 31. After the soft summer ended and the part-timers with jobs returned to work, lobstermen's souls could go to the devil.

And so summer Sundays became our day of rest, and because we were fishermen, we rested best by going fishing. We didn't do this in quest of adventure or seeking a white-headed whale with a wrinkled brow and a crooked jaw and three holes punctured in his starboard fluke. We had no gold Spanish ounce to nail to our masts; we barely had two quarters to rub together. We did pass the measure a fair amount, though it was Narragansett short-necks and not rum as hot as Satan's hoof quaffed from the sockets of keen harpoons. Which, actually, we did have of a sort.

What we did is drift over the flats in my nine-foot pram between the fertile outfalls of Belfast's sardine cannery and its poultry processors, a beer in one hand and a frog gig in the other, while spearing flounders the size of dessert plates, sometimes even dinner plates. When tide or turbidity veiled our prey, we bounced sparrow-egg sinkers and little long-shank Limericks baited with chunks of fat hen clams dug from the reeking mudflats.

Every time we'd feel that tentative tap-tap tug, we'd get as excited as little kids. And it wasn't just the prospect of flounder in the skillet and maybe even a surplus to swap for more Narragansetts at the Bi-Rite Market. For some reason we felt a fuzzyheaded metaphorical connection with a fish born like all fish, swimming upright on edge with eyes on each side of its head, until one day it decides that having eyes just like everyone else simply won't do, so it takes to its bed and reclines through life, twisting its skull sideways and migrating its eyeballs, the better to spot both predator and prey.

In a way we were transmutated fish—an East Tennessean and a blue-collar Bostonian who had somehow ended up lobster fishing in Maine, both of us less from a spirit of Captain's Courageous adventure than from the simple need to earn a living that didn't involve stitching shoes, canning sardines, eviscerating poultry, or asking a tourist if she wanted french fries with her clam roll.

David and I had both recently emerged from the '60s—spindled, folded, and transmutated in the familiar pharmaceutical ways and in others that may be less directly familiar depending on your draft number, socioeconomic status, and whether you had, as a former vice president and purported fly fisherman once said about military service in those days, other priorities.

My transmutation came in a top-secret naval communications center, where in my duties I sometimes read messages between important national leaders that an impressionable True Believer ought not to have read. David's came in the doorway of an Air Cavalry Huey spraying the tree line with a .50 caliber while Jefferson Airplane and the screams of the wounded blared through his headphones.

David had a lot more transmutation to deal with than I did. I merely found out that leaders lie. David found out that teenagers die for those lies. Or they survive with scars that never quite heal—not even aided by a whole vast ocean of short-neck Narragansetts or an island-studded bay filled with flounders.

After lobstering ended around Thanksgiving I spent winters at home and cut wood, built lobster traps, and watched *Schoolhouse*

Rock with my toddler son. "It's only a bill," we'd sing. "Conjunction Junction, what's your function?" And so with time my superficial wounds healed, or at least scabbed over.

David's wounds were much deeper and never healed. He often spent winters on Georges Bank working on the last of the old Eastern-rigged side-draggers fishing out of Provincetown, Chatham, and New Bedford for scallops, for cod, and especially, when times were good, for flounder. *Yellowtails*, David would say. *There's nothing like a yellowtail flounder.*

And now more than a third of a century has somehow flashed past. The *Mary R* and the *Lucy B* are both long gone—sold off, obsolete, withered to dry husks beneath tattered tarps and burned to ashes on the tide flats. Belfast's sardine cannery is gone, the poultry packers and shoemakers are gone, and most of the blue-collar jobs and the people who held them are gone. David is gone, his Agent Orange riddled ashes quite literally sleeping with the fishes beneath the cold gray waters of Penobscot Bay. And the flounder are gone, too, at least from our end of the bay.

No one knows why, or perhaps the officials who do know why would rather not say—the mercury-seeping Superfund site upriver, all those emerald-green waterfront lawns fertilized and weeded and debugged by hired guns wearing hazmat suits, the occasional oil spills from the tankers and the fuel terminal, the leaky chemical plant, or maybe the grandfathered waterfront septic systems straight-piping summer people's shit into the bay.

It's an additive condition, they say. It's not one thing; it's every-thing. Don't eat the lobster tomalley from our bay, they say. Or the striped bass. Or the mussels and clams and whelks and snails. PCBs! Dioxin! Mercury! Oh my.

The advisories don't mention flounder. Why bother? But they aren't completely gone, and maybe, just maybe, they're coming back. Because a few years ago I saw a kid who didn't know that all the flounder are gone catch one from the town wharf. It was no bigger than his tiny hand, but it was a sure-enough flounder.

A few weeks later, I saw a cormorant near the wharf trying to swallow a flounder—beyond demitasse and verging into saucer size. A week later, drifting along the mudflats with my watchful eyes stuffed inelegantly down my peapod's outboard-motor well, I saw them. One here, one there: beady little eyes staring back from the bottom. A fish that looked at nature red in tooth and claw and PCB, and thought it best to hunker down on the bottom and wait things out.

I caught my first that afternoon—a winter flounder, four inches short of the minimum legal size of twelve inches. But a week after that, at our little town's annual lobster-boat races, an old friend took me aside and, with the kind of confidence reserved for his debit card's PIN or exactly how much turbo-boost old so-and-so was pushing through his race engine, he said, "They're a-comin' back some old strong over there," and he gestured with his hat brim toward a particular cove on a distant island with a name I won't mention, but for which I set sail one morning with the wind on my beam and my heart in my mouth.

I'd tell you how it went, but my hypos have gotten the upper hand of me quite enough already.

35. *Cod Stock*

T HERE WAS NOTHING MELVILLEAN ABOUT OUR dawn-patrol departure from the foggy coast of Maine. Despite the dour weather, we didn't suffer from a damp, drizzly November in our souls, nor do we seek a substitute for pistol and ball. We had simply accounted it high time to get to sea for the age-old reason that we were hungry for fish, and like the Basques, the French, and the English, who began fishing these waters nearly five centuries ago, we expected to fill our hold with cod, the googly-eyed bottom-feeders that brought Europeans to North America long before they came looking for a northwest passage or cities of gold or the freedom to persecute those of different ethnicity or religion.

Cod certainly lured my ancestors to the Gulf of Maine. And it was cod that lured Dave Teufel and Jerry Gibbs and me out into the fog on a chilly June morning almost four centuries later. As we cleared the harbor and the coffee kicked in, the conversation strayed from the fishing conventions of techniques and tackle and into the merits of crumbs versus batter, evaporated milk versus cream, Crown Pilot Biscuits versus Vermont Common Crackers.

And why not? Few fish are more culinarily useful than cod. Few freeze as well or better retain their mild, meaty flavor when cured by salt and sun. Cod are the beef of the sea, the fish everyone who likes fish likes to eat, the essential ingredient in fish and chips, in that splendid mélange of garlic and potatoes and pureed salt cod known as *brandade*, in that New England ubiquity, chowder—"Chowder for breakfast, and chowder for dinner, and chowder for supper," wrote Melville in *Moby-Dick* of a Nantucket chowder queen bearing the name and location, but not the occupation, of another of my scaly ancestors, "till you began to look for fish-bones coming through your clothes."

So what if they fight with the tenacity of a hip-boot? So what if they rival the goosefish for sheer unlovableness? Codfish, as we say in Maine, eat real good. Shouldn't that be enough to drag three fly fishermen from warm beds and out into the chill Maine fog for an unrepentant day atop the food chain? I mean, even devout catch-and-releasers have to eat.

We were headed toward a submerged hillock called Tanta, a thirty-mile run from Teuf's place back in Harpswell. According to Walter Rich's 1929 book *Fishing Grounds of the Gulf of Maine*, Tanta is "2 to 3 miles in diameter and has depths of about 40 fathoms over a bottom of broken ground of rocks and gravel. This is a spring and summer fishing ground for cod . . . Herring and mackerel usually are present."

One of Teuf's friends was out there yesterday looking for bluefin tuna and saw lots of herring. With herring, you get cod. And with cod you get, well, us for one thing. A big Portland-based bottom dragger, for another.

It's a crowded ocean, and thanks to GPS and sonar it harbors few secrets—especially few in the Gulf of Maine, where fishermen long ago charted its submarine topography by sounding with lead weights attached to long, long lines—toss by tedious toss.

The very names of these fertile concentrators of fish conjure wooden ships and iron men: The Bounties, Inner Kettle, Three-Dory Ridge, Cod Ridge, Pollock Hub, Haddock Nubble.

In the old days you followed your compass to the fishing grounds, cast the log, and ran out your time—*For Fippennies, run fifty-nine miles south by east three-quarter east from the Cuckolds, nine hours and a bit, full and by.* Everywhere you probed the bottom with tallow-armed lead—*forty-five fathoms and black gravel,* the leadsman sings out while examining the tallow and counting the fathoms marked on the sounding line, and over the halibut gear goes.

Nowadays we punch in numbers on the GPS and set the depth alarm on the sonar. We pick out individual rocks on its glowing screen and see fish clustered just above them and herring shoals fifteen fathoms down.

A statistician's spreadsheet graphing the growth of fishing technology against the decline of fish populations looks like the Cross of Saint Andrew. Researchers at the University of New Hampshire estimate that Gulf of Maine cod stocks are only 3 percent of their pre-European numbers and have declined more than 90 percent since the 1950s, which was about when sonar began to move from the war on submarines to the war on fish and about when ever-bigger bottom draggers began replacing small boats setting gillnets or a half-dozen tubs of trawl—bottom-tending long-lines stored in half-barrels, for you inlanders.

Of course when tub trawling began replacing hand lining in the 1860s, and when gillnets began replacing tub trawls in the 1880s, cranky old diehards predicted the fishery's imminent collapse, too. But there's a world of difference between a thirty-six-foot boat fishing a 400-hook long-line or 400 fathoms of gillnet and a 120-foot dragger vacuuming the bottom at four and a half knots. The net's 150-foot maw is spread by a pair of steel doors as big as king-size beds plowing twin furrows through mud deposited by the glaciers, with the heavy rock-hopper rollers on its foot rope crushing everything in its path, including deep-water corals that need centuries to grow. After a half-century of relentless bottom dragging many of these jagged, ragged, coral-studded seamounts that have nurtured marine life beyond imagining since the glaciers retreated have been planed as smooth as marble slabs and left nearly as lifeless.

Not that Teuf and Jerry and I were technologically pure. We weren't burning a hundred gallons of diesel per hour like our Portland friend, though we likely fed Teuf's yowling Yamaha thirty or forty gallons of gasoline before the day ended. But if we limited out at ten cod each, we'd be buying our families' winter fish for around a dollar a pound—nearly a dollar less than the dragger's cod will bring at the wholesale auction and five dollars less than fish-market retail. And, like our ancestors who came here with hand lines, tub trawls, and gillnets, we won't be obliterating the very nurseries meant to provide fish—and fishing—long after we've become ancestors ourselves. In our minds we justified our actions, which is what humans mostly do.

Still, we had our own technological revolution onboard. Teuf and I were armed as cod fishermen have been since the 1920s: with broom-stick boat rods, 4/0 reels the size of coffee cans spooled with thick fifty-pound-test line, and a pound and a half of chrome-plated lead jig trailing a treble hook. Jerry had a skinny graphite casting rod, a tiny Shimano level-wind reel spooled with gossamer forty-pound-test superbraid and a tiny, at least by offshore standards, six-ounce jig with a single hook.

Teuf and I—a couple of experienced offshore guys—didn't think Jerry's dinky little jig would tend bottom in the Gulf of Maine's fierce currents or that his toy tackle would withstand winching up a good codfish from 240 feet down.

Teuf and I, of course, were dead wrong. Our fat monofilament billowed downcurrent and dragged our big jigs along with it while Jerry's tiny jig with its thread-like line arrowed for the bottom and stayed there. And while we methodically ground up our codfish like the dead weights they were, Jerry pumped and played his cod like proper game fish. Which, unfettered by a pound and a half of lead stuck in their jaws and forty fathoms of heavy mono dragging in the current, they were. Jerry didn't just catch more fish than us; he worked less at it and had more fun doing it. This, of course, filled us with technological envy and silent resolve to come back for next year's cod stock suitably armed, the perennial reaction of fishermen everywhere anytime anyone outfishes them.

Finally the tide turned and the wind began to make from the southeast, and it was time to head back for Harpswell. Four hours of jigging put around twenty codfish between six and twelve pounds in the fish box and another dozen or so undersize fish back over the side. Not great fishing by any means but not bad in these pinched times. And plenty to feed our three families their winter's fish.

The Portland dragger had dissolved into the gathering fog, but from the way the gulls were screaming in the distance I'm guessing he'd hauled back and was culling through the catch—sorting by size and species: no cod under twenty-two inches, no haddock under nineteen, no more than six hundred pounds of cod for the trip that was legally allowed that year, although as of 2015, the cod catch is limited to two hundred pounds for commercial boats and none at all for recreational anglers. Like bottom draggers throughout the Gulf of Maine, he was shoveling back into the sea everything too small or too unmarketable or, like the crushed and mangled lobsters, simply illegal to catch with bottom trawls but which bottom trawls inevitably catch—shoveling back the deepwater corals, the sea slugs, the starfish, the unbelievable wealth of life for which there is no market but for which there was, before it was towed for two hours in the sausage funnel of the big net's cod-end, a purpose and a future.

There's no premeditated evil in all this. Like fishermen up and down the coast, the dragger's skipper was simply trying to navigate the Byzantine tangle of federal and state regulations that strive to preserve both fish and fishermen and are essentially doing neither.

I wonder what our ancestors would think of fishing today. Would my ninth great-grandfather Phillip Babb, the fishing master of Maine and New Hampshire's Isles of Shoals from the 1640s through the 1670s, admire the technological advances that allow three men to replace a hundred? The regulations that favor big corporate-owned draggers over owner-operated gillnetters and long-liners? Or would he turn away in shame after seeing a vast ecosystem and a way of life destroyed in a single lifetime?

36. *The Vision Thing*

Whether sparked by yellow chalk scratching through first-grade fog or the Clark Kent spectacles that transformed that fog into a chalkboard with instructive writing or the parental insistence that my amblyopia would correct itself if only I would make my lazy eye sit up straight and look where it's going and wear its embarrassing eye patch, I've always envied people who can see the hard-to-see.

Especially fish, which are harder to see than practically anything more corporeal than ghosts and leprechauns. Who hasn't heard the defeated tone of a guide on the bonefish flats who realizes that no matter how many times he says, "Ten o'clock, Sixty feet, Three big bones tailing left to right," his dimwitted sport will cast to the three mangrove shoots six feet astern?

But it isn't entirely our fault. Prey species are forever contriving unfair ways not to be seen. Brook trout disappeared into the dappled green forest streams by evolving backs covered with forest-green dapplings. Bonefish got themselves chrome-plated to reflect the shining expanse of skinny tropical flats straight back into hostile eyes. Small soft creatures like herring flock together with thousands of other small soft creatures—all of them saying, "Eat them, not me," and most of them getting away with it. Species that grow from toothsome young prey into large toothy predators look for hangouts where even larger and toothier predators won't prey on them.

Take striped bass and flats, for example. When stripers were young and tender, ospreys and herons made skinny sunlit flats into dangerous neighborhoods. But when they reach a certain size stripers no longer fear aerial assault, and the shallow clear flats are mostly free of the seals and sharks and stern trawlers and soft plastic Slug-Gos that can make deeper, faster water nervously unrestful even for a fifty-pounder.

As most saltwater fishermen know, striped bass are creatures of the twilight, of movement, of tide rips and swirling bait schools and crashing surf. This makes striper anglers creatures of pre-dawn departures and midnight shoreline stumbles and of live-lining mackerel, deep-drifting eels, and trolling plugs the size of policemen's nightsticks. Fly-fishing for stripers, like the striper itself, is pure brutality: heavy depth-charge fly lines and ginormous flies and rod-shattering strikes and enough adrenaline to turn a pack of PETA pacifists into foie-gras-eating ax murderers.

Which is why a rippled expanse of alluvial ooze overlain by a few feet of transparent seawater is about the last place a standard-issue striper fisherman might look for a striper, especially with the sun burning high in a cloudless sky.

But that's exactly where we went looking for them, we being fish-mag editors Dave Klausmeyer and Joe Healy fishing with Eric Wallace and Mac McKeever on a skinny backwater flat on a bright sunny day—the very time when normal Maine striper fishermen were snoozing in the shade after having flamed out on a dawn tide in one of the big brackish rivers or along the near-shore islands, casting into the rips and the surf while jockeying for position with all those other boatloads of coffee-cranked striper fishermen casting into the rips and the surf.

Out there on the windless late-morning flats, it was just us and the sun and the seagulls and the gray stern granite and green pointed firs hemming a small secluded cove. Joe and I fished with Eric, one of only a few Maine guides who specialize in flat-fishing for stripers, and it was a dislocating experience. I'd look

back from the postcard view of coastal Maine to see Eric up on
the poling platform with his sunblock and sunglasses and, "Get
ready, good fish at two o'clock about sixty feet off." I'd narrow my
eyes and roll them around, and slowly a striper would materialize.
And then I'd snap out of my no-worries-mon Bahamian bonefish trance and launch a mighty dawn-patrol striper cast that hit
the water like an osprey and scared the bejesus out of that striper,
then we'd ghost along looking for another to frighten away, with
me chanting under my breath, "I'm bonefishing for stripers, I'm
bonefishing for stripers. Everybody say Aummmmm."

Along with nurturing my inner calm, I was also trying to
remember the mechanics of spotting fish. You do this, as anglers
all should know, not by looking for fish—stripers, with their
mirrored sides traced by waving lines, can be as invisible as baby
bonefish even when pushing forty pounds—but by looking for the
suggestions of fish. At a distance, you see not the striper but the
impression of a striper: its shadow on the bottom, the flick of a
fin, the flex of a tail, the dart of a jaw snarfing a green crab, grass
shrimp, or sand eel.

Compared with the hyperactive tent revival of striper fishing in
the surf, sight-fishing the mirrored flats is Zen: the quest becomes
its own reward. Like dry-fly fishing, it's a form of aesthetic self-
denial that slows your pulse and makes you *see*.

But it isn't a way to run up numbers. For the day, we each boated
one fish and lost another. With a dawn assault on a big tidal river,
that would be an official defeat. But for flats fishing in Maine it
was a success—and possibly the birth of an addiction.

There's always a genesis moment when something new materi-
alizes from the fog. Anglers to the south won't see fly-fishing the
flats for stripers as anything new—the big flats off Cape Cod's
Monomoy Island or Long Island's Great South Bay have long
been home to a minority cult of flats-fishers. But here in Maine,
stripers on the flats have been pretty much invisible, and fishing
for them the way they need to be fished for, which is to say slowly
and carefully without even a trolling motor's cautioning whisper,
is beyond novel.

Mac McKeever, the senior PR wallah at L.L. Bean, is the first person I know to have done it, though I know other people who were rumored to have done it but didn't want anyone to know. Like most significant discoveries, Mac's was an accident.

"Ten or so years ago," he said, "I was pulling my skiff at a boat ramp, and a telephone worker was having lunch and asked how I did. I told him I'd caught a few fish here and there, and he said he was working high atop a pole at a nearby bluff overlooking a shallow white sand flat, and he'd seen loads of fish milling around in the skinny water. I went over there, and sure enough, the flats were haired over with the things—some big ones, too! I've been on them ever since, at first climbing atop coolers and then library step stools or teetering on the outboard's cowling to try for a better vantage point to spot fish."

Finally Mac got a proper poling platform made for his sixteen-foot Aquasport, and now he spends his days fishing the Pine Tree State Caribbean-style: long light leaders, little crab flies, and clock-face casting. "Pretty neat stuff," Mac says. "Clear shallow water, light sand, and black-backed stripers hunting for crabs." And a few—a very few—anglers on the flats hunting for stripers.

A year later, Jerry Gibbs and I met Mac at a different beach—his original beach, the lineman's beach—at the leisurely hour of half past eight, a time dictated in part by the high-noon low tide and more significantly by the sight-fishing necessity of high flooding sunlight. Which, as is typical with a trip planned well in advance, didn't arrive.

With intermittent cloud cover and the hot southern breath of a looming storm, even Mac had difficulty spotting fish before they spotted us. Through the morning we saw more than thirty stripers, most past twenty inches and a few past three feet. I managed a cast to only one taking fish, and when he turned on the fly with his open mouth, he spotted the boat and flushed like a partridge. The lesson: flats-fishing for stripers is a choose-your-day kind of thing. If the weather's right, you go; if it isn't, you go do something else. Unless you've driven 125 miles through coastal Maine tourist traffic to fish. Then, you go anyway.

And I learned another lesson: Stalking those fish and getting that single, turning, almost-a-take in skinny transparent water was as exciting as dragging a dozen depth-charged stripers from the foaming deep. Perhaps that's a personal vision not everyone can see. But then, not everyone needs to.

A few weeks later, sparked by a near connection with what was here all along, if only blinkered eyes could see, I revisited a few neglected flats not far from home, where bluff-top observations with high-powered binoculars revealed drifting shadows too big to be mackerel and too reposeful to be sturgeon.

In just the right light, I could envision a big Hudson Bay freighter canoe ghosting along with its motor kicked up beneath a simple poling platform made from aluminum pipe bent in a friendly nearby muffler shop, a scrawny old man leaning on a long black push-pole and shading his eyes from the noonday sun. He sees something moving, eases the pole into its rest, and then slowly lifts his fly rod and casts.

It might be a good striper in my vision—I hope so, anyway. Or it might be a stick of pulpwood drowned in the mudflat since river-driving days. It probably doesn't really matter. In either case the electric anticipation is pretty much the same.

37. *Victory at Sea*

FOR OBSCURE PSYCHOLOGICAL AND PHYSIOLOG-
ical reasons, the voices in my head imagine they're disk jockeys
hired to soundtrack my every move. So when Jerry Gibbs and I
met Mac McKeever and Jeff Miller at the wharf and we headed
down the river and out into Maine's Casco Bay by dawn's early
light, it was no surprise when the voices cued up Richard Rodgers
and Robert Russell Bennett's unapologetically bombastic score
from *Victory at Sea*, the Emmy-Award-winning documentary
about World War II's epic naval battles that resounded across
nearly every television on the planet from 1952 well into the 1960s.

That seemed appropriate enough given that we were headed
some twenty-odd miles offshore in a smallish outboard trend-
ing into harm's way and seeking battle with the wily bluefin tuna
based on intelligence reports that said, They're Out There.

Which was a relief, because for obscure hydro- and ichthyological reasons this was the year the big schools of stripers and bluefish that reliably provide the Maine coast's summer entertainment
chose instead to play a summer-long engagement on the Jersey
Shore.

By August, things had grown so dire that local television news
crews were interviewing sorrowful state officials about the striper
shortage's economic impact with backstories about idle attendants

at shoreside gas docks, empty-pocketed bait-and-tackle dealers, out-of-work guides, and idle anglers in shadowy saloons angrily speculating about just what Those People south of Cape Cod were up to.

There's nothing worse than thinking someone else is rolling in undeserved riches while you stew in a pool of deprivation. The next thing you know, the voices in your head are telling you to invade Manchuria and the Dutch East Indies or maybe lead a motorized infantry assault on the Vince Lombardi Service Area at Exit 18 of the New Jersey Turnpike as a diversion for the main invasion by sea through Barnegat Bay and Toms River.

Worse, what few stripers and bluefish did bother to come north arrived accompanied by the highest gas prices ever seen and some of the largest concentrations of baitfish seen in many years. The result was that on those rare occasions when you could actually afford enough gas to go out and look for stripers and bluefish and you actually found some, you could rarely get the voices in their heads to believe it's worth their while to chase down your artfully tied Bunker Fly when they could simply yawn and inhale yet another brace of menhaden or blueback herring without flicking a fin.

All of which made the arrival of bluefin tuna off our coast a Big Deal. And not just any bluefin tuna, but big schools of fishable-size bluefin tuna—twenty, forty, eighty pounds—something you have a reasonable chance of hooking and boating on a fly rod without latching onto one of those five-hundred-pounders that hardly notices it's hooked whether you're bent double over a straining twelve-weight fly rod or are strapped to a fighting chair and grinding a deep-sea reel the size of a chum bucket.

We arrived on the grounds just as the sun split the horizon, and had no sooner readied our rods than we spotted our first school of bluefins tearing up the ocean. Jeff punched the throttle, and we sped off to get in front of them, but before they resurfaced, the ten- to fifteen-knot northwest wind predicted by our government intelligence sources piped quickly past twenty-five and headed for thirty. With the sea in such a stew, chasing visible schools of tuna slid quickly off the maneuvering table.

Jeff, ever-resourceful and newly afflicted with bluefin fever, streamed astern an enormous spreader rig that looked as though he'd dragged a spring-tooth harrow through a 42nd Street sex-toy shop, and we set out to search the sea in a methodical and lurid manner. And we found nothing except that the cruel sea, excited by the northwesterlies that had failed to follow the script and lay down after that first sun's-up rush, found equal amusement in cats-cradling Jeff's fish-fluffers and in making our lives lumpily uncomfortable. Finally we bottled up our bravado and slunk home, four damply defeated men with drooping rods. The voices in my head selected something considerably less triumphalist for a soundtrack than the theme song from *Victory At Sea*. I forget what it was. Possibly that Gillian Welch song about an East Tennessee coal miner stuck down in a deep dark hole.

The next morning, well before first light and off on our own, Jerry and I crept downstairs while trying not to disturb his wife, Judy, enjoying the innocent slumber of the non-angling-obsessed, and we trailered his big flats boat to the launch ramp in Yarmouth. With picket lines of wading birds reporting our movements to their air cover circling overhead, we eased down the twisting Royal River toward the dawn and the bay and all those familiar spots where Jerry reliably finds stripers and blues.

All that day and half the next we rushed from likely place to likely place, casting this fly and that fly and nearly all our other flies nonstop from sunup to suppertime, and for our efforts we got but one touch: a half-hearted feather-tug from a big bluefish lazing along like an aqua-park porpoise.

Unwilling to surrender, we headed for bluer water past Great Chebeague and Long Island, Cliff and Jewell, Inner Green and Outer Green. We cast here, cast there, and studied Jerry's big LCD fish-finder, all the while marking fish like crazy just off the bottom. Finally, down went the fly rods and out came the jigging rods—we are, after all, fishermen and not strictly fly fishermen—and began bouncing Butterfly Jigs off the bottom with a couple of small flies cantilevered off the leaders on droppers.

Thus, having suffered through trials and tribulations and been transformed in classic monomythical fashion, we vanquished The Great Skunk, and to celebrate, Richard Rodgers and Russell Bennett fired up the NBC Symphony Orchestra right where they'd left off two days before, all trombones and trumpets and too much timpani.

Did we break our backs muscling in broad-shouldered striped bass, hunkered on the bottom scrounging green crabs and short lobsters? Well, not exactly. Did we battle fierce ravening bluefish chasing mackerel into the eelgrass? Not so much. Did we derrick up a halibut the size of a barn door or even a bath mat? Don't we wish. Did we fill the boat with brawny bottom-feeding codfish, haddock, pollock? Not quite—well, maybe that last one, a bit.

What we caught were a couple dozen snappy, scrappy little harbor pollock ranging from six to sixteen inches (Great eating!); a fourteen-inch cunner (Big for a cunner this far north!); a two-inch sculpin (My smallest fish ever on a fly! If you don't count the dragonfly nymph that ate a BWO emerger on Slough Creek in Yellowstone, and if you count a dragonfly as a fish and a Japanese Sabiki rig as a fly.); a live Cliona sponge about four inches across (My first ever Poriferan on hook and line!); and the trophy of the day, at least if you measure trophy by how long it took to lever it off the bottom and by how much of a bend it put in my rod: a horse mussel easily five inches across (my largest ever mollusk on an artificial lure!).

On our way back to Jerry's we stopped to fill his gas tanks, depleted by two days of feeding his Yamaha 250. As the dial spun well into triple digits before the decimal point and I nervously fingered my credit card, I could distinctly hear Maine's own Rudy Vallée singing *Brother, Can You Spare a Dime.*

But that night's harbor-pollock dinner was all kinds of tasty, as long as we didn't trouble ourselves with the thought that, for the same money, we could have eaten dozens of Bagaduce oysters and a whole saddle of sea-island lamb, and if we figured in the cost of Jerry's boat and motor and tow vehicle we could have added *foi gras* and white truffles and a 95-rated bottle of *Pouilly-Fuiss*é. We didn't, of course—real fishermen don't do amortization tables.

The real kicker came early the next morning, when I crawled from my own bed a hundred-odd miles northeast and settled on my own couch with my own coffee in my own cup and turned on the television and watched our local public-access cable channel's Harbor-Cam, which runs live in tandem with the morning's marine weather forecast.

And there, right in front of the camera, twenty-odd yards off the Belfast public landing and its early-morning joggers and tai chi practitioners, were a couple of dozen enormous cow stripers with dorsals like dinghy sails methodically surrounding a huge school of herring and chopping them to bits.

I laughed almost as hard as I did when Jerry, the long-time fishing editor of *Outdoor Life*, landed a six-inch pollock, and the fishing columnist of *Gray's Sporting Journal* quickly followed with a four-inch sponge.

I don't care what the voices in my head say or what music they play: that was way more fun than stripers.

38. *Great Expectations*

T HEY WERE SITTING ON THE BANK COMPLAIN-
ing about how hard it is for an honest guy to make a living these
days, how peckish one gets when the baitfish don't show, and how
unfair life can be for those whose very existence depends on the
ocean's fickle bounty. We certainly sympathized, as our own great
expectations were being likewise thwarted by the cruel sea.

Of course it was mostly my fault.

I'd arrived on Maine's Casco Bay with a cooler full of ice
and the intention to whack a slot-limit striper for the table. I
do this once or twice a year, which seems reasonably responsible
for an omnivorous angler. Usually these aren't premeditated acts
of piscicide but a clean-up-on-aisle-three vultching of fish that
messily swallow a fly and will soon be as dead as Monty Python's
parrot, no matter how tenderly released. But nothing says intention like a cooler full of ice, and nothing jinxes a fishing trip like
intentions.

Doubtless all those gulls and cormorants and herons and
ospreys kvetching on the bank blamed their poor fishing less on
me promising my wife a striper for supper than on a stiff onshore
wind prolonging the period of slack water at high tide, which
meant the scattered schools of juvenile herring they were awaiting hadn't yet begun to bunch up in the not-yet-swirling current,

where they could be harried into easy edibility by slashing striped bass.

After an hour of fruitless cruising and casting we finally spotted a small silver basketball of bait bouncing slowly along the shoreline, but as nothing was chasing them we did what the birds had hoped to do: headed for home and supper.

As last night's leftovers warmed and the tardy ebb finally began to overpower the building southeast wind, we kept walking to the porch to see if the birds' supper for tonight might be ready and therefore our supper for tomorrow. Just at sunset the birds lifted off and began dive-bombing the shoreline, our cue to set the oven to *Keep Warm* and fire up the boat, because birds, unlike humans, never lie about the fishing.

Sure enough, a school of striped bass had a shoal of bait pinned against the ragged shoreline and were chasing them so enthusiastically that one precocious teenager turned two high-altitude somersaults and became briefly terrestrial.

There was some disappointment on the culinary front, as these stripers were clearly ending just south of Maine's twenty- to twenty-six-inch slot limit. (In 2015 it's one fish over twenty-eight inches.) But it's a sorry angler indeed who's disappointed by dozens of feeding fish that pull hard and shake their heads and otherwise go ramming around with the sort of reckless fervor that sends people fishing instead of to the market.

For the next half-hour the birds literally gorged on bait, and Teuf and I figuratively gorged on schoolies. I had an easy dozen, Teuf a few less because he decided to try a popper in mid-bite for the entertainment value, and by the time he was ready to be entertained the bite was almost over. Still, I envied the surface muggings his popper got, not that I was unhappy with the subsurface muggings of my slinky olive-and-white Deceiver.

Those little schoolies weren't the striped-bass supper we'd hoped for, and there was some family dynamics disappointments that all the big bruisers Teuf's brother had boasted of catching here last week had lit out for the territories, as big stripers tend to do when summer wanes or someone shows up with an expectant cooler. But we weren't disappointed in the schoolies themselves—all around eighteen inches, strong, fat, eager, and huge fun on our little fly rods. And the birds were happy with all that savaged bait.

Of course not all predators are so easily amused, as we found the next day in a distant cove known for its big stripers.

They were sitting on the bank complaining about how hard it is for an honest guy to catch enough fish for a meal these days, what with all the damned regulations and the damned seals and the damned ospreys and eagles and shags and now all these damned bluefish—a complaint they emphasized by cranking in yet another eight-pound specimen of the fightingest fish in the sea, stomping on its head, ripping the hook from its throat, and booting it back into the bloody surf like a deflated soccer ball.

We felt no sympathy for these picky predators surrounded by dead and dying bluefish and wished we could drown them in the cruel sea. At the risk of sounding all snooty-fly-fisher-boy, the three anglers on shore were of a different species, with their surf rods and live mackerel and big coolers rapidly emptying of beer to make room for slot-limit stripers—or better yet, over-forty-inch cows, one of which you could remove from the gene pool every day in Maine in those days, thanks to regulations governed more by politics than by the biological certainty that large size is an inherited trait.

"Seen any stripahs?" one called toward our boat.

"Not today," we replied. "Bluefish?"

"All ovah. Try a poppah," another hollered, inviting us to help them rid the seas of vermin.

Not a bad suggestion, we figured, as we had been casting heavy flies on sinking lines in hopes of finding a big striper down deep tidying up the table scraps from all those binging bluefish. This was a good theory except for one thing: it required the presence of big stripers.

Like many philosophically dissimilar species, bluefish and stripers don't especially enjoy each other's company. To stretch a metaphor past its breaking point, imagine huge shoals of mackerel and herring as the fare at a white-linen fund-raiser, and striped bass as a group of portly Rotarians bellying up to the buffet. And then the doors burst open and in roars a bunch of bikers with bones through their noses and threatening tattoos, and they rush to the table and gobble everything in sight while the Rotarians blot their brows and drift off quietly to the all-you-can-eat at KFC.

In their 1953 classic *Fishes of the Gulf of Maine*, biologists Henry Bigelow and William Schroeder called bluefish "perhaps the most ferocious and bloodthirsty fish in the sea." Seventy years earlier, pioneering ichthyologist George Brown Goode wrote that the bluefish are "not content with what they eat, which is itself of enormous quantity, [they] rush ravenously through the closely crowded schools, cutting and tearing the living fish as they go, and leaving in their wake the mangled fragments."

Averting our eyes from the wanton slaughter, it's hard to imagine a species better designed to entertain anglers—not to mention scavenging birds. And for anyone with modest kitchen skills or the address of a truly gifted seafood restaurant, it's hard to imagine a better seasonal meal—roasted whole with tomatoes and onions and basil or filleted and quickly grilled with a flutter of lemon zest, their unctuous cheeks breaded and fried like scallops. Not to mention that bluefish contain enough omega-3 fatty acids to counteract a whole barrel of KFC. If you're not at the bottom of the food chain, what's not to love about bluefish? So we whacked a couple on the head, bled them carefully—essential for a fish that must be eaten perfectly fresh to be eaten at all—and slipped them into the waiting cooler.

"You guys eat them things?" the alpha-angler hollered, followed by speculative mutters among his friends about other things we might enjoy eating or predilections we might pursue.

Predilections? Two different species met alongshore in a time of diminished expectations, and thanks to blind adherence to personal predilections only one would be eating fish for supper.

39. *Bangor Bonefish*

It had been an ugly winter here in New England. Nothing unusual there, of course. All those iconic images from Currier & Ives and Grandma Moses showing carefree New Englanders dashing through the snow in one-horse open sleighs share one thing in common: people dashing through snow. For half the year, that's what we do up here. Which for a couple of months is all lovely and traditional and olde Newe Englandey, but by the time you finally haul the Christmas tree to the dump and purge the brain of its relics of "Jingle Bells" and "White Christmas," wintertime life in olde Newe Englande simply becomes old.

But that's why airplanes were invented.

Strictly speaking, Orville and Wilbur didn't build that first flying machine so winter-weary northerners could go bonefishing at Andros Island, Ascension Bay, or Ambergris Caye, but for icebound anglers who can't warm to ice fishing, it's hard to imagine a better use for a 737 or an A320.

This, however, was a minority opinion among the madding crowds at Bangor International Airport the day of the big blizzard. Inversely ordered by the number of persons expressing an opinion and the volume with which they expressed it, airplanes were invented so:

5. Grandparents could visit their grandchildren.

4. Business executives could become internationally intrusive micromanagers.

3. Families could enjoy expensively unmemorable moments at Disney World.

2. Spring-breaking college students could shed their inhibitions and undergarments in Cancun and Negril and bring home unfortunate tattoos to horrify their parents and souvenir syndromes to amuse their family physicians.

Who might well have been found among the fifth and smallest group, the handful of veteran travelers sitting quietly in remote corners of the terminal patiently awaiting whatever was going to happen instead of besieging gate agents with unanswerable questions and threats of comic emptiness.

Though complete strangers, we knew each other by our uniforms—faded pastel shirts with large pockets and clever venting, thin tan trousers, sunglasses on keepers, long-billed caps, and salt-stained Top-Siders. We carried well-worn daypacks from Simms and Patagonia accessorized with scarred rod tubes and lightweight breathable rainwear, and we eyed each other with silent recognition like wallflowers at an eighth-grade party—both too cool and too withdrawn to make social overtures beyond a discrete nod and an occasional mutual roll of the eyes as yet another irate grandparent/executive/family/spring breaker flung unintentionally hilarious insults at the implacable parapets of Delta/American/Northwest/Continental/US Air.

That airplanes were neither leaving nor arriving was not, as the gate agents impatiently pointed out, their fault. When I left home at three in the morning it was just beginning to snow in earnest, and at nine o'clock it was snowing sideways at two to three inches per hour with the wind gusting well past fifty knots. According to the omnipresent CNN Airport News, air travel all over the east was paralyzed thanks to this enormous snowstorm. According to the FAA's web page that tracks flight delays, it doesn't take an enormous snowstorm to paralyze air travel these days. A minor thunderstorm in Chicago or Atlanta can ground the whole system, and even on a nice sunny day you can see "Departures are experiencing taxi delays greater than 45 minutes and/or arrivals are experiencing airborne holding delays greater than 45 minutes" splotched across nearly every major airport in the country.

Airlines blame the weather and the FAA's antiquated traffic-handling system. The FAA blames the weather and the airlines' trend toward replacing fewer, larger, emptier planes with more frequent, smaller, fuller, and thus more profitable planes. The long-suffering public, mindful that ten years ago a thunderstorm in one city didn't bring the entire airline industry to a halt, blames everyone and everything, and as usual the public has it nailed.

Also as usual, the problem that morning was in distant airports, not Bangor. With one of the world's longest runways, built to loft A-bomb-bearing B52s at the USSR and now home to a strategically important aerial refueling wing, BGR is well equipped with top-drawer snow-removal equipment plowing to and fro in *corps de ballet* unison, clearing the way for the very large planes filled with very young, and some not so very young, soldiers that even in that monster snowstorm were stopping here en route to or from the Middle East for fuel and a pee and homemade chocolate-chip cookies, dispensed by a group of enthusiastic elderly veterans who turn up around the clock to show these young and not-so-young soldiers that someone in America cares in more tangible ways than wearing an American flag as a lapel pin.

A fresh planeload had recently arrived, and from their pale faces and nervous braggadocio it was clear they were outbound. On the inbound flights they're sunburned and silent and slightly jumpy—just as you'd expect, given where they've been and what they've been doing. They're also damned glad to be here in Maine, however briefly, and to see the first openly friendly faces they've seen in a year or more.

Whether or not we brothers and sisters of the rod cases and salt-stained Top-Siders were glad to be there in wintertime New

England was another matter entirely. Ever since the Thanksgiving turkey became leftover sandwiches we've been plotting our escapes—practicing our tropical-casting skills in the backyard while wearing goose-down parkas and snowshoes, reading and rereading the various bonefish gurus in print and online, spending unconscionable amounts of money on tackle we'll fish at best once a year, and endlessly tying flies of no possible use within two thousand miles of where we've chosen to live.

Some of us occasionally think of upping sticks and moving where the fish live this time of year—carefully ignoring that we live where rod-cased tourists arrive from all around the world to fish for brook trout, landlocked salmon, smallmouth, and stripers—and that although northern New England may suffer through six months of winter we're only occasionally beset by hurricanes, earthquakes, volcanoes, and third-world politics, and never, at least so far, by dengue fever and filariasis.

It is an inborn human trait, this grass-is-greener-elsewhere syndrome. It's how our particular crowd spread across the globe from a small valley in Africa, and it's what fills the skies with airplanes full of our distant relatives, and distant markets with fresh faces and fresh money, providing middle-class jobs in places like Andros Island, where middle-class jobs might otherwise be as rare as a snowstorm.

Tourism, I was surprised to discover, is the world's largest industry—the planet's principal employer at a trillion dollars per year. The two hundred thousand people living in the Bahamas, the little country this snowstorm was keeping me from visiting, are visited by 1.6 million of their distant cousins annually. In many places around the world, including Maine in these days of industrial decay, tourism isn't just a strong portion of the economy. It *is* the economy.

I know icy rivers in Labrador and Quebec and muddy ocean flats in the Bahamas and Belize and places all around the world where the only attraction is fish, and the only buffer between poverty and mild prosperity is a planeload of keen anglers from Minneapolis or Lewiston or Manchester or London. Yet I sometimes wonder if we focus too much on squeezing more milk from a nicely sustainable system and too little time worrying how to keep the cow alive and healthy.

It's difficult to avoid wondering just how many of those young and not-so-young people wearing uniforms of desert camouflage were on their way to where they're going because so many of us wearing other uniforms were on our way to where we're going, burning tons of fossil fuel in our relentless search for novelty, entertainment, business, far-reaching family, or brighter, faster fish.

With my face pressed against the cold glass, I watched the snowplows in their Sisyphean battle and the big planes come and go and the little planes neither coming nor going. It was hard not to imagine bonefish on distant tropical flats—hard not to yearn for that first fibrillation as my rusty casting finally connects with that first electric bonefish, the line and leader cutting a furrow of silver spray across the aqua sea, the flamingos lifting off in protest looking impossibly pink against impossibly blue. The long winter of anticipation, deprivation, and preparation was all coming together in one magical connection between stalker and stalkee— the stalker enjoying everything about the experience as much as anyone could ever enjoy anything; the stalkee not enjoying anything about it at all; the two briefly connecting thanks to the original labors of Orville and Wilbur Wright and the ongoing efforts of tens of thousands of young and not-so-young people wearing desert camouflage whose job, in the end, is to keep that oil flowing.

Air travel is the goose that laid the golden egg or, in the case of the Top-Sider-wearing wallflowers, the silver fish. Only that wouldn't be happening for me, according to the flight-cancellation board. There was only one flight a week to my island, and what bonefish I'd catch that year would have to come vicariously from the runway at Bangor International Airport, where the silver furrows in the flats were cut by bright yellow plows pushing swirling white snow, and the big planes coming and going filled with young and not-so-young people whose sacrifices I hope we all appreciate.

40. *Ten Years After*

Of the several ways of recalibrating a New Englander's reflexes and predatory strategies for fly-casting successfully to bonefish, a week of Atlantic salmon fishing in New Brunswick isn't one of them. Casting methodically to the same lies day after day from the armchair comfort of a Sharpe canoe then mending so the fly swings past its invisible target at the only speed salmon care to see no more prepares you for snap-shot wing-shooting to speeding bonefish from a panga's bouncing foredeck than tossing crickets with a cane pole to farm-pond blue-gills prepares you to fly-fish for blue marlin off Australia.

Yet despite my efforts at self-handicapping, that first morning fishing out of Tranquility Bay Lodge on Ambergris Caye, Belize, I managed to boat four or five bones, lose two, and frighten hundreds. The few my tweedy, sleepy casting managed not to flush beyond gunning range were the usual Belizean bones of a pound or three, but bonefish of any size were welcome indeed in the stiff and unpredictable winds the laws of chance thought fitting to toss our way.

Aside from the usual rustiness that comes with a sudden change of venue, the morning carried its own integral déjà vu, a novel situation for that subspecies of humanity known as a fish-writer, which for complicated professional reasons seldom revisits

the scenes of past crimes. Still, ten years ago almost to the week I
had been here on this very flat casting these very flies even more
ineffectually to the ancestors of these very same bonefish. Then as
now, the wind and overcast sky had posed climatological obstacles
by blowing a steady twenty to twenty-five knots and gusting well
over thirty and making fly-casting less an act of recreational pre-
dation than of blind faith.

Given this, we—we being Shannon and Dave and later in the
afternoon our friend Joe, who had prepared for his own bonefish
trip by missing his plane from Maine—decided to spend the rest
of the afternoon in a more relaxing, pop-the-top-on-a-cold-malt-
beverage sort of way, so we baited up some commandeered spinning rods and unrepentantly tossed chunks of sardines at reef fish
just inside the world's second longest barrier reef.

The afternoon's tally: a yellowtail, a mutton snapper, a small
grouper, and a five-foot barracuda that so badly wanted a small
jack struggling at the end of my line that it felt cruel to deny him.
And so after three reel-burning runs and a half-dozen photoge-
nic leaps that made the previous week's Atlantic salmon seem
almost sedated, the barracuda joined the yellowtail, the mutton
snapper, and the small grouper as our dinner guests. Which we
enjoyed very much thanks to the talented kitchen staff of the
Tackle Box Sea Bar, a fishermen's hangout teetering on pilings a
hundred feet from shore and overlooking a strategic pinch-in of
the barrier reef.

But we didn't fly all the way to Belize merely to prey upon
reef fish, no matter how talented the kitchen staff was at preparing them. Levering our overstuffed frames away from the dining
table, we waddled out onto the deck, cantilevered ourselves over
the sea, and saw plenty of what had brought us here: large shoals
of baitfish, drawn by the bar's lights and swept down on the current, and a continuously cycling armada of predators preying on
them—jetting needlefish, slashing barracuda, large rays cruising
like stealth bombers, and, just at the edge of the light, a half-
dozen huge tarpon with their enormous eyes glinting back in an
I'm-beyond-casting-range insouciance.

There, we said, pointing with our Belikins. *That's why we've come here.* Because in the summer on Ambergris Caye the resident tarpon haunt the mangroves back in the lagoon, and the big migratory tarpon move onto the flats that stretch twenty miles toward the mainland. And soon, we thought, we would board our pangas and hoist big rods and fling big flies in their general direction, with the hopes that one would bite and then whup our pale Yankee asses in a most entertaining fashion.

And then the weather took a turn for the worse, and we fled from the bar to our comfortable cabanas. As the rain and wind and sand and the occasional thundering coconut blasted away at our doors and windows, we thought of the wonders of the tropics, how being here brought one so close to nature, and how the last time we saw a storm blow like this was in a 1940s movie where the island's inhabitants had to strip Dorothy Lamour of her sarong and stuff her down a volcano to make it stop.

But lacking both a suitable sacrifice and a volcano, the storm didn't stop, and the next day dawned tougher in some ways than the day before, with gustier winds that ranged from flat calm to thirty knots and seemed purposefully mischievous about direction, like naughty children leaping from behind furniture and shouting "Boo!" while you're fumbling for the defibrillator. And as a special bonus, we faced a solid gray overcast that made spotting fish before they spotted us difficult for even our seasoned Belizean guides, never mind our windburned Yankee eyes.

By lunch I'd caught one, and Joe two, and Dave three, and Shannon a couple including a fat four-pounder that was, if I remember correctly, the big bone for the week.

We could see the tarpon flats fifteen miles downwind, and we reconciled ourselves to the reality that even if we could make it there without taking green seas over the stern, we probably couldn't spot fish, and would have one helluva wet and bouncy ride back to boot. So with tarpon and sight-fishing off the table, we were reduced to casting into deeper mud clouds and hoping for the best.

Which, come to think of it, wasn't all that bad, because although the next day brought intermittent thunderstorms and overcast followed by a final decisive transformation to bright blue skies, puffy cumulus, and gusty northeasterlies, we could at least see well enough to sight-fish in the lee of the Caye. We worked our way from pod of fish to pod of fish, taking three or four each in satisfying sight-fishing fashion, and frightening a great many more in less satisfying sight-fishing fashion, and taking a half-dozen or so each from deep-water muds that, while perhaps less satisfying as exercises in sight-fishing, were certainly adequate compensation when measured by the sound of fly reels spinning merrily around, their buzzing sometimes even drowning out the constant sound of hotels and houses being built as Ambergris Caye, like the rest of the world, prepares to receive more visitors.

For things had changed on Ambergris Caye ten years after my first visit. The local metropolis of San Pedro—four thousand souls year-round—is far less sleepy than it once was. It is now less the kind of place where you might wander into a bar and find Sydney Greenstreet plotting foggy-ethics larceny with Humphrey Bogart and far more on the verge of becoming one of those coiffed and manicured modern tourist destinations where loud pale people photograph themselves enjoying their credit cards. But somehow in all the growth San Pedro managed to remain a small friendly place where you can walk around and feel at home, and in this day and time that's a rare and comforting thing.

The old hand-powered ferry to the north island was gone, alas, replaced by a new steel bridge across which the occasional golf-cart purposefully trundles, automobiles still being banned from the island north of San Pedro. Construction was evident everywhere, and the spoils of economic growth were filtering down to the lowest aspiration-level of Ambergris society: dredging sand with shovels and buckets into eighteen-foot pangas and selling it by the boatload to boutique concrete producers. But this is no different from anywhere else on our crowded planet, where the definition of paradise must be ever more flexible depending on whether you're a visiting Yankee fly fisher hoping to go Gauguin or a local guide, restaurateur, hotelier, or taxi driver hoping to earn the kind of living that needn't be modified by the compound adjective "third-world."

And the bonefish of Belize hadn't changed—still skittish, still fond of small pink-nosed Gotchas tied with arctic fox fur and discreet touches of flash, and still capable of bending an eight-weight fly rod and twirling a reel spool in a most soul-satisfying fashion. And they're still always there, ghosting across the flats, and still always welcome, especially when the tarpon flats are tantalizingly weathered just out of reach.

The people of the Caye hadn't changed, either—as kind and concerned and humorous as anyone you will ever find. And when you leave Ambergris Caye, you still feel that you couldn't possibly *not* go back. And that it ought to be a lot sooner than ten years after.

41. *Birthday Bones*

I DIDN'T KNOW WHETHER TO BLAME THE bright Bahamian sun for broiling the brains of a winter-pale northerner stalking bonefish flats and mangrove creeks or whether it was all those bonefish over the past week—all of them, every flashing, slashing one of them burned as bright and silvery into my mind as the big chrome bumper of the 1949 Buick I closely encountered on the bicycle I got for my sixth birthday. Or maybe it was simply the inevitable synaptic erosion of someone born the same year as that Buick, someone who increasingly disremembers how to tie knots he's tied for sixty years. Or maybe it was just a touch too much wine or all those hellfire-hot bird peppers Les pounded into the cracked conch at supper.

Whatever scrambled my cerebrum, I was losing five points off my already-eroded IQ because I couldn't keep straight whether diamonds follow spades as trump and whether I ought to bid high and try to win or bid low and try to lose, thereby actually winning in this odd English card game called Contract Whist.

But at least I'd remembered, unlike Patrick, not to speak in a bogus Punjabi accent until after diamonds become trumps—an automatic loss of ten points in a new rule Jonathan imposed to restore a measure of decorum here in the homey lounge at Acklins Island Lodge. This despite his own intermittent lapses

into Lerner and Loewe, a temporal-lobe digression we all mindlessly followed like coyotes hallooing at the moon: spurred, no
doubt, by the boundless shoals of bonefish a few miles north in
Lovely Bay, a place so perfectly named it had cast its spell and left
us dazed and searching loudly for a room somewhere with one
enormous chair . . . "Oh wouldn't it," we melodically asked Les,
the lodge manager and chef de cuisine, "be loverly?"

At which Les shook his head and left for the night, muttering
something about the crazy English that failed to exempt me, the
token American. The guides had left already, and The Birch had
gone off with them pub-crawling in a place that had, as near as
we could tell, no actual pubs. But he felt the drums calling, or so
he said—calling the Caribbean blood of his father, a Church of
England Vicar from Tobago who'd married a high-born English
Rose—and he ran off into the night baying at the moon and being
Birchie. We were sitting cozily around the table with warm faces,
warm hands, and warm feet—sunburned, actually—reliving the
day, inventing bizarre handicapping rules for Whist, engaging in
recreational vituperation in affected accents, and generally laughing ourselves silly.

For it was, after all, a party. Brains was turning forty, and to
celebrate this epochal watershed he gathered together a pod of
his friends—me, Jonathan, Patrick, Rod, Birchie—for a week of
bonefishing on Acklins Island in the Bahamas. What better way
to celebrate this chronological dividing line between ascent and
descent than to go fishing with people who you know will relentlessly make fun of everything, including you?

It was an eclectic group—five Oxbridge Englishmen and an
East Tennessee hillbilly—collectively aggregated into multiple
occupations: two magazine editors, four writers, one lapsed crafter
of Tudor furniture, one rehabilitator of ravaged chalk streams, one
rehabilitator of ravaged cartilage and bone.

Over the week this motley crew had relentlessly ravaged the
local bonefish population, or at least briefly annoyed them.
While deducting another ten points from Patrick of the Punjab,
Jonathan, our mathematically deft scorekeeper at Whist and at

fishing, announced that over the course of this week the six of us had collectively caught 375 bonefish, not counting naughties, meaning bonefish hoisted from deep-water muds and not spotted in clear shallow water and specifically targeted. Jonathan, the editor of that august English sporting magazine *The Field* and thus the acknowledged arbiter of proper form, declined to keep score on the week's naughties but hazarded a guess of somewhere over fifty.

Anglers believe all fish are gifts and that bonefish are rare and special gifts, but during this weeklong celebration of Brains' eventual demise we were all well blessed. In Copperfieldian terms, Brains had a memorable birthday. And so had we all, with scene after scene flashing through our collective memories like slides from an over-produced PowerPoint presentation.

Flash: Flats-stalking beneath a sweeping sky in slow half-step, the strains of Elgar's "Pomp and Circumstance" impossible to suppress. The flats were lifeless except for a turtle the size of a twenty-dollar pizza, dodging and weaving in a dazzling display of evolutionary perfection achieved 280 million years ago. Then patches of nervous water shimmer far to windward. Muscles tense, brows furrow. At last sickle-scything fins materialize in range, and then that first hopeful cast, that first tentative strip, that first *foom*, that inevitable *yaaaaaaaaaah!*

Flash: Birchie stings his first ever bonefish and instantly transforms from blasé English chalk stream druid into a bonefish madman—Mister Toad's Wild Ride with screaming drags and rifle-shot casts and every inch the mania of Toad seeing his first ever motorcar, "O bliss! O poop-poop! O my! O my!"

Flash: Bouncing along in JJ's boat and pivoting around an otherworldly patch of the deepest indigo set in a featureless expanse of pale jade—a blue hole, one of the Bight of Acklins' seventy-two portals into a network of limestone caverns as labyrinthine as the Catacombs of Paris and as deep as a Cornish tin mine. They burrow right under the island to the sea, jetting a fountain of seawater on the incoming tide and flushing like a toilet on the ebb. No one truly knows what fish live down there, but no one ever stops imagining.

Flash: As Brains watches, a lemon shark snips the stern half from a bonefish following his fly, and an hour later I find its head being tugged along by a brown-and-yellow mantis shrimp as big as a keeper lobster. When I venture too near, it whacks my wading boot with a blow I feel into my teeth.

Flash: At a chokepoint between Lovely Bay and a tidal inlet, a silver river of bonefish flows past like a herring boat discharging its catch, more bonefish than anyone could ever imagine exists on the planet, never mind in one little Bahamian backwater. We cast once, twice, and they evaporate into the ether.

Flash: On a narrow strip of swimming-pool-blue flat sand-wiched between a deep purple channel and thick green mangroves, Rod and I and a half-dozen lemon sharks await the oncoming tide and its flush of incoming bones. I assume the position in a mangrove-sheltered corner, and the bonefish come at me from all directions. I take only five, though all were over five pounds and two considerably over, but I could have taken fifty had I evolved eyes in the back of my head, for when I'd be intent on a school coming in fast from the east, another school would be coming in just as fast from the west, and when I'd cast toward the pod I could see, the pod I couldn't see would flush like quail and tem-porarily vacuum the flat of life.

Flash: Rebuilding a leader macraméd by midcast indecision. Standing stock-still for a good five minutes, messing around in my tackle bag and trying to remember how to tie a blood knot while finding another fly the right size and weight and color. Finally finishing and looking up to find myself entirely enclosed within a huge school of feeding bonefish, nuzzling against my knees like a flock of chickens pecking at grain. When I move my head they explode in all directions, leaving me dripping wet and murmuring, "Holy shit, holy shit," like a mantra.

Flash: Skulking along small tidal creeks after bonefish cruis-ing alone or in pairs, an action so much like fishing an English chalk stream that we're almost surprised to see green herons and

mangroves instead of swans and ranunculus—although trying
for the delicate brown trout of the softly subtle Hampshire Meon
or John Constable's Wiltshire Avon couldn't be less like battling
bones in these narrow mangrove-delineated channels, where you
abandon delicacy in favor of cable-stout leaders and a hook-setting
technique akin to jerking a tablecloth from beneath a place setting.

Flash: The image, just a few hours ago, of three broad schools
of bones ruffling the waters in Delectable Bay and Birchie and
me knocking up three consecutive doubles. Our laughter pealed
across the flats and frightened an air-wing of shocking pink fla-
mingoes into flight. To cap the perfect day of a perfect week, the
sight of three enormous bonefish—eight, maybe nine pounds—
cruising slowly along as we waded ashore from Doug's boat with
our unrigged rods clamped under our arms. The big bones turned
to examine us solemnly, and then casually, almost contemptu-
ously, they flipped us off and resumed their evening meander.

We all remember snapshots from our birthdays—that special
present, those friends gathered around a cake aflame with can-
dles, the embarrassing singing of The Song, the tender glances
from loved ones, and the feeling of well-being and satisfaction at
having lived another year despite the odds.

But this was a birthday we'll all remember—one we'll almost
certainly never forget.

PART SIX

Signs and Portents

Cut if you will, with Sleep's dull knife,
Each day to half its length, my friend,—
The years that Time take off my life,
He'll take from off the other end!
                    — Edna St. Vincent Millay

42. *Sailors Take Warning*

Peer up the paternal stem of my family tree, and before the résumés vanish in the mists of time you'll see a policeman, two masons, two farmers, a miller, three planters, a fishing master, and three sea captains. Beyond a last name and a Y chromosome, they share one thing common with most of our ancestors: outdoors occupations ruled by weather.

According to the 2000 census, 80 percent of Americans live in urban or suburban areas, and except for brief recreational expeditions into the vast open spaces, we live and work mostly indoors. To us, weather is a helpful television program advising us to take along an umbrella, leave early for work, or run for shelter. But only two or three generations ago, weather was a personal thing for us all, and our ability to predict its actions determined how we lived our lives and whether we'd produce descendants.

Which is why it's puzzling that so many of today's immensely knowledgeable anglers risk unsuccessful fishing, or even involuntary pruning from their own family trees, simply because they don't know tomorrow's weather unless the Weather Channel tells them about it.

Not to knock the Weather Channel. Before the 1960s, when meteorologists got computers, eyes-in-the-sky satellites, and Doppler radar, weather prediction was an even more imperfect

science than it is today. An hour before the Great Hurricane of
1938 roared ashore and killed seven hundred people from New
York to New Hampshire, official weather forecasts still called for
cloudy skies and gusty winds.

Nowadays we swipe across our iPhones and watch the live-
action radar approach of everything from regional showers to
national disasters. In most settled areas, we can listen to government weather broadcasts on pocket-sized radios and even receive
automated alerts of hazardous weather for our specific location.
But the pace of local weather often outruns regional forecasts, and
in the backcountry, weather-radio coverage can be unreliable to
nonexistent, never mind smartphone service, which leaves you up
that ancestral tree protected only by your own observations and
knowledge. And poetry.

"Red skies at morning, sailors take warning; red skies at night,
sailor's delight," dates back to Biblical times. But unlike such
antique flapdoodle as whistling for a wind or consulting wood-
chucks about the probable onset of spring, this old saw is accurate
roughly 70 percent of the time.

In the northern hemisphere, weather moves mostly from west
to east—weather being revolving areas of high or low atmospheric pressure. In the northern hemisphere, high-pressure systems revolve clockwise and mostly mean dry, nice weather. Low-
pressure systems revolve counterclockwise and mostly mean the
opposite.

We see a red sunset because the sun's low-angle rays refract
through the dry, dusty air of a high-pressure area to our west. If
those rays get lost in the moisture-laden clouds of an oncoming
low-pressure area, we see a gray or yellow sky.

A red sunrise means high pressure has passed to our east and
the low-angle sun is illuminating clouds approaching behind it.
A violently red sunrise means the air to our east is saturated with
moisture and portends a substantial storm, often moving from
south to north, as in a northeaster or a hurricane. As Lieutenant
William Bligh wrote in his log during the epic voyage of the
Bounty's launch, one day the sun "rose very firey and Red, a sure

indication of a Severe Gale." So severe a gale that the crew jettisoned most of their belongings and baled nonstop for days, and Captain Bligh and company very nearly perished before Charles Laughton, Trevor Howard, and Anthony Hopkins got to say, "This is mutiny, Mr. Christian."

But we can't always rely on old sayings to keep us safe from bad weather. I attempted to predict countless storms based on whether cows were lying down in the fields or standing and moving about until I realized that cows know nothing about weather or anything else, except where and when to expect the silage cart. But some useful bits of weather lore have survived science's skeptical glare, and the intrepid angler could memorize them in less time than it takes to tie a dozen of the Hot Fly du jour—and likely fish more successfully to boot.

Most of these come down to us from our mariner ancestors, because more than anyone else sailors were, and are, at the weather's mercy. But if you've ever tried to cast a heavy striper fly on a deep-sink shooting head with a crosswind gusting past twenty-five knots, you'll realize that fly fishers are equally in the climatological crosshairs.

- *Mare's tails and mackerel scales say next day you will shorten sail.* High thin cirrus clouds blown into the shapes of horse's tails typically precede a low-pressure system by a good twenty-four hours, and when they transform into fish-scaly-looking cirrocumulus then to a thicker and lower blanket of altocumulus, you can figure no more than twelve hours before things ugly up.
- *Rain before wind, halyards, sheets and braces mind; wind before rain, soon you may make sail again.* A low-pressure system typically arrives with a gentle rain that builds in intensity accompanied by a rising wind. In tidal waters, conditions almost always change with the turn of the tide. But a blast of wind followed by rain usually comes from a local thunderstorm, a brief event of an hour or less. A useful wrinkle and just as true: *Long foretold, long last. Short notice, soon will pass.* An even more useful

wrinkle for us fisher-folks: *Clouds a-gathering thick and fast, keep sharp eyes on sail and mast. Clouds that slowly onward crawl say shoot your lines and nets and trawl.*

- *Backing winds say storms are nigh, but veering winds will clear the sky.* Veering winds trend clockwise and say high pressure. Backing winds spin counterclockwise and say low pressure. According to Buys-Ballot's Law, named after a pioneering nineteenth-century Dutch meteorologist, not a Congressional election, if you stand in the northern hemisphere with your back to the wind and extend your arms, your left hand points to low pressure and your right to high pressure. South of the Line it's the opposite.

- *A halo ringing moon or sun says rain's approaching on the run.* And in a more specific but not necessarily more accurate variation: *Ring around the moon, rain by noon; ring around the sun, rain by dawn.* A glowing halo around the moon or the sun means its light is refracted through a veil of high-altitude ice crystals, the leading edge of a low-pressure system spreading over your area. Expect rain and increasing wind. Fish early and hard, as fish tend to feed up before weather changes. Then beat the storm back to camp and read a good book.

- *Campfire smoke a-lofting high says pleasant days and clear blue skies. Campfire smoke a-rolling low says rains will come on with a blow.* Smoke is a primitive barometer, as it rises unfettered in high pressure and hugs the ground in low pressure. This is surprisingly accurate even for tracking short-term fluctuations in atmospheric pressure.

- *Seagull, seagull, sit on the sand. It's never good weather when you're on land.* This is accurate only if there are no seaside fast-food joints, where you'll find as many panhandling gulls on a fine day as a dirty one. But seagulls are far more at home in the air than on the hard, and when they're lined up on the beach with their hands in their pockets, it's best to pay attention. Gulls are way smarter than cows.

- *If grass is dry at morning light, twill surely rain before the night. If grass is damp and pearled with dew, it shall never rain on you.*

Well, never is a strong word. A dewless morning doesn't always mean it'll rain before dark. It does usually mean it'll rain within twenty-four hours, though. Of course in the age of Gore-Tex rain is but a minor diversion for anglers. What worries us is wind and, even more, lightning.

- *Beware those bolts from north or west, toward south or east the bolts be best.* Lightning is more fun to watch than to encounter, especially with rods made of graphite, a near-perfect conductor of electricity. Fiberglass and bamboo are insulators, if you need to manufacture justification for a nice cane rod. Lightning to your north or west says you're in the storm's path, and it's best to flipper your float-tube ashore and make yourself small. Lightning to your south or east should pass you safely by. You can estimate how far off the storm is in miles by counting the seconds between flash and boom and dividing by five. Will Ryan, Tom Fuller, and I once sat out a lightning storm high on the shoulder of Maine's iron-rich Mount Katahdin, where the flashes and booms arrived simultaneously above, below, and on all sides for more than an hour. As the Bible says, we were sore afraid.

Learning more about weather, like learning more about fishing, is its own reward. Spotting an oncoming storm using the knowledge of your intrepid forebears is just as gratifying as catching a trout on their antique rods and obsolete flies, which lends a flush of pleasure and a solid connection with a slower-paced life from which we all grow ever distant.

43. *Autumn Leaves*

No CHANGE OF SEASON IS SO DRAMATIC AS the shift from summer to autumn. The first snow of winter, the first robin of spring, the first sugar-and-gold corn of summer—none packs the sheer emotional impact of the deciduous trees' winter-long retirement from photosynthesis. No sooner do the great forests of New England blossom from chlorophyllous greens into a variegated patchwork of red and gold than the gray roads fill with carloads of marveling leaf-peepers, *oohing* and *aahing* and dabbing at misty eyes.

As the leaves begin to fall, nostalgia for warm summers lost and chill winters ahead fill our every thought, and Johnny Mercer's syrupy reimagining of Jacques Prévert's gloomy poem "The Dead Leaves" oozes through airwaves and elevators and food courts across the land. "The falling leaves drift by the windows," the crooners relentlessly croon—Frank Sinatra and Nat King Cole, Andy Williams and Yves Montand, Montovani and Muzak, too. "Since you went away the days grow long," they metaphorically lament. Who cares that autumn days actually grow shorter when lost loves want lamenting?

Sift through the literature of autumn and you'll find endless lamentations, from Mr. Browning's "appeal to sympathy for its decay" to Mrs. Browning's loss of youth on "chilling autumn wind." But as a fisherman I find myself more in tune with Albert Camus, for whom "Autumn is a second spring where every leaf is a flower." Because when autumn arrives, those solar-powered little factories that toiled all summer converting water and carbon dioxide into sugar to nourish the tree that bore them now enjoy a second and equally important life when they drift by the window and into water to nourish the entire aquatic food chain.

Big fish eat little fish, and little fish eat bugs, and bugs eat, well, the autumn leaves of red and gold—either directly, in the case of crayfish and stoneflies and other largish invertebrates that munch and crunch those fallen leaves like socialites at a salad bar; semi-directly, with tiny filter feeders like net-spinning caddis and blackfly larvae that sift minute leftovers drifting with the current; or indirectly, with diatoms and algae and aquatic plants busily extracting nutrition from the leaves' residual carbohydrates and minerals extracted by the tree from deep within the soil. In headwater streams, anywhere from 60 to nearly 100 percent of the total organic nutrients arrive courtesy of falling leaves.

Gifford Pinchot, founder of the US Forest Service and conservationist co-father with preservationist John Muir of the bipolar American environmental movement, had it right when he said, "The connection between forests and rivers is like that between father and son. No forests, no rivers." Pinchot was talking about the way forests, with their leaky-roof canopies and spongy organic soils, absorb great gouts of rainwater and dole it out to watersheds in steadily digestible quantities. But you can extend his analogy to say the connection between falling leaves and fish is like that between mother and child: no falling leaves, no fish.

Show me a stream with no trees or other seasonally replenished sources of organic debris, and I'll show you a stream not worth fishing. Show me a piece of waterfront property where a water-loving homeowner cut the stream-bank trees and barbered the tangled underbrush into a burnished green lawn, and I'll show you a waterfront-property owner who doesn't love the stream anywhere near so much as he thought he did when he was carving out an attractive view.

With the trees gone, our homeowner's little bit-o-paradise now lies open to the sun, and what had been cool shady water thick with aquatic insects and fish is now a warm torpid tea thick with algae and thinned of oxygen—a Saharan barrier to upstream and downstream passage for cool-water fish like trout and salmon, except in times of flood.

With the tangled bankside growth replaced by shallow-rooted nonnative grasses, seasonal changes in water levels nibble away at banks, and instead of the nourishment and shelter of falling leaves and twigs and the occasional whole tree born down by wind and old age, the stream now receives a constant infusion of inorganic silt that smothers the eggs of aquatic insects and fish and further erodes the great wealth of beautiful life that drew our homeowner here in the first place.

Given the devastation wrought by cutting bankside trees and undergrowth, it's probably best not to think about how the stream and its web of life are affected by the high-nitrogen fertilizers and broad-spectrum weed killers that perpetuate our homeowner's sterile emerald lawn.

So trees and leaves are good for fish and, by extension, fishing, but not all trees and leaves are created equal. Evergreens such as pine, spruce, fir, and hemlock provide valuable shade, and their habit of shedding lower limbs as the crown spreads and reaches for the sun provides a self-replenishing store of woody debris. But because the evergreens retain their skinny leaves all year, they provide a stream with little in the way of nutrients, and what few leaves they do shed wash quickly and ineffectually away.

Mighty oaks provide shelter and shade as well, but most oaks dislike the wet ground found near water, and their leaves, like evergreen leaves, are acidic and evidently unpalatable, for come spring you'll find them thickly matted and mostly intact in backwaters and eddies, providing the stream's small benthic creatures with shelter but not much nutrition.

A far better indicator of good fishing is a thick stand of birch, poplar, cottonwood, or alder, which shades the stream, stabilizes its banks, and refreshes it with showers of spent flowers, leaves, and twigs. In addition, their thin bark and sugar-laden cambium attract beavers from far and wide.

Beavers, like most life-forms driven by complex biological urges to reshape landscapes to their liking, are a mixed blessing. As thin waters deepen behind the dam, concentrating nutrients from beaver cuttings and fallen leaves, new beaver ponds can have magical effects on the fishing in small forest streams. Over time, however, as the beavers cut the surrounding trees ever farther back from the water and the rising water table drowns the roots of those few trees they spare, many beaver ponds—particularly those spreading across broad, low-slope valleys—become warmer and shallower before ultimately becoming bogs, then meadows, and then, over the course of a century or more, new forests.

One of the earlier trees to pioneer these new forests is, conveniently, the fisherman's best friend—a tree that thrives on the soggy banks of beaver ponds and bogs and armors its trunk in thick bark that beavers don't enjoy if they can find anything else. It's a tree that grows throughout the eastern US from Maine to Michigan and down into Tennessee and north Georgia, and, thanks to rampant cutting of higher-value species, is increasing in stem density throughout its range by more than 30 percent each year. Moreover, it's a tree that mines the subsoil for minerals more effectively than any other tree I know of, and it grows quickly and regenerates readily from seeds or stumps. This tree almost infallibly leads fishermen to good fishing just as it leads us assuredly into autumn with its bright red foliage that might begin heralding the fall of the year as early as mid-August here along Maine's Penobscot River.

I refer, if you haven't already guessed, to the red maple, whose soft, nutrient-packed leaves flutter down in carpets and whose tolerance for acidic soil and wet feet makes it perfectly at home in environs where its loftier, more delicate, and ever so famous cousin, the sugar maple, cannot thrive.

Red maples are hard to spot at a distance in the seamless green forests of summer, and you'll need to hike closer until you spot their red twigs and characteristic leaves, which look like simplified versions of the sugar-maple leaf on the Canadian flag only with the indented divisions between lobes sharply pointed instead of rounded. In the autumn, their bright red foliage shines forth like a beacon, and from miles away it's hard to mistake them for anything else.

When the autumn leaves of red and gold begin to drift by your window this year, you might consider forgoing the seasonal gloominess of Mercer and Prévert and follow Mrs. Browning. Go sit upon a lofty hill and turn your eyes around, "Where waving woods and waters wild / Do hymn an autumn sound." And Lewis Carroll, who advises us, "In autumn, when the leaves are brown, Take pen and ink, and write it down."

Doubtless he meant autumnal red, only it didn't rhyme. But when you return in the spring to those red maples you admired in the fall, you will find their leaves living new lives reincarnated as the best things leaves can aspire to become: fish.

44. *Upland Heaven*

I'M PROBABLY NOT THE WORLD'S WORST BIRD hunter, but when I can count a stellar season's total take on the surviving fingers of a careless carpenter's hand, it sure seems that way. To be good at something, whether it's fishing, snooker, wing-shooting, or psychokinetic levitation, you must (1) do it a lot and (2) pay attention to what you're doing. By some measures of bird hunting, I marginally qualify under category 1, but from where I'm unsuccessfully attempting to mystically lift from my office chair, I can't even see category 2.

Like most folk with easily diverted brains, I can function in real life only by consistently following a schedule. I rise at five and write until six, then I eat breakfast and read the news and triage the to-do list and get back to work by seven—editing or writing as the publishing calendar dictates—until I break for lunch around half-past eleven. After lunch I might walk to the post office and the corner store, then I might split kindling and fill the wood box or work in the garden according to the season. Then, weather and workload permitting, I go off and do something.

From May until brooks and streams close on September 30, I try to go fishing. From October until the end of December I try to go bird hunting. When bird season closes I sharpen the chainsaw and cut next winter's firewood. Then, after fidgeting through the holidays, the bleak bitter winter, and the sploshy spring floods, I start fishing again.

Altogether this makes for a full year with a minimum of time wasted wondering what to do—which is what I used to do before I followed a consistent schedule.

Being a fish-writer, expeditions are always coming along to interject inconsistency. Summers are typically full of these—day trips or overnights or four-day weekends where I kiss off writing and editing and just go fishing. Because the issues of *Gray's Sporting Journal* cluster in seasonal clumps, I had a lot of free days in late winter and midsummer, a handful in the spring, and very few in the fall. Which means that, although I could fish like a retiree most of the summer, I had to strictly follow routine, or things that must be done simply wouldn't get done.

Even in the busy-busy autumn, I could manage a few breaks. There was the obligatory September trip out west to the fly-fishing retailer show, which usually included an extracurricular fishing trip with friends in Oregon, Montana, or Colorado, and in one particularly reckless year, all three. In October there was the annual landlocked salmon trip to northern Maine, where a few rivers remain open until month's end, and my friends and I can have a last go at pretending we're still in our semi-durable forties.

But mostly the fall of the year sees me sitting at the keyboard every day from seven until half-past eleven, and those afternoons not ruined by looming deadlines or crappy weather will see me heading for the woods out back to hunt birds.

My wife, who still nurses a culinary grudge against catch-and-release fishing and knows there's no such thing as catch-and-release bird hunting, calls this "taking the shotgun for a walk to the brook." She refuses to call it hunting. Hunting, she reminds me, is meant to have tangible results.

Angling's softhearted new ethos has broadly redefined tangible results. If I slip out back for an hour on a busy afternoon and fish the same stretch of homey little trout brook I always fish and catch and release a couple of the same bejeweled little brook trout I almost always catch, I will have achieved the tangible results that modern-day fly fishers theoretically live for. If I have a few extra hours, and trailer the boat down to the bay and spend the afternoon casting my flies at the rips without ever once sticking a striper, I'll at least have spent an afternoon breathing salt air in the company of gulls and ospreys and seals and porpoises and maybe, if I'm lucky, a pilot whale or a humpback or some tropical exotic swept inshore by the Gulf Stream and the incrementally warming ocean. Even if I stick a dozen good stripers and choose not to bring home a legal-length fish for the grill because none was badly hooked or played out, I'll still have tangible results, if you'll permit me to call a sunburn, a leader burn, and a contented smile tangible.

But when I come home from wandering the woods with my shotgun—which happens to be, as the gun-writers say, a "6¼-pound 16-gauge with 30-inch barrels shooting an ounce of #8s"—I'm expected to offer up a tastily tangible brace of partridge or woodcock and not some fuzzy-headed tale involving the cinematographic death spirals of poplar leaves I blasted well astern of the partridge that flushed when my mind and eyes were elsewhere.

Where they were, of course, was on the brook.

I try to hunt the upland aspens and overgrown orchards where I know the partridge likely are, but like eroded rock I am drawn downhill to water, and if I see a bird it's less because I've skillfully stalked one in its thorny lair than because I've stumbled on one when we were both on our way elsewhere. And if I actually shoot one, it's less the result of tightly focused wing-shooting than good luck for me and bad luck for the bird.

It isn't that I'm a bad shot. In fact, I shoot this gun—a pretty side-by-side made by Ignacio Ugartechea to fit my oddly constructed body, which has atop its shoulders an edifice my boyhood barber said looked like a Slinky doing something nasty to a watermelon—better than I ever dreamed I could. It's just that it's hard to shoot well when your mind turns like a dowsing wand toward water.

No matter where I wander in the little wild kingdom composed of our woodlot and those of our neighbors, the brook runs

tangibly through it—at the downhill end of every seep and every
gully or ravine or depression in the earth. Wherever I go I can
smell it. I can hear it. And I can never, ever, resist its call.

I know there are birds around. In March I saw four fat partridge clambering all over the old apple trees that shade our house,
peering in our windows and snipping buds like little chickens-
o-the-trees. In May I heard them drumming in the woods as I
fished the Hendrickson hatch. In July I saw their little spotted
chicks scurrying around the old cellar hole chasing electric-blue
damselflies. And now they're grown and are probably feeding in
the old apple orchard behind the graveyard or in the poplar jungle that sprouted from the neighbor's clear-cut. And yet here I
sit beside the brook, the elegant blued steel and swirling Spanish
walnut shining bright against a funereal hemlock while I search
the current for spawning trout, for caddis larvae, for stoneflies on
the move—for anything at all that is in, of, or under the water.
And only when it grows too dark to see will I notice I have spent
two hours not hunting but merely sitting by the brook achieving
nothing tangible at all, even though I do this a lot and always pay
attention to what I'm doing—or not doing, depending on who's
categorizing.

As Harlan Hubbard wrote in *Shantyboat: A River Way of Life*,
"Who can long watch the ceaseless lapsing of a river's current
without conceiving a desire to set himself adrift, and, like the
driftwood which glides past, float with the stream clear to the
final ocean?"

Not me, anyway. Because the human body is made mostly of
water, water draws us toward itself with the same unconscious
magnetism that draws newborns to their mothers. Without water
to drink, we die. Without water to look upon, our spirits die. We
travel toward water, alongside water, over water. We vacation
beside water, upon water, in water. It brings us our lives, carries
away our wastes. We cannot pass by water without looking at it
and into it, and therefore into ourselves.

Sometimes I imagine I might learn to focus my scattered mind
enough to lift off from this mossy gneiss divan of mine to hover

briefly and then glide upstream into the mist, as the antigravity offspring of Saint Izaak of Walton and a magic-carpeted Buddha. I would just float along smiling at the little brook and its cache of familiar trout. And when I reach the damp hillside of its beginnings I will turn, sink, and, in a different and less tangible form, let the little brook carry me far out to sea, where I will finally become what I'm mostly made of.

45. *A Few Prosaic Days*

I HATE AUTUMN, BY WHICH I MEAN I LOVE autumn so much I dread its arrival for knowing how briefly it will stay.

Pleasant seasons are always too short and the miserable ones too long, even where they predictably divide into quarter-slices of the annual pie: a warm spring, a hot summer, a cool autumn, a cold winter. Sadly, many places that interest anglers often follow less equitable schemes.

Except in rogue years, summer doesn't reliably arrive here in Midcoast Maine until the second week of June, and by the second week of August it's already painting the swamp maples red and reminding us to take along a sweater and consider an evening fire and get that woodpile out from under its tarp and into the shed. The first full moon in September typically brings the first frost, and a few weeks later we can expect the first hard freeze. The first tentative snowflakes often arrive before Halloween, and by Thanksgiving our first plowable snow says winter is icummen in, to "freezeth river, turneth liver," and rammeth wind until ice-out. Most years this seasonal unlocking begins around mid-April, though I've fished in June with snow on my hat and my optimistic tomato seedlings frozen black in their cages.

With so much of the northern calendar appropriated by less deserving seasons, autumn, the loveliest time of the year no matter where you live, must crowd into "A few prosaic days / A little this side of the snow / And that side of the Haze," if I may swap winter-angry Ezra Pound for quietly autumnal Emily Dickinson.

Our few prosaic days are a time of diminishing time, a relentless narrowing of the window through which undeferable tasks must be undeferably shoved, from filling the woodshed to mounting the snowplow to squeezing in those last few fishing trips of the year.

Especially those last few fishing trips of the year.

In the spring, every nice day invites you to go fishing. And should other tasks intrude, no matter, another nice day will soon come tripping along as the northern hemisphere tilts toward the sun and adds warmth and minutes to every day in a lovely predictable progression.

Come summer, the days blur softly together. Go fishing today, go fishing tomorrow, and if you miss a day or two or even five from work or storms or other unavoidable impedimenta, no big deal—there's plenty of time next week to go a-Waltoning.

But in autumn, every day the weather worsens, every day the daylight shortens, every week the lawbook terminates another fishing season—there go the streams, there go the ponds, there go the rivers but for two, then there they go, too. Every autumn hour spent with the dentist or the computer or the chainsaw is an hour forever gone from the fishable remainders until an epoch-distant spring.

Of course, once winter rammeth in and shutteth northern-tier fishing beneath the ice, a healthy credit card can whisk the weary to bonefish-land or permit-land—or even bluegill- and bassland if the credit card is still woozy from the Great Recession. And for northern anglers, there's always a hut waiting out there on the windswept ice, inviting us to jig hopefully down a hole, fending off the cold with Allen's Coffee Brandy and those neon-red Maine wieners that glow like Rudolph's nose.

Alas, the ice and its stoic anticipation never quite quickened my pulse even when I was a drinking man. And the escalating

indignities of modern air travel keep raising the price for those
pricey weeks in paradise. Soon, a TSA defender will ask me to
explain all the string and sharp objects in my carry-on. And
I, having paid twelve hundred dollars for a narrow seat in the
screaming infant section and one hundred dollars to check my
bags, having a narrowing window to make my one connecting
flight to the islands, having waited three unapologetic hours for
the equipment to arrive, will say, "Yes, I was totally planning to
hogtie the crew with fly line and poke them full of Crazy Charlies
unless they pancake the plane into a bonefish flat." And then I
will be taken away to a cold gray room filled with unsmiling faces
and unlubricated latex gloves.

And so I spend my increasingly creaky winters remembering what I did when it wasn't winter and I wasn't so creaky, and
because we remember best what happened last, I particularly
remember autumns, the wellhead of rose-colored antifreeze that
keeps my motor running as I push three feet of hard gray snow
down the driveway, my lanky shanks frozen to the tractor seat,
snotcicles pending from my nostrils like Father Frost.

The previous years' memories mostly involved decent small-
stream trout fishing, a one-month season cubed by Maine's coldest and wettest summer ever. But as poetic as it is, catching small
trout on small rods in three months of chill April drizzle doesn't
quite warehouse the kind of balmy memories needed to suppress
images of wintering in a central Florida doublewide. For that cure,
New Englanders need a stronger physic.

Some years, our last-chance winter-proofing has been a final
trip with the usual suspects to the usual spot—a small wild river
in north-central Maine connecting two large lakes, a popular
autumn rendezvous for brook trout and landlocked salmon gathering to perpetuate their species, and restricted in October to
catch-and-release fly-fishing.

In the autumn of 2009 it was just Will and me, our usual crowd
recently thinned by the usual middle-aged reasons: failing health,
family commitments, un-deferrable work, or an unscheduled exit.
At the last minute, we were joined by our friend Danny Legere,

perhaps the best guide in Maine, his clientele recently thinned by the horrible weather, the horrible economy, and the horrible new frugality.

Conditions weren't ideal—cold and windy and raining build-an-Ark buckets—yet the river ran counterintuitively low, the upriver dam having squeezed shut to alleviate downriver flooding. But in Maine, waiting for ideal autumn fishing conditions means never fishing in autumn, so we hiked the three miles to where the river becomes a lake and fished our way back upstream, not exactly knocking them dead but having a good time, sour weather be damned.

Will, who remembers these things much better than I do these days, said we each caught one good salmon and maybe a few smaller trout by the time we huddled beneath the cedars for damp sandwiches. Then Danny headed home for honey-do duties, and Will and I fished back up to the truck. Along the way we caught a few decent salmon—Will had a twenty-incher—but compared with previous years, there was nothing especially memorable.

The next day was much better: very cold, very windy, and undecidedly sunny with bars of iron-gray clouds sweeping across a cobalt sky. We had Danny's drift boat, and the river pretty much to ourselves.

After a modestly productive morning dredging big ugly nymphs and big neon strike indicators, we spent a pleasant hour anchored at the tail of the Beach Pool, casting size-twenty-four emergers to the afternoon blue-wing olive hatch. The fish were rising just above the lip in a tapestry of narrow seams, and if you got closer than sixty or seventy feet or edged into their seam, they'd stop rising. For a decent float, we needed a downstream curve cast and lots of tricky line mending, with the wind gusting upward of twenty knots and the sun strobing on and off with the clouds.

Danny finally hooked a good one on a beautiful cast that caught a lull in the wind and hooked around just right, and then he busted the 6X tippet with a heave-ho streamer strike. And then I had one on but lost it because my long slack-line cast had just enough slack to yield a drag-free drift and way too much to set the hook. And then Will caught one by ignoring all this impossible-cast, invisible-fly insanity and swam a pair of porky wet flies across the tail-out on a short stout leader.

But the vision that stayed with me as I pushed snow down the driveway a few months later was a nice male brook trout Will caught—sixteen or seventeen inches, fat as a bass and wearing all the colors of autumn: the greens and reds and oranges and blacks and blues and whites of the hemlock and cedar, maples and ashes, and the hard dark shadows and intense sky and racing clouds, with the trout frozen alongside the boat in one of those narrow God-beams of sunlight that photographers spend their lives chasing.

That was memory enough for that winter—perhaps because, as payback for the previous year's nine feet of snow and nine days of summer, that particular winter ended in January and our spring arrived in March. When I should have been watching ice and floods remodeling the neighborhood brooks, I watched instead brook trout rising to caddis hatching a full two months too soon.

The week after opening day, when folks in the Old Confederacy were shoveling snow and declaring global warming an inconvenient hoax, I slipped into a free-running Maine brook wearing a light sweater and hip-boots and caught six nice trout on a dry fly.

46. *Locking Up*

THE FIRST THING YOU NOTICE IS THAT YOUR fly line no longer shoots through the guides with the soft sibilance of silk but with the bumpity-bump of barbed wire. The second thing you notice is that your fingers can no longer form a clinch knot. And then you notice other signs, like a gradual thickening of water as it flows around rocks, which despite their immovable mass follow the thermometer downhill five times faster than the water passing by. Stay on the river a while longer, and you may notice those rocks growing transparent rings and becoming miniature Saturns all ready for the junior-high science fair. Then slowly the rings spread out and join others, and the river flows in ever-narrowing channels until finally only a hollow gurgle says it's still flowing at all.

What's happening is obvious to people throughout the north. Like our neighbors stowing away barbecue grills and yard art, redirecting the mail and loading the Buick for the annual migration to Florida, the waterways are locking up for the winter. But unlike the migratory neighbors and the long vees of Canada geese *ka-lunking* their way to warmer surroundings, the waterways aren't going anywhere; they're staying right here and toughing it out beneath a sheath of floating ice that, for the rest of the winter, will shield what lives within from what lives without.

And what lives within is everything that interests anglers—caddis larvae and mayfly nymphs, stoneflies and dragonflies, dace and chubs, bass and trout, suckers and salmon. After a long season of being pestered by relentless predators from herons and otters to me and thee, winter brings the inhabitants of northern rivers a welcome time-out.

Up on the snowy riverbank, there's no visible evidence of what lies beneath, but all those hatches we fussed over in the spring and summer have borne fruit, so to speak, and below the insulating ice, nestled beneath rocks and the salad bar of fallen leaves, the inspirations for our favorite trout flies feed and bide their time, waiting for spring to bring a brief and dramatic opportunity to live for a few days in a different form and a different environment.

The wood turtles I saw last summer near the river now hibernate beneath its ice, where in the running water they find dissolved oxygen and relief from the frigid air. The frogs are there, too, breathing through their skins and dreaming of whatever it is frogs dream of. Hopefully bugs and not a formaldehyde-scented afterlife involving a shaky scalpel and a pair of gagging, giggling teenagers in third-period Biology.

Overwintering anglers needing a more tangible aquatic-insect fix can sometimes find it wandering around on the late-winter ice in the form of small dark stoneflies, perfect miniatures of the great fluttering *Pteronarcyidae* of midsummer and perfect reminders that not all life conforms to expectations.

Chief among local species that don't conform to expectations is the Atlantic salmon, which is just as confounding in winter as in fishing season. A small nearby river of my acquaintance has a tiny remnant population of salmon—six returned to build redds last year—and in the winter I sometimes visit the big deep pools and imagine salmon finning quietly beneath the ice on the sheltered bottom, just biding their time until ice-out and the annual migration to the feeding grounds off Labrador and Greenland. But according to University of New Brunswick researchers who radio-tagged salmon on the Miramichi in the fall and tracked them through the winter, where you'd expect the salmon to be isn't necessarily where they are.

In cold weather, shallow riffles leading into deep pools become giant Slurpee machines, and this endless frazil ice, as scientists call it, accumulates like cholesterol in arteries and fills these seemingly placid overwintering retreats with slush that constricts and sharpens the flow.

So before local retailers even begin hanging Christmas decorations, Atlantic salmon have already begun heading for saltwater, and it doesn't matter whether they're thirty miles or three miles from the sea. Most spend the winter near head of the tide, where twice-daily infusions of salt water minimize ice formation. What few salmon winter upriver do so at frazil-free zones near the mouths of tributaries, or in current-free backwaters where you'd never find a self-respecting salmon in fishing season. Here they wait for winter to end, dreaming, perhaps, of new ways to confound the expectations of anglers.

Back by the fireside, crouched over a vise winding up tiny black stoneflies for no other reason than we saw one crawling on the ice and feel some visceral need to imitate it, northern anglers wait for winter to end, too. About the time the schools have used up their snow days and the town road commissioners are worrying whether their salt-and-sand piles will last the season, what few neighbors haven't fled to Florida until Memorial Day begin asking each other the same questions. "Will it ever stop snowing?" "Will it ever warm up?" "Will winter never end?"

The expected answer is, "It always has." Except for this one time.

It was 1816, known variously as the year without a summer and eighteen-hundred and froze to death. Blame the unhappy coincidence of the lowest sunspot activity ever recorded and, the summer before, Earth's largest volcanic eruption—Mount Tambora in Indonesia—in more than ten thousand years. The planetary blanket of volcanic ash—a minor version of which we experienced in the 1991 eruption of Mount Pinatubo in the Philippines—brought the northeast a killing frost and snowfall every month that year. Newly shorn sheep froze in the fields. Migratory birds dropped from the air like stones. Crops failed throughout the region. Livestock starved. People starved. And the survivors began pouring from New England into the newly opened lands to the west, a one-way migration that wouldn't reverse for more than a century and a half.

"Maybe this time will be like that one time," is a thought that furrows pessimistic brows around New England firesides from Thanksgiving through Easter. As we hang Christmas decorations we begin thinking maybe this time we should migrate—permanently like our predecessors or temporarily like our neighbors and the geese.

Every year, while mounting the snowblower on the tractor and stuffing the woodshed full to the rafters, I wonder if I ought instead to mount the little fish boat on its trailer and stuff the pickup with sandals and shorts and fly rods and boxes filled with Crazy Charlies and Gotchas and follow my neighbors and the great honking vees of geese south toward a softer, gentler life in sunnier climes—a place where people fish through the winter in free-flowing water instead of dangling baits through holes in the ice or walking the frozen banks of a locked-up river that only a short while ago we fished daily but won't fish again for a very long time.

Of course, like lots of northerners possessing flexible employment and a certain level of disposable income, I do get down into palm-tree country for a week or so most winters. And afterward, as I shovel the truck from its airport snowbank and head for home with my skin burned boiled-lobster red and my mind burning with images of bonefish and permit and palm trees, I remember something wise a migratory friend once told me. In a week, you can only sample the fishing in a new place; to truly learn it, you have to live there.

As I head for home from the airport, my eyes barely register the ice-covered roads and canyons of dingy snow. Instead they see a middle-aged man in sandals and shorts and a moth-eaten T-shirt twisting up a fresh batch of Gotchas on the veranda of a rickety shanty boat tucked away in some secluded corner of Florida Bay or a beachfront shack on a backwater island in the Bahamas. A basket of crabs, chicken-necked from the warm shallows, waits for the pot to boil, and the scent of Old Bay Seasoning fills the air. An effortless squadron of pelicans glides by on the warm breeze. A Red Stripe fresh from the icebox pearls with condensation and dampens a postcard from a neighbor toughing it out back home. On its face is a lobster wearing earmuffs and on its back is an account of the latest weather-related horror—how many trees came down in the ice, how long the power was out, how they managed the process of elimination when the septic tank froze solid. It ends, as expected, with the nonmigratory New Englander's universal malediction: *If you can't take winter, you don't deserve summer.*

Maybe that's why I haven't yet made the break and locked up the house when winter locks up the rivers, following the neighbors and the geese toward secluded salt marshes with their endless sunshine, endless seafood, and endless opportunities to truly learn the fishing someplace new and different.

Maybe it's that fear that you truly don't deserve a New England summer unless you suffer through the winter. Or maybe it's the fear that, like some of those neighbors and so many of those geese, I won't quite make it to that secluded salt marsh in the bright sunny South, and I'll end up spending the winter waddling around a golf course in New Jersey.

47. *A Theory of Evolution*

GIERACH'S E-MAIL CAME IN THE NICK OF time: late January, suicide season, the gray Maine winter howling like Grendel at the gates of Heorot, Izaak Walton's admonition to go a-angling and study to be quiet feeling as faraway as the next millennium.

"We should plan a fishing trip," John wrote from the depths of a Rocky Mountain blizzard.

"I'm all ears," typed I, my fingers numb from shoveling snow and my brain a spumoni of frozen pipes, a shrinking wood pile, and the new calendar from Red's Automotive that claimed I was somehow closer to seventy than sixty. "But it has to be cheap because I'm, uh, pondering retirement. Though you didn't hear that from me."

"A cheap trip for you," John wrote, "would be something in your region about which I know next to nothing."

A cheap fishing trip in my region? Through the snow squalls came the peeping and cheeping of a distant spring. The drifted driveway transformed into a winding river. Mayflies hatched from windswept ripples. In the lee of the snowblower, a dun floated on its nymphal shuck and a nice salmon rose from behind a tractor tire and ate it.

Fishing restoreth the soul, they say, and travel broadens the mind and expands your horizons. But fishing without traveling

offers similar benefits without drilling a four-figure cavity in your
bank balance or enduring four hours of 27B explaining to 27A the
theocratic wonders of Fox News. Plus, for whatever reason, I fish
better in the East.

Maybe many years of fishing familiar places have left me
thinking I'm a halfway decent fisherman, in the same way that
singing *Siegfried* in the shower makes me imagine I'm a halfway
decent heldentenor buttering up Brünnhilde for a bit of hide the
braunschweiger and not a tone-deaf Elmer Fudd twying to kill
da wabbit.

Maybe it's the intimidation factor. All those brawling western
rivers filled with brawling western trout that spurn effete eastern
flies and shatter wussy eastern fly rods, then knock off our tweed
caps and Harry Potter glasses and grind them into the purple sage.

Maybe. But I'm not that kind of Easterner. I may have been
born with a book in one hand and a fly rod in the other, but I grew
up in a hardscrabble little town in the East Tennessee hills and
have lived a hardscrabble life for more than forty years in a raw-
knuckle corner of Maine, which has its own brawling rivers filled
with wild brook trout measured in pounds and hyperkinetic landlocked salmon that peel reels bare before you even realize you've
hooked one.

So what I'm thinking is, it's the scenery.

It's not that we don't have scenery in the East. It's just that our
scenery tends to be ancient, eroded, and greenly concealed behind
endless trees. But beneath the wide-open skies of the Rocky
Mountain West, the scenery is raw and new and in-your-face
and impossible to hide, impossible to ignore. Wherever you look,
there it is—behind you, in front of you, all around. The Front
Range. The Absarokas. The Crazies. San Juans. Wind Rivers.
Beartooths. Beaverheads. Bighorns. Name a western mountain
range, and I've lost a good trout gawking at it.

But the worst offenders—or, seen another way, the best offenders—are the Grand Tetons. As a lifelong member of the seventh
grade, I feel a filial bond with those nineteenth-century French
voyageurs who *Alouetted* and *Frère Jacquesed* their way into Jackson

Hole, looked up from the fruited plains at those purple mountains' majesty, and said *Wouah, Gros Nichons!* Followed closely by *Putain d'merde*: there's *three* of 'em.

On my first trip to Jackson Hole I couldn't tear my eyes away from the polymastian magnificence of Teewinot, Owen, and Grand Teton, thrusting a mile and more from the valley floor— Brünnhilde's granitic bustier dominatrixing the skyline. I nearly did a face-plant doddering down the jetway, nearly fell out of the drift boat trying to keep them in sight, and missed cast after cast and strike after strike, as mesmerized as a scrawny seventh-grader tossed into the girls' locker room, a goober-brained Gomer Pyle endlessly going, "Golleeee!"

After a few days I finally absorbed enough scenery to spot a really good fish rising in a secluded slough, with a small tree-covered bluff blocking the view and another blocking the restless wind that incessantly blew. It was twenty feet farther than I can usually cast with a twenty-foot upstream reach-mend I usually can't do, hitting a small moving target I usually can't hit. But somehow everything worked out, and a hungry snout pierced the film, snarfed my tiny Adams Parachute, and headed for the open river.

After a long bulldogging run and much pumping and grinding, I muscled him close enough to see nearly two feet of bronze-and-scarlet cutthroat frothing the back-eddy like a Mixmaster. Then he got a good look at my aviator shades and Searsport Lobsterboat Races cap, and roadrunnered around the corner and into the river with me in Wile E. Coyote pursuit. And there, towering over the landscape and rim-fired by the sinking sun, stood Brünnhilde's triple-brass breastplate. Worse, across the slough at a marshy rule of thirds point stood a moose and her twin calves sipping from the pewter river while far overhead a golden eagle soared along an opposing diagonal of sun-gilt cumuli—a Mother Nature tableau as precisely composed as a Constable or a Turner or a Hamm's beer commercial.

Result: one slack jaw, one slack line, one big cutthroat gone bye-bye.

So I was thinking a local trip about which I know a little something and John knows next to nothing might be just the ticket, even though our last trip, two years before, had also been here in Maine. It had been arranged by filmmaker Carter Davidson, and included stays in the posh Bethel Inn, homey Bosebuck Mountain Camps, and a rustic cabin on the Rapid River at Aldro French's Forest Lodge, once the home of writer Louise Dickinson Rich of *We Took to the Woods* fame.

Rods in hand, we took to the upper Androscoggin and caught suspicious browns, eager rainbows, and the largest and fiercest chub I've ever seen.

We took to the Rapid and caught nice brook trout and landlocked salmon and some of those invasive smallmouth bass that threaten to turn America's premier wild brook trout fishery into the newest stop on the Bassmasters Trophy Trail.

We took to the Magalloway and caught some very nice salmon at Little Boy Falls, where in 1878 a New York attorney and fly-fishing author named Henry P. Wells first fished his famous Parmachenee Belle and where in 1997 I photographed fly-tackle historian A.J. Campbell catching a wild snapping brook trout passing eighteen inches on a Parmachenee Belle he tied, wielding a seven-and-a-half-foot Kosmic cane fly rod he restored, which had been built in the 1890s for just this sort of fishing by three soon-to-be-famous Maine rod-builders named Edwards, Thomas, and Payne.

"Well," I told John, "we could try the West Branch of the Penobscot in June again." This is my home water, so to speak, and June is when I'm usually there, but the fishing and the weather have been iffy in recent years, and when John and I fished it a dozen or so Junes ago we'd found it dispiritingly tough. Plus, in a major bird-flip to the calendar and all those songs filled with blossoms and butterflies and gooey rhymes for June, it snowed.

"Or we could try the East Outlet in September." This is where I try to be in the autumn, when the weather tends to be more respectful of the calendar but the fishing, depending as it does on water flow and the timely arrival of autumn rains, tends toward on-or-off streaky. And though the East Outlet of Moosehead Lake can be crowded, it has the twin advantages of being both back-yard-familiar and a two-and-a-half-hour drive from the house, and the disadvantage of being an unforgiving river to wade, especially if you're closer to seventy than sixty.

"Or I could email my guide friend Danny Legere and see if he has any bright ideas."

Which is how John and Danny and I found ourselves in mid-September deep within northern Maine's vast industrial forest, over-stuffing two twenty-foot canoes with tents and cots and coolers and folding chairs until we looked like the Joads fleeing the Dustbowl.

We shoved off into a soft foggy drizzle, the three of us shoe-horned into nooks and crannies in Danny's square-stern Mad River, its four-horse Yamaha humming a mindless tune and tow-ing our freight canoe, a Tripper XL made of what Old Town calls Royalex and crusty old Mainers call Tupperware, bound eight miles down the upper West Branch of the Penobscot for a camp-site just beyond Big Island.

By sheer coincidence it was the same week Henry David Thoreau traveled this route in 1853. He, his cousin George Thatcher, and their Penobscot Indian guide, Joe Attean, rode the stagecoach from Bangor to Greenville, took the steamer forty miles up Moosehead Lake to Northeast Carry, trekked two miles overland into the Penobscot, paddled a birch-bark canoe ten or so miles down to Chesuncook Village at the head of the lake, then turned around and poled back. The account of this trip, published in 1858 in *The Atlantic* as "Chesuncook," became the center third of his epic book *The Maine Woods* in 1864.

We passed the small island where Thoreau spent a restless night rolled in a blanket before a roaring fire, and we glided between the same dark walls of dog-hair spruce overtopped here and there by soaring white pines and the flaming grace notes of autumn maples, the same high steep banks cut into amusement-park water-slides every few hundred yards by twelve thousand years of amphibious moose—the same wild land that guided Thoreau's immortal pen 161 years ago.

In this half of the nation's most heavily forested state, "all mossy and moosey" for many thousands of square miles, it's almost impossible not to get carried away by the great transcendentalist's brand of wilderness mysticism. Unless you walk a half-mile from the river through the black dripping forest and emerge into the patchwork of regenerating old clear-cuts and newer shelter-wood cuts and mature timber waiting its turn to become houses and newspapers and magazines and books. Or you're simply a crusty old Mainer.

Thoreau may be the spiritual godfather of America's environmental movement, a profound influence on writers and thinkers from Marcel Proust and Ernest Hemingway to Mahatma Gandhi and Martin Luther King, but to some old Mainers I've fished with, the sainted author of *Walden* and "On Civil Disobedience" was simply "that friggin' hippie who built a playhouse in Waldo Emahson's backyahd." And somehow or other—they shake their heads—"he managed to get lost on Mud Pond Carry."

In the account of his 1857 expedition "The Allegash and the East Branch," Thoreau wrote that, "The Indian was greatly surprised that we should have taken what he called a 'tow' (*i.e.*, tote or toting or supply) road, instead of a carry path—that we had not followed his tracks—said it was 'strange,' and evidently thought little of our woodcraft."

* * *

I was thinking about Thoreau and his woodcraft as we passed the inlet of Ragmuff Stream, where Thoreau and Thatcher stopped to fry some trout for lunch and stew in abandonment-issue juices because their guide wandered off scouting for moose and didn't return for an hour and a half. When he died in 1862, Thoreau's last words were "Indian" and "moose," and I wondered if Thoreau went searching for his AWOL guide in the afterlife and if Chief Attean—for Joseph was both the last hereditary chief of the Penobscots and the first popularly elected tribal chief—had really gone looking for moose or had just needed a break from Thoreau's relentless "suckling at the very teats of nature's pine-clad bosom."

By Thoreau's account, "his Indian" was a man of few words, which got me thinking that the first crusty old Mainers hadn't evolved from those dour seventeenth-century European settlers but had arrived with the moose when the glaciers melted—unchanged and unchangeable, their acerbic opinions about know-it-all motormouths from away becoming calcified by the onset of puberty.

The first historical record of endemic Maine crustiness dates from 1524, when Giovanni da Verrazano was exploring the Atlantic coast from Florida to New Brunswick. After two frolicsome weeks with the friendly Wampanoag of Rhode Island, Verrazano and company headed for Maine. Spying some locals watching from a cliff near the mouth of the Kennebec River, Verrazano made grandiloquent gestures of friendship and trade. Which the locals greeted with "all signs of discourtesy and disdain . . . displaying their buttocks and laughing immoderately." And so Verrazano, the very first tourist to be mooned in Maine, labeled his map of the Maine Coast *Terra Onde di Mala Gente*: Land of Bad People.

Soon we began to see a scattering of campsites notched into the forest—big tents, taut tarps sheltering rustic picnic tables, neatly stacked firewood, and classic wood-and-canvas canoes pulled up against the steep bank. Then the long stretch of skinny rocky dead-water quickened, and the channel narrowed and turned twistier and rockier and, to my eyes, not always evident until we eddied out, a mile later, into the slack water below Big Island.

This was to be our home for the next five days—a snug campsite called Smart's, named for Myron Smart, the crusty old guide and canoe builder who camped here for many years, fishing for the big landlocked salmon that begin running upriver from Chesuncook Lake when the autumn rains bring that first push of high water.

Forty-some years ago, as a budding photographer accompanying a friend who wrote newspaper articles about colorful Maine characters, I met Myron in his Milo canoe shop. Then in his eighties, Myron was supplementing his retirement by building wood-and-canvas canoes and ash paddles in his garage. He began guiding in 1915, trapped beaver, worked as a logger during ox-team and river-driving days, became a game warden, and was widely famous for his woodcraft and campsite cuisine.

As my friend asked journalistic questions and scribbled in his notebook, I stuck my camera in Myron's face from various artsy angles and chattered away about Thoreau and woodcraft and fly-fishing and other things I thought I knew something about—a typical know-it-all motormouth from away.

I was in my early twenties, newly moved to Maine, newly and dejectedly divorced from my brainiac Boston wife, wandering in mind and focus—an aspiring photographer or an aspiring guitar player or a Thoreauvian back-to-the-lander depending on which day you asked: a textbook example of what Anthony Trollope called a "hobbledehoy." I admired the canoe Myron was finishing, a workmanlike twenty-footer meant to transport two people and all their gear into the Maine woods, upriver or down, over skinny water or deep, flat or fast, with a minimum of fuss and effort. He offered to build me one for six hundred dollars, if I remember correctly, but that was more than a month's pay for me. Besides, what did I need with a canoe? I'd spent my formative years waist-deep in roaring East Tennessee trout streams and face-down in the pages of *Field & Stream*, *Outdoor Life*, and *Sports Afield*, where real fly fishermen waded chest-high through brawny rivers. Only the most indolent and decrepit anglers lounged about in canoes, dangling their sad, limp lines in stagnant ponds.

* * *

As we lugged our gear up the bank and erected the tents and set up the kitchen and stretched the big tarp over the picnic table, Danny told us about coming to this remote stretch of the river way back when he first started his Maine Guide Flyshop in Greenville. Then and now, the Fox Hole is a tight, closed society. To get here—and, more importantly, to get back upriver to your truck—you need to know what you're doing. Danny kept coming back, a young man eager to learn, and after a few years the old guys began to nod in his direction, lift a hand to wave, and eventually actually

talk to him. "We was waitin' to see if you was a wookie." Once
accepted, they showed him the channels, the lies, and how to pole
a canoe upriver and down through thin fast water where a paddle
is worse than useless and an outboard motor needs a Pez dispenser
filled with shear pins.

Few objects of human manufacture are more evolutionarily
appropriate than the canoe, and it reached its highest form right
here in Maine and eastern Canada. The white birch whose bark
formed the canoe's skin grew largest here. A labyrinth of long
rocky rivers and short woodland streams connecting small ponds
and huge lakes made possible rapid, long-distance travel for families and all their belongings.

A Wabanaki family might spend their summers on the sea-
coast fishing, clamming, and hunting seals and porpoises, the
cool afternoon sea breeze holding at bay the clouds of blackflies
and mosquitoes that make a misery of summer in upland Maine.
When the frost smote the wingéd vampires and the leaves began
to turn, they'd load their canoes and head upriver to spend their
winters deep within the sheltering forest, trapping fur and hunting moose and dodging the howling ocean gales that savage the
naked coast.

The extent of this birch bark highway is an eye-opener to the
uninitiated. To get seriously initiated, pop $12.95 for a copy of
Above the Gravel Bar: The Native Canoe Routes of Maine by David
S. Cook—historian, teacher, and, when he was growing up,
Myron Smart's next-door neighbor and protégé. From Myron's
old campsite we could paddle 140 miles straight downriver to my
home on Penobscot Bay. Or pole upriver forty or so miles to the
North Branch of the Penobscot, carry a few miles overland into
a tributary of the Chaudière, and paddle downstream to Quebec
City. A different carry from the North Branch takes us into the
headwaters of the St. John, where we could paddle downstream
to the Grand, pole upriver, then carry into the Restigouche and
on down to Chaleur Bay and the Gaspé Peninsula. Or we could
pole up the Tobique and carry into the Miramichi and the Gulf of
St. Lawrence or continue on down the St. John past Fredericton

to the Bay of Fundy. Or we could paddle seven miles downriver from our campsite to Chesuncook Lake, pole up Caucomgomoc Stream, and portage into the Allagash River on Thoreau's Mud Pond Carry of 1857. From there we could head downriver to the St. John or carry into the Fish River and then into the St. Croix and downriver to the twin cities of Calais, Maine, and St. Stephen, New Brunswick. In this neck of the woods, the possibilities are endless if you've got a good canoe and know how to use it.

I first saw a canoe paddled by someone who truly knew how forty-some years ago and thirty-some miles downriver in the Big Eddy. It was a Trout Unlimited campout, and well-dressed doctors and lawyers from Bangor manhandled their shiny synthetic canoes around the eddy, dropping anchor above mid-pool seams and casting long picturesque lines to rising salmon. Through their midst glided a big wood-and-canvas canoe with a scrawny little old man in the stern flicking it around like a feather with no perceptible effort from his long ash paddle while his young friend in the bow cast a short precise line into the rapids at the head of the pool. My first thought was how the *hell* does that creaking geezer do that? And my next thought was, could I?

As it happened, I couldn't, at least not for a while. Life, as it tends to do, got in the way, and for the next six years I hauled lobster traps and the six years after I drove a lobster truck, and in my spare time I waded rivers and streams the way I learned as a boy— somehow, along the way, evolving into a fledgling fish-writer. Newly possessed of a purpose, a whiff of disposable income, and the dim awareness of something called a tax deduction, I stopped in southern Maine at Kittery Trading Post on my way home from the weekly lobster run to New Jersey and found KTP's annual scratch-and-dent canoe sale underway. An hour later I drove off with a barely blemished sixteen-foot Mad River Explorer balanced atop a hundred empty lobster crates and the slushy remains of two tons of ice.

The canoe salesman was young, knowledgeable, and so enthusiastic it bordered on evangelical. He showed off clippings of a manic mesomorph pushing an Explorer to a national whitewater

poling championship and of noted wilderness paddlers championing the new canoe in books and magazine articles. The Explorer
was the latest thing, the bee's knees, the lobster's waistcoat, and
only a month's pay marked down from a month and a half's. Of
course, any crusty old Mainer worth his yellow-eye beans could
have told me its shiny shallow-V bottom was too tippy and flexy
and slick to stand in comfortably, and the canoe itself was too short
to pole and paddle in the relaxed and energy-efficient manner of
crusty old Mainers and the Native peoples who taught them. But
what did they know? I was barely out of my hobbledehoy twenties,
and those old farts were so frozen in time that some still fished
with split-bamboo fly rods.

* * *

With the campsite shipshape, the drizzle abating, and a leisurely
lunch under our belts, John wanted to get acquainted with the
river in the full-immersion fashion of wading anglers everywhere,
so he slipped into the Home Pool at Smart's and began working
out line while Danny and I headed a half-mile upriver to Myron's
Run.

I'd never fished this stretch of the Penobscot before, and as we
anchored the canoe and eased into the hip-deep water, I looked
out across the river seeking fresh new scenery but seeing only my
backyard.

Living your life within the scenery of a nature conservancy calendar has a wealth of aesthetic advantages with one wet-blan-
ket disadvantage: sooner or later, it ceases to be scenery. On the
bright side, it means that once you stop marveling at the dewdrops
on the spruce needles you can get on with the business at hand,
whether turning part of the scenery into next winter's firewood or
asking Danny what fly he'd recommend. Which turned out to be
a streamer invented by a crusty old Mainer for this very stretch of
water to gull the ancestors of these very fish.

Landlocked salmon are eccentric feeders—the two biggest
I've taken both ate Beadhead Pheasant Tail nymphs not much

bigger than this 9. But their daily meat and three is the rainbow smelt, an iridescent pencil of flashy energy whose spring spawning runs flow up rivers like pipelines of molten silver. All the classic old Maine streamers—Grey Ghost, Black Ghost, Nine-Three, Ballou Special, Supervisor, Pink Lady—were designed to imitate smelt, long and skinny and flashy as a rainbow. The fly I tied on was typical, a slim orange body ribbed with silver, a variegated underwing of red, white, and blue bucktail topped with a white puff of marabou that undulates underwater like a mermaid's tresses.

"It's got all the essentials," its crusty old creator had said. "Form, flash, and action."

"Sounds like a Montreal whore," said his crusty old friend. And that became its name.

Undistracted by the scenery that looks too much like my backyard to be scenery, I fished the Whore with the unconcerned concentration of an angler who's done this many times and knows what to expect. Within a few hours, I landed six landlocks between sixteen and twenty inches. Several more tossed the hook, including one with broad shoulders that released itself in a theatrical leap even the Russian judge would've scored a perfect 10.0.

It's no wonder landlocked salmon are Maine's signature fish. "As a game fish they have no equal," wrote H.O. Stanley and E.M. Stillwell in their 1874 report as Maine's Commissioners of Fish and Fisheries. "We have caught many fresh and sea salmon in our day, but nothing that we have ever hooked on to can equal one of these fishes in his electric like leaps and runs."

For this, Maine anglers can thank a quirk of evolution. Essentially, landlocked salmon are simply Atlantic salmon that no longer go to sea. Some say the retreat of the glaciers locked them forever in their home waters, but the four Maine river systems with original populations of landlocks—the Penobscot, the St. Croix, the Union, and the Presumpscot—all maintained their connections with the ocean until late in the eighteenth century, when know-it-all folks from away began beavering-up un-navigable dams. Current thinking says that long before

the dam-building craze, isolated groups of Atlantic salmon collectively decided to stay safe t'home eatin' smelt and forgo the
annual eighteen-hundred-mile swim to Greenland, with its hungry gauntlet of seals and sharks and whales countering its bounty
of arctic shrimp.

That night, without a trace of irony, Danny cooked shrimp
scampi over the fire, then we leaned back in our folding chairs—
three crusty old farts talking about fishing and admiring the stars
while drinking beer my son made and eating wild blueberry pie
Danny's wife made. In the morning we crawled out of our sleeping bags and ate sunny-up eggs my ducks laid and then suited up
for serious fishing.

* * *

John and Danny headed upriver in the canoe while I fished a
Montreal Whore down through the Home Pool and didn't get a
look. Even before the days of catch-and-release, salmon were as
notorious as three-year-olds for eating only the thoroughly familiar—except when they'd eat only the new and novel. Twenty or so
years ago, Maine salmon that had seen only big flashy streamers
or drifting dry flies began to see heavily weighted nymphs rolling along the bottom. And ate them like shrimp at a free buffet.
These days almost everyone fishes weighted nymphs, but a few
outliers have found that salmon grown suspicious of nymphs and
streamers sometimes chase small swinging wet flies like kittens
after a yarn ball.

And so I fished down through the pool again with a pair of wet
flies and took enthusiastic salmon of twelve, fourteen, and seventeen inches before running out of fishable water. Encouraged, I
hijacked the freight canoe, paddled across the run, and took three
sixteen-inch salmon, a fourteen, and two chubs. The chubs ate a
delicate mayfly emerger tied when my eyes and hands still worked
well enough to tie delicate mayfly emergers; the salmon ate a rag-
gedy soft-hackle of the type even shaky old fumblers can tie, its
unkempt collar of umber partridge extending well past the hook's

bend, its scant orange body wound from Pearsall's silk spun in the same English factory since 1795.

To repurpose a line from Mole and Ratty, there is nothing half so much worth doing as simply catching fish with our ancestors' tackle. If I could transport that fly to third-century Dalmatia, the temper and sharpness of its Japanese hook might have surprised Roman Emperor Diocletian, recently retired from office to spend his golden years fishing a private trout stream, but the pattern itself would have been as familiar as a wine jug.

Unfortunately, salmon are immune to nostalgia, because after lunch the three of us swung wet flies down the river and couldn't buy a fish—not even a chub—though we tempted some fourteen-inch seventh-graders with the Whore.

Another group of anglers were having a late lunch at their downriver campsite, and we paused to pass howdies and swap the weekend edition of the *Bangor Daily News* for three garden-ripe tomatoes and a tip on the hot fly du jour—a newish streamer called the Blue Streak, which featured beneath its come-hither wing of white marabou an underwing made of that Bunsen-burner-blue tinsel most commonly seen in wigs worn by ironic teenagers at Halloween parties and overweight men at football games.

It was an interesting crowd, several generations of friends and family who'd been coming here for many years and who fished their enormous Maine streamers the same way Messrs. Payne, Thomas, and Edwards fished them in the 1880s: sitting amidships in anchored canoes with their rods tracking long methodical swings enlivened with subtle rhythmic pumps.

Their rods may have been modern graphite and there were four-horse outboards hanging sidesaddle on their canoes, but mixed in with the usual Tupperware Trippers were canoes made by Mainers as famous in some circles as Payne, Thomas, and Edwards. One looked to be an E.M. White, and another, Danny said, was a Fred Reckerds—I don't know my vintage canoes the way I should. But I do know that if I could transport one of those canoes to this same spot five hundred years ago, the locals would have been surprised only by its watertight skin of green canvas instead of amber birch bark. In evolutionary terms, the Eastern woodland canoe achieved perfection before the New World ever discovered it was new.

After a semi-successful afternoon with wet flies and small fast-moving streamers, we headed back upriver and found the extended family all out fishing—most were into good salmon. One guy shakily said he'd lost the biggest fish he'd ever hooked. "I couldn't move it; I couldn't hold it." He wanted to say thirty inches, but seemed unwilling to commit to what we all knew was possible. A thirty-inch salmon weighs between eight and ten pounds, and Maine's biggest ever landlock, caught in Sebago Lake in 1907, weighed a few ounces over twenty-two.

These days a good fish is closer to twenty inches than twenty pounds, but many folks have hooked landlocks of more than six pounds. I've landed two between six and seven, and on one unforgettable day I hooked one much bigger. Four of us were fishing the West Branch above the Telos Bridge, two on each side, and I'd just cast to a small pocket in heavy water when my rod slammed into a half-hoop. A second later my line was all gone along with half my backing, and on the opposite bank an immense salmon hung in the sun on a fadeaway jumpshot and spat my Pheasant Tail at Chucky Ringer's face.

* * *

The midnight pee arced into frosted ferns beneath an unfiltered ocean of stars, but at dawn the wind came sou'west and brought clouds and unseasonable warmth. Danny and John headed downriver in the Kevlar square-stern, and I followed behind paddling the Tupperware Tripper, the plan being to take a break from our modernized tactics and go old-school like our neighbors, with sinking lines, slow swings, and bigger streamers.

Freshly armed with a Blue Streak, and casting toward a granite palisade where tannic water swirled into a root-beer float the size of a bond-trader's bathtub, I took a fourteen-incher, three sixteens, and a fierce leaper that my adrenaline initially measured at twenty-four and calm retrospect adjusted to twenty once I'd tweezed out the hook and briefly cradled her in the current. In the next hole down, beneath the ghost of a pine perforated by generations of woodpeckers, I boated a solid twenty-one-incher and lost an honest two-footer in the heavy water at the tail-out, where a younger version of me might have followed, a throbbing rod in one hand and a flailing paddle in the other.

But such a paddle to be flailing: a stubby plastic-and-aluminum spatula of the semi-disposable whitewater-rafting variety that Danny'd found floating facedown in the West Branch. A proper paddle hadn't been on my packing list, but I'd have swapped two extra sweaters and my spare fly rod for the six-foot ash paddle I carved one winter and the twelve-foot spruce pole I cut off my woodlot and shod from the dusty boxful of cast-iron pole shoes Danny scored when Titcomb's General Store went belly-up back in the 1980s.

I went belly-up a lot back in the 1980s as I taught myself to pole and paddle by watching old guys who'd learned from their grandfathers. Then I practiced their moves far from judgy eyes, like a teenager learning to dance watching *American Bandstand*. Slowly and damply I evolved into a fair-to-middlin' canoe-man, and after the weekly three-day lobster run to New Jersey I'd find an interesting new spot, pole the canoe upstream for a few miles, eat lunch, and then drop back downriver, standing and snubbing with the pole, anchoring to fish likely water, and making mental notes for my next fish-column in the *Maine Sportsman*.

Then life got in the way, as life tends to do. While a new full-time gig editing boating books brought the twin novelties of a lower-middle-class income and health insurance, it also left scant time for aimless explorations in the canoe. Seven years later, after a lateral move from editing boating books in an office thirty miles away to editing fishing and hunting books at home, I began writing the column for *Gray's Sporting Journal*, and my vehicle for explorations became an airliner. A few years later another lateral move found me editing *Gray's* as well, and seventeen and a half years later I looked up from untangling a thorny passage to see a cheesy muscle-car calendar from Red's Automotive that (1) claimed I was closer to seventy than sixty, and (2) implied that I'd spent almost half my life sitting in front of a computer pruning other peoples' adverbs.

Not that I've any regrets. Done properly—which is to say help-fully, carefully, invisibly—editing is a noble calling. But done properly it also consumes a lot of time and mental bandwidth—so much, in fact, that I didn't notice a winter gale had toppled a seventy-foot white pine across the spine of my canoe until the tree was Swiss-cheesed to tinder by generations of carpenter ants.

So when I found myself noodling around on the upper West Branch in a spatula-propelled Tupperware Tripper, I was sur-prised to find I could still thread my way through foamy chutes and twisty channels, eddy out into the lee of boulders and drop anchor more or less where I was aiming. Given a pole, a decent paddle, and a lightweight sidesaddle outboard, I could imagine a man of a certain age extending his angling years past the point when wading fast brawny rivers evolves from a pleasurable physi-cal challenge into a micro-tragedy on the six o'clock news.

* * *

Overnight a cold front roared through along with, according to John and Danny, an amorous bull moose bellowing for his Brünnhilde. I missed the moose thanks to a little blue pill my doctor said would let me sleep even with a river filled with fish only a few steps away, but with hard frost encrusting table, tents, canoes, and waders, the cold front was impossible to miss.

We stoked the fire and lingered long over duck eggs and cof-fee, eyeing our icy waders and watching our new neighbors try for an early salmon from the steamy waters of the Home Pool. They'd arrived yesterday, Steve Cole and a young relative, and were camped across the back-channel on the island. Steve and Danny and I'd fished together up in Ungava a few years back, and I was glad to see him, in part because he came visiting last night with a pan of biscuits hot from his father's old reflector

oven, in part because he comes factory-equipped with the crusti-
est of Maine accents—"we got three saam'n on the Ho-wah"—
and in part because I admired the way his canoe sat the water,
how quickly it turned, how handily it bore the weight of them
and their gear and their sidesaddle Yamaha without squatting
or pitching. Steve said a fellow called Asa Gallupe built it up
in Aroostook County in the 1940s or early '50s, and while his
ash pole was new, his maple paddle was the same one his father
guided with in the 1950s. It looked just like the one I carved
back in the 1980s from a drawing made by canoe historian Edwin
Tappan Adney in the 1880s of a Passamaquoddy paddle that
likely hadn't changed since the 1480s.

Admiring the Gallupe's cedar ribs and planks glowing with age,
I became dangerously suspicious that a Tupperware Tripper, while
immensely practical as a low-maintenance fishing tool and floating wheelchair, might be insufficiently aesthetic for a guy who
likes cane rods, dusty books, cast-iron skillets, and wool shirts.

This being our last full day, we headed upriver towing the
Tupperware Tripper with the expressed intention of fishing our
way back to camp and with the unexpressed hope that the violent
change of weather had only winged the fishing and not torpedoed
it at the waterline. At the head of Big Island, Danny stopped to
visit with a friend who said he'd landed two good ones earlier and
had just lost the only fly they'd eat to a real monster. Was Danny
coming back in on Monday? And would he bring along a dozen
Golden Retrievers?

"A dozen what?" I asked, looking at the golden retriever resting his friendly head against the bow seat of a classic wood-and-
canvas E.M. White.

We continued on upriver into the dead-water then drifted back
throughout the day fishing every riffle and run and pool with
everything in our boxes—wet flies, nymphs, dry flies, a Gray
Ghost, a Blue Streak, the Whore—everything except a Golden
Retriever. Danny didn't have one, and I'd never heard of one,
though within my lizard brain was a vague tickle of something,
somewhere.

Late in the afternoon we made it back to camp, having covered lots of water and seen lots of scenery and had lots of laughs. What we hadn't had lots of was fish. John caught three or four small salmon, and I technically avoided an outright skunk with two chubs. I had, however, enjoyed flicking the big Tupperware Tripper around the riffles and rips almost like I knew what I was doing. Except when a sharp gust caught that slab-sided hull and, despite much flailing with the plastic spatula, sent it skittering across the river like a water strider.

* * *

The next morning—our last morning—dawned beneath a soggy gray blanket. In a few weeks, we'd learn this was Maine's third driest September following its twelfth driest August, but for now we knew only that the clouds were oozing, the winds were squirrely, and the river was showing its bones. Low water meant few fresh salmon were moving up from the lake, and the fish already in the river had seen a lot of flies. Still, fishermen fish whatever the prospects, so John waded into the Home Pool and began working out line in his precise, methodical way, and Danny and I attacked the pocket-water below camp from the canoe. We tried streamers, we tried soft hackles, and after a helluva lot of casting we'd each caught a fifteen-inch salmon.

"What was that fly your friend with the golden retriever lost to the monster?"

"A Golden Retriever."

Danny dug through his boxes again and finally found one, a beadhead Woolly Bugger-looking thing with a tuft of tan marabou for a tail and a red thread body overwrapped with flashy cappuccino-colored Estaz chenille. It looked like a naughty stage prop for a Montreal Whore, but Danny's friend had taken two good salmon and lost a real monster on one. Could it be the next new thing? We fished it through the same water we'd just fished with our old reliables and . . . and . . . and . . . the salmon boiled on it and streaked after it and cartwheeled into the air like mahi-mahi slaughtering ballyhoo. The fishing was so manic my intracranial accountant couldn't track numbers and size, so I'm only guessing somewhere north of a dozen and south of two dozen; I can say with more assurance that all were between fifteen and seventeen inches—not monsters, by any means, but wild as bears. Danny and I aren't your high-fiving sort of people and certainly aren't buttocks-displayers, but we did spend the better part of an hour laughing immoderately.

That evening we unloaded the truck at Danny's fly shop in Greenville, and because John and I were staying a few more days to fish the East Outlet, I raided the Golden Retriever bins for a dozen in three different sizes. Having the hot fly du jour is as much one of our crowd's East Outlet traditions as staying at the Indian Hill Motel, eating breakfast at Auntie M's, and stuffing our backpacks with dagwoods from Jamieson's Market.

We parked near the bridge where we always park, and with our snap-crackle-and-pop knees lobbying for an easy day, we hoofed a mile and a half downriver to a favorite pool with plans to fish slowly back to the truck in plenty of time for the fried-clam special at Flatlanders.

Somehow, a mile and a half is a lot farther than it used to be. And even with the drought the river seemed rougher and slicker and faster. Colonel John Montresor, a British engineer who mapped the region in the 1760s, wrote that the East Outlet was "narrow, deep, and full of rocks. To go back or gain the shore was equally impossible. . . . The descent everywhere [is] so great, that the river runs with vast rapidity."

We started at Old Reliable, where over the years my friends and I have caught hundreds of salmon, including my largest, a six-and-a-half-pounder. The fish came fast—John got a salmon on nymphs in the glide, and my Golden Retriever took a sixteen-inch salmon and a fourteen-inch brook trout from the curl. Optimism blossomed like bluets in the rain. So we cast and we cast and we cast some more. We changed flies—John to wet flies, me to a bigger Golden Retriever then to a smaller—and we cast again. And again. And again.

Over the course of a long day fishing our way back to the truck, John caught two brook trout—a sixteen- and a thirteen-incher, if memory serves—and that was pretty much it. The best part of the day came over lunch at the Cedars, eating Henry's dagwoods and watching the water go by, two creaking geezers grateful we can still hobble around inside the scenery and do what we do. While we still can.

* * *

Over fried clams at Flatlanders, we formulated a theory that with the river so low, the salmon might be closer to the lake, so for the next day we determined to bushwhack three miles to the outlet and fish back up. If we still can.

I'd love to say it was a perfect day and that the salmon were so ferocious we had to hide behind trees to tie on our flies. But the best I can say is that the forty-knot gusts cracked so many limbs off the trees we couldn't hear our knees. Casting downstream into the wind was YouTube-ridiculous. Casting upstream, a mere flip of the fly would send it sailing to the backing knot.

We weren't skunked, though. For a full day of hard fishing we caught maybe half a dozen salmon and half a dozen brook trout to sixteen inches with John doing a little better on his wet flies and me doing a little worse on my Golden Retriever—the hot new fly that had driven the Fox Hole salmon wild but, for reasons not then clear, left the East Outlet salmon underwhelmed.

Six months later, I snowshoed to the summer office to collect a Golden Retriever to set beside the keyboard and refresh my memory for this chapter, and while the fly boxes were out, I did a rough inventory of slots that needed filling for the upcoming season. There, tucked away in a secondary nymph box, was a Golden Retriever, and back came the memories.

Years ago I'd fished the East Outlet with Jim Finn, a good fisherman, a super-nice guy, and the Golden Retriever's creator. Jim owned a fly shop in Virginia and had come to Maine one October with Tom Rosenbauer and Jim Lepage. He caught a nice salmon at the Cedars, as I recall, and handed me one of his flies. It's practically the only fly he fishes, he said—anywhere and everywhere. He'd caught more than forty species on that fly in both fresh and salt water. I emailed him and said, "Hey, guess what," and he said that for the past four or five years he's been selling Golden Retrievers like crazy in Maine and that Maine fly shops can't keep them in stock. The *Northwoods Sporting Journal*'s editor V. Paul Reynolds wrote an article about them and then had Jim as a guest on his radio show, *Maine Outdoors*, to talk about the fly's lethal versatility.

The Golden Retriever may have been late-breaking news to me and the isolated salmon on the remote Fox Hole, but on the easily accessible East Outlet they're as familiar to the fish as Jamo's dagwoods are to the fishermen.

* * *

After a certain age, chasing the next new thing becomes ridiculous. I mean, how would you even know? I think of my pickup truck and my chainsaw as new, though the paper trail says I bought both during the Bush administration. When folks ask where I live, I tell them it's the new house in the field across from the bottle-redemption center, though we started building our new house in 1979, when gas was eighty-six cents a gallon, interest rates were 15 percent, a new house cost $50,000, and the average wage was $17,500. That year I hauled 300 lobster traps a day from a wooden boat built in Friendship, Maine, in 1939, and my social security statement says I cleared $3,750. That year the average computer was the size of a chest freezer, and the e-mails that made it possible for me to sit in Maine for eighteen years editing a magazine based in Georgia were only a propeller-head's theory on a yellow legal pad. These days I think of e-mail as the latest greatest thing, but my thirty-something son finds e-mail so laughably antique he won't even use it. He and his friends prefer something thumbable on their shiny new smartphones, but I'm too old to know what it is.

I do know I ain't gettin' no younger, and if I mean to fish to the bitter end of my threescore and ten, I need to evolve. Or at least adapt. So all winter I've been perusing the paddle-boats section of the Maine Bible, otherwise known as *Uncle Henry's Swap-or-Sell*. In theory I'm looking for a twenty-foot Old Town Tripper XL, pretty much the standard for a big-river canoe back when Old Town still made them. They won't win any beauty contests, they feel and smell like those Tupperware tubs in the back of the fridge, and are as slick inside as an East Outlet ledge, but they're also indestructible and maintenance-free, weigh a little more than one hundred pounds, and can haul three-quarters of a ton of stuff you probably don't need anywhere you want to go—by pole, paddle, or a sidesaddle outboard. Everybody who knows anything about fishing in northern New England knows that. Which means you can figure on spending most of a social-security check for a Tripper XL these days, assuming you can find one.

What's mostly in the ads are shiny plastic kayaks and shiny plastic canoes meant to haul picnicking families across a quiet pond, aluminum canoes that boom down the rapids like an oil can and stick to rocks like flypaper, or tripping canoes that have been modernized too far from their roots and are too small to support the weight of a sidesaddle outboard. Mixed in with these ads are a scattering of dangerously aesthetic options, like an eighteen-and-a-half foot E.M. White "all-original and always stored inside" and a twenty-foot Fred Templeton whose "gunnels and fiberglass need attention" and three different twenty-foot Fred Reckerds, one needing new canvas, another needing some "TLC," and another "just restored by Island Falls Canoe." The prices range from three-quarters of a social security check plus a whole lot of fiddly shop-work to two social security checks and most of a third. Still, at a certain point an angler really needs a nice place to sit down and fish. While he still can.

Maybe that's how it'll all end, impracticality and constant maintenance be damned. I'm writing this in the middle of the worst Maine winter since 1962, but if I hold my head just right I can peer out past the snowbanks and see myself sitting amidships in a classic wood-and-canvas canoe with its varnished ribs and planks glowing in the sun and my rod tracking long methodical swings through a sweeping pool, enlivening a long flashy streamer with subtle rhythmic pumps of a liver-spotted hand.

He looks happy, that scrawny little old man. No longer a hobbledehoy, though maybe still a bit of a motormouth know-it-all from away. Fully at home in that nature conservancy scenery, living in a calendar, spending his time a-angling, and studying to be crusty.

48. *One More Cast*

THERE ISN'T AN ANGLER ANYWHERE WHO hasn't said to a friend, parent, spouse, or simply to himself: one more cast. Just one more cast and I'll go.

The day has been long and arduous, and whether you've worn yourself out catching fish or not catching fish doesn't matter. You've spent a portion of your life lost in the intricacies of angling, and at some point you have to head for the landing, for the truck, for camp, for home.

We stretch the day as long as we can, with our irresponsible selves cutting small bargains with our responsible selves: just one more good fish, one more any fish, one more strike, one more rise, one more bat plucking caddis from the sky. Finally, when we can no longer even pretend we imagine a hatch, a rise, or the location of our fly, it comes down to one more cast.

I can't remember the last time I caught a fish on that last hopeless cast. Maybe I never have. But as long as anglers have been anglers, we keep making just one more cast long after it makes sense.

Writing is like that, too. The brilliant debut, the anemic sophomore embarrassment, the workaholic mid-career adequacies, the drain-circling spiral into repetitive irrelevance. The trick with writing, with fishing, with everything, really, is knowing when it's time to go.

Which is a roundabout way of explaining why, as editor of *Gray's Sporting Journal*, I fired myself from the best gig in all of fish-writing.

The writer-me maintains that I could have kept spinning out new adventures when the clotted editorial calendar permitted and recycling old adventures when the clotted editorial calendar didn't, that with age comes wisdom and perspective, and that not all modern fish-writing must pass first through airport security. But the editor-me wanted an angling columnist unencumbered by calendars, inboxes, competing foci, jaded hindsight, and contracting horizons.

Editor-me wouldn't have minded the 2002 edition of writer-me hanging around another ten years, but that version had long passed its sell-by date. Blame an escalating series of sinus surgeries that finally came to a head, so to speak, at the Lahey Clinic in Boston in 2008 and left me, for want of a better term, inadequately carbureted. Blame a knee damaged while fishing the Beaverkill in 2003, damaged again fishing the Colorado Rockies in 2006, and yet again in Arctic Quebec in 2007. Blame that knee for letting go but good while fording the flooded upper East Outlet of the Kennebec in October of 2010, for coming as close to drowning me as anything had since I was twelve years old and fell into the tailrace of Fort Loudon Dam on the Tennessee River, leaving me then with nightmares about the water closing over my face and the white light at the end of a tunnel, and in 2010 with both confidence and cartilage forever encumbered and a solemn vow never again to hoot and jeer at a three-hundred-pound NFL lineman squalling like a colicky baby because he tore his wittle hamstwing.

Blame that editorial calendar. Back when *Gray's* did its final page-proofing with a blue pencil, a pack of yellow Post-Its, and a four-hour phone call, the year's calendar was as reliably regular as a vegetarian, and I'd fill those vast white spaces between red-blocked commitments by couch-surfing the minor English chalk streams, or driving aimlessly around eastern Canada or the Western USA, or boarding an airliner with fly rod in hand bound for someplace new and exciting to wet a line and write about it.

Then, gradually, overwhelmingly, Complete Computerization gnawed that reliably geometric calendar into an exploding-Crayola-phase Jackson Pollock. A week-long bonefish trip to the Seychelles, you say? I can just about make it the third week of February if the plane has Wi-Fi and I only stay four days.

Blame an increasingly parochial mind, which I first encountered while standing hip-deep in one of the world's great salmon and steelhead rivers swinging a green-and-purple fly the size of a mackerel while worrying I was missing the first run of green-and-purple mackerel back home in Maine. Blame a mind increasingly preoccupied with flounder, sunfish, and white perch. With endlessly sniffing up some blue-line trout brook animating a small cane rod and a nondescript pair of flies, knowing full well that I can't write in a pay-the-bills sort of way about blue-line trout fishing with small cane rods more than once every five or six years—never mind writing about mackerel, flounder, sunfish, and white perch. Blame a mind that finally understands Nick Lyons' farewell "Seasonable Angler" column in *Fly Fisherman*, where Nick wrote that he looked forward to going fishing simply because he wanted to go fishing and not because he needed something new to write about.

Blame the actuarial tables in an article I read about folks of a certain age needing to prepare their finances for retirement. According to their data, if I want to finish the collection of fishing essays I've been thinking about for seven years, not to mention commit the unsalable act of midlist literary fiction I've been meaning to write for far longer than that, I'd better get cracking. And soon.

Blame a lot of things, including the dread of someday finding that I checked off most of the years on my actuarial tables while seated at a keyboard trying to write those books and edit a magazine and write a magazine column, too.

Blame the long sunny afternoon and soft-focus evening I spent fishing an anonymous blue-line trout brook, bouncing down through the hills of Nowhere, Maine, toward its merger with a minor river running into the unimportant arm of an insignificant estuary feeding a backwater chunk of the North Atlantic.

A different sort of actuarial table told me I'd better go visit this neglected old friend for one last cast. A guy I know said a guy we both know will soon be moving in equipment—a feller-buncher, a delimber, a grapple skidder, and a bunk-trailer to haul sawlogs and pulp to the mill. And not for one of those targeted harvests so many of us small landowners must do to thin mature timber and pay our property taxes, but a full-on liquidation logging that leaves behind a moonscape and a housing development, the fate of too many blue-line trout brooks that once ran through primeval forest, then through a family's farmland, then through a family's woodlot, and finally through a family's neglected financial liability, conveniently situated within commuting distance of a city with twenty-first-century jobs.

So one last cast on a stream I once fished a dozen times a year and now haven't seen in a dozen years, though I've thought of it often while standing hip-deep in some of the world's great fly-fishing water.

Everything was pretty much where I left it. Those cool drooping hemlocks and the broad-arrow pines, the soft red maples and the gleaming yellow birches smelling of wintergreen. The colossal pile of midstream granite that looks like the Incredible Hulk taking a dump, and always held the best trout in the brook back in the days when I fished only here and places like it, and the Madison and the Yellowstone, the George and the Tree, the Meon and the Dee, the Teifi and the Usk, the Matane and the Miramichi, the York and the Dartmouth, and the Grand and Petite Cascapedias were merely thin blue lines on distant maps.

And so I waited there in the fading light, feeding the mosquitoes and letting the pool recover its equilibrium after a stupid cast that caught its smallest trout and put the fear of actuarial tables into its biggest, scribbling in my notebook the bones of a story I expected would become yet another *Gray's* column about the unassuming joys of small-stream trout fishing that writer-me hoped to sneak past editor-me.

Instead, it became the rationale for this book that I've been thinking about for the past seven years, and something I'd been trying to ignore these past few years: that we all have a last cast waiting for us somewhere. The trick is knowing when it arrives.